MW00721050

Real-Resumes For Customer Service Jobs

...including real resumes used to change careers
and resumes used to gain federal employment

Anne McKinney, Editor

PREP PUBLISHING

FAYETTEVILLE, NC

PREP Publishing

1110 ½ Hay Street

Fayetteville, NC 28305

(910) 483-6611

Copyright © 2005 by Anne McKinney

All rights reserved under International and Pan-American Copyright Conventions. No part of this book may be reproduced or copied in any form or by any means–graphic, electronic, or mechanical, including photocopying, taping, or information storage and retrieval systems– without written permission from the publisher, except by a reviewer, who may quote brief passages in a review. Published in the United States by PREP Publishing.

Library of Congress Cataloging-in-Publication Data

Real-resumes for customer service jobs : including real resumes used to change careers and transfer skills to other industries / Anne McKinney, editor.
   p. cm. -- (Real-resumes series)
 ISBN 1-885288-44-1
 1. Resumes (Employment) I. McKinney, Anne, 1948- II. Series.

 HF5383.R39584 2005
 650.14'2--dc22   2005043113

Printed in the United States of America

PREP Publishing

Business and Career Series:

Judeo-Christian Ethics Series:

Contents

Real-Resumes For Customer Service Jobs

Anne McKinney, Editor

A WORD FROM THE EDITOR:
ABOUT THE REAL-RESUMES SERIES

Welcome to the Real-Resumes Series. The Real-Resumes Series is a series of books which have been developed based on the experiences of real job hunters and which target specialized fields or types of resumes. As the editor of the series, I have carefully selected resumes and cover letters (with names and other key data disguised, of course) which have been used successfully in real job hunts. That's what we mean by "Real-Resumes." What you see in this book are *real* resumes and cover letters which helped real people get ahead in their careers.

We hope the superior samples will help you manage your current job campaign and your career so that you will find work aligned to your career interests.

The Real-Resumes Series is based on the work of the country's oldest resume-preparation company known as PREP Resumes. If you would like a free information packet describing the company's resume preparation services, call 910-483-6611 or write to PREP at 1110½ Hay Street, Fayetteville, NC 28305. If you have a job hunting experience you would like to share with our staff at the Real-Resumes Series, please contact us at preppub@aol.com or visit our website at www.prep-pub.com.

The resumes and cover letters in this book are designed to be of most value to people already in a job hunt or contemplating a career change. If we could give you one word of advice about your career, here's what we would say: Manage your career and don't stumble from job to job in an incoherent pattern. Try to find work that interests you, and then identify prosperous industries which need work performed of the type you want to do. Learn early in your working life that a great resume and cover letter can blow doors open for you and help you maximize your salary.

As the editor of this book, I would like to give you some tips on how to make the best use of the information you will find here. Because you are considering a career change, you already understand the concept of managing your career for maximum enjoyment and self-fulfillment. The purpose of this book is to provide expert tools and advice so that you *can* manage your career. Inside these pages you will find resumes and cover letters that will help you find not just a job but the type of work you want to do.

Overview of the Book
Every resume and cover letter in this book actually worked. And most of the resumes and cover letters have common features: most are one-page, most are in the chronological format, and most resumes are accompanied by a companion cover letter. In this section you will find helpful advice about job hunting. Step One begins with a discussion of why employers prefer the one-page, chronological resume. In Step Two you are introduced to the direct approach and to the proper format for a cover letter. In Step Three you learn the 14 main reasons why job hunters are not offered the jobs they want, and you learn the six key areas employers focus on when they interview you. Step Four gives nuts-and-bolts advice on how to handle the interview, send a follow-up letter after an interview, and negotiate your salary.

The cover letter plays such a critical role in a career change. You will learn from the experts how to format your cover letters and you will see suggested language to use in particular career-change situations. It has been said that "A picture is worth a thousand words" and, for that reason, you will see numerous examples of effective cover letters used by real individuals to change fields, functions, and industries.

The most important part of the book is the Real-Resumes section. Some of the individuals whose resumes and cover letters you see spent a lengthy career in an industry they loved. Then there are resumes and cover letters of people who wanted a change but who probably wanted to remain in their industry. Many of you will be especially interested by the resumes and cover letters of individuals who knew they definitely wanted a career change but had no idea what they wanted to do next. Other resumes and cover letters show individuals who knew they wanted to change fields and had a pretty good idea of what they wanted to do next.

Whatever your field, and whatever your circumstances, you'll find resumes and cover letters that will "show you the ropes" in terms of successfully changing jobs and switching careers.

Before you proceed further, think about why you picked up this book.
- Are you dissatisfied with the type of work you are now doing?
- Would you like to change careers, change companies, or change industries?
- Are you satisfied with your industry but not with your niche or function within it?
- Do you want to transfer your skills to a new product or service?
- Even if you have excelled in your field, have you "had enough"? Would you like the stimulation of a new challenge?
- Are you aware of the importance of a great cover letter but unsure of how to write one?
- Are you preparing to launch a second career after retirement?
- Have you been downsized, or do you anticipate becoming a victim of downsizing?
- Do you need expert advice on how to plan and implement a job campaign that will open the maximum number of doors?
- Do you want to make sure you handle an interview to your maximum advantage?

Introduction:
The Art of
Changing
Jobs...
and Finding
New Careers

- Would you like to master the techniques of negotiating salary and benefits?
- Do you want to learn the secrets and shortcuts of professional resume writers?

Using the Direct Approach

As you consider the possibility of a job hunt or career change, you need to be aware that most people end up having at least three distinctly different careers in their working lifetimes, and often those careers are different from each other. Yet people usually stumble through each job campaign, unsure of what they should be doing. Whether you find yourself voluntarily or unexpectedly in a job hunt, the direct approach is the job hunting strategy most likely to yield a full-time permanent job. The direct approach is an active, take-the-initiative style of job hunting in which you choose your next employer rather than relying on responding to ads, using employment agencies, or depending on other methods of finding jobs. You will learn how to use the direct approach in this book, and you will see that an effective cover letter is a critical ingredient in using the direct approach.

Lack of Industry Experience Not a Major Barrier to Entering New Field

"Lack of experience" is often the last reason people are not offered jobs, according to the companies who do the hiring. If you are changing careers, you will be glad to learn that experienced professionals often are selling "potential" rather than experience in a job hunt. Companies look for personal qualities that they know tend to be present in their most effective professionals, such as communication skills, initiative, persistence, organizational and time management skills, and creativity. Frequently companies are trying to discover "personality type," "talent," "ability," "aptitude," and "potential" rather than seeking actual hands-on experience, so your resume should be designed to aggressively present your accomplishments. Attitude, enthusiasm, personality, and a track record of achievements in any type of work are the primary "indicators of success" which employers are seeking, and you will see numerous examples in this book of resumes written in an all-purpose fashion so that the professional can approach various industries and companies.

The Art of Using References in a Job Hunt

You probably already know that you need to provide references during a job hunt, but you may not be sure of how and when to use references for maximum advantage. You can use references very creatively during a job hunt to call attention to your strengths and make yourself "stand out." Your references will rarely get you a job, no matter how impressive the names, but the way you use references can boost the employer's confidence in you and lead to a job offer in the least time.

You should ask from three to five people, including people who have supervised you, if you can use them as a reference during your job hunt. You may not be able to ask your current boss since your job hunt is probably confidential.

A common question in resume preparation is: "Do I need to put my references on my resume?" No, you don't. Even if you create a references page at the same time you prepare your resume, you don't need to mail, e-mail, or fax your references page with the resume and cover letter. Usually the potential employer is not interested in references until he meets you, so the earliest you need to have references ready is at the first interview. Obviously there are exceptions to this standard rule of thumb; sometimes an ad will ask you to send references with your first response. Wait until the employer requests references before providing them.

The "direct approach" is the style of job hunting most likely to yield the maximum number of job interviews.

Using references in a skillful fashion in your job hunt will inspire confidence in prospective employers and help you "close the sale" after interviews.

An excellent attention-getting technique is to take to the first interview not just a page of references (giving names, addresses, and telephone numbers) but an actual letter of reference written by someone who knows you well and who preferably has supervised or employed you. A professional way to close the first interview is to thank the interviewer, shake his or her hand, and then say you'd like to give him or her a copy of a letter of reference from a previous employer. Hopefully you already made a good impression during the interview, but you'll "close the sale" in a dynamic fashion if you leave a letter praising you and your accomplishments. For that reason, it's a good idea to ask supervisors during your final weeks in a job if they will provide you with a written letter of recommendation which you can use in future job hunts. Most employers will oblige, and you will have a letter that has a useful "shelf life" of many years. Such a letter often gives the prospective employer enough confidence in his opinion of you that he may forego checking out other references and decide to offer you the job on the spot or in the next few days.

With regard to references, it's best to provide the names and addresses of people who have supervised you or observed you in a work situation.

Whom should you ask to serve as references? References should be people who have known or supervised you in a professional, academic, or work situation. References with big titles, like school superintendent or congressman, are fine, but remind busy people when you get to the interview stage that they may be contacted soon. Make sure the busy official recognizes your name and has instant positive recall of you! If you're asked to provide references on a formal company application, you can simply transcribe names from your references list. In summary, follow this rule in using references: If you've got them, flaunt them! If you've obtained well-written letters of reference, make sure you find a polite way to push those references under the nose of the interviewer so he or she can hear someone other than you describing your strengths. Your references probably won't ever get you a job, but glowing letters of reference can give you credibility and visibility that can make you stand out among candidates with similar credentials and potential!

The approach taken by this book is to (1) help you master the proven best techniques of conducting a job hunt and (2) show you how to stand out in a job hunt through your resume, cover letter, interviewing skills, as well as the way in which you present your references and follow up on interviews. Now, the best way to "get in the mood" for writing your own resume and cover letter is to select samples from the Table of Contents that interest you and then read them. A great resume is a "photograph," usually on one page, of an individual. If you wish to seek professional advice in preparing your resume, you may contact one of the professional writers at Professional Resume & Employment Publishing (PREP) for a brief free consultation by calling 1-910-483-6611.

Part One: Some Advice About Your Job Hunt

What if you don't know what you want to do?

Your job hunt will be more comfortable if you can figure out what type of work you want to do. But you are not alone if you have no idea what you want to do next! You may have knowledge and skills in certain areas but want to get into another type of work. What *The Wall Street Journal* has discovered in its research on careers is that most of us end up having at least three distinctly different careers in our working lives; it seems that, even if we really like a particular kind of activity, twenty years of doing it is enough for most of us and we want to move on to something else!

Figure out what interests you and you will hold the key to a successful job hunt and working career. (And be prepared for your interests to change over time!)

That's why we strongly believe that you need to spend some time figuring out *what interests you* rather than taking an inventory of the skills you have. You may have skills that you simply don't want to use, but if you can build your career on the things that interest you, you will be more likely to be happy and satisfied in your job. Realize, too, that interests can change over time; the activities that interest you now may not be the ones that interested you years ago. For example, some professionals may decide that they've had enough of retail sales and want a job selling another product or service, even though they have earned a reputation for being an excellent retail manager. We strongly believe that interests rather than skills should be the determining factor in deciding what types of jobs you want to apply for and what directions you explore in your job hunt. Obviously one cannot be a lawyer without a law degree or a secretary without secretarial skills; but a professional can embark on a next career as a financial consultant, property manager, plant manager, production supervisor, retail manager, or other occupation if he/she has a strong interest in that type of work and can provide a resume that clearly demonstrates past excellent performance in *any* field and *potential* to excel in another field. As you will see later in this book, "lack of exact experience" is the last reason why people are turned down for the jobs they apply for.

How can you have a resume prepared if you don't know what you want to do?

You may be wondering how you can have a resume prepared if you don't know what you want to do next. The approach to resume writing which PREP, the country's oldest resume-preparation company, has used successfully for many years is to develop an "all-purpose" resume that translates your skills, experience, and accomplishments into language employers can understand. What most people need in a job hunt is a versatile resume that will allow them to apply for numerous types of jobs. For example, you may want to apply for a job in pharmaceutical sales but you may also want to have a resume that will be versatile enough for you to apply for jobs in the construction, financial services, or automotive industries.

"Lack of exact experience" is the last reason people are turned down for the jobs for which they apply.

Based on more than 20 years of serving job hunters, we at PREP have found that your best approach to job hunting is **an all-purpose resume** and **specific cover letters tailored to specific fields** rather than using the approach of trying to create different resumes for every job. If you are remaining in your field, you may not even need more than one "all-purpose" cover letter, although the cover letter rather than the resume is the place to communicate your interest in a narrow or specific field. An all-purpose resume and cover letter that translate your experience and accomplishments into plain English are the tools that will maximize the number of doors which open for you while permitting you to "fish" in the widest range of job areas.

Your resume will provide the script for your job interview.
When you get down to it, your resume has a simple job to do: Its purpose is to blow as many doors open as possible and to make as many people as possible want to meet you. So a well-written resume that really "sells" you is a key that will create opportunities for you in a job hunt.

This statistic explains why: The typical newspaper advertisement for a job opening receives more than 245 replies. And normally only 10 or 12 will be invited to an interview.

But here's another purpose of the resume: it provides the "script" the employer uses when he interviews you. If your resume has been written in such a way that your strengths and achievements are revealed, that's what you'll end up talking about at the job interview. Since the resume will govern what you get asked about at your interviews, you can't overestimate the importance of making sure your resume makes you look and sound as good as you are.

So what is a "good" resume?
Very literally, your resume should motivate the person reading it to dial the phone number or e-mail the screen name you have put on the resume. When you are relocating, you should put a local phone number on your resume if your physical address is several states away; employers are more likely to dial a local telephone number than a long-distance number when they're looking for potential employees.

If you have a resume already, look at it objectively. Is it a limp, colorless "laundry list" of your job titles and duties? Or does it "paint a picture" of your skills, abilities, and accomplishments in a way that would make someone want to meet you? Can people understand what you're saying? If you are attempting to change fields or industries, can potential employers see that your skills and knowledge are transferable to other environments? For example, have you described accomplishments which reveal your problem-solving abilities or communication skills?

How long should your resume be?
One page, maybe two. Usually only people in the academic community have a resume (which they usually call a *curriculum vitae*) longer than one or two pages. Remember that your resume is almost always accompanied by a cover letter, and a potential employer does not want to read more than two or three pages about a total stranger in order to decide if he wants to meet that person! Besides, don't forget that the more you tell someone about yourself, the more opportunity you are providing for the employer to screen you out at the "first-cut" stage. A resume should be concise and exciting and designed to make the reader want to meet you in person!

Should resumes be functional or chronological?
Employers almost always prefer a chronological resume; in other words, an employer will find a resume easier to read if it is immediately apparent what your current or most recent job is, what you did before that, and so forth, in reverse chronological order. A resume that goes back in detail for the last ten years of employment will generally satisfy the employer's curiosity about your background. Employment more than ten years old can be shown even more briefly in an "Other Experience" section at the end of your "Experience" section. Remember that your intention is not to tell everything you've done but to "hit the high points" and especially impress the employer with what you learned, contributed, or accomplished in each job you describe.

Your resume is the "script" for your job interviews. Make sure you put on your resume what you want to talk about or be asked about at the job interview.

The one-page resume in chronological format is the format preferred by most employers.

Once you get your resume, what do you do with it?

You will be using your resume to answer ads, as a tool to use in talking with friends and relatives about your job search, and, most importantly, in using the "direct approach" described in this book.

When you mail your resume, always send a "cover letter."

A "cover letter," sometimes called a "resume letter" or "letter of interest," is a letter that accompanies and introduces your resume. Your cover letter is a way of personalizing the resume by sending it to the specific person you think you might want to work for at each company. Your cover letter should contain a few highlights from your resume—just enough to make someone want to meet you. Cover letters should always be typed or word processed on a computer—never handwritten.

Never mail or fax your resume without a cover letter.

1. Learn the art of answering ads.

There is an "art," part of which can be learned, in using your "bestselling" resume to reply to advertisements.

Sometimes an exciting job lurks behind a boring ad that someone dictated in a hurry, so reply to any ad that interests you. Don't worry that you aren't "25 years old with an MBA" like the ad asks for. Employers will always make compromises in their requirements if they think you're the "best fit" overall.

What about ads that ask for "salary requirements?"

What if the ad you're answering asks for "salary requirements?" The first rule is to avoid committing yourself in writing at that point to a specific salary. You don't want to "lock yourself in."

There are two ways to handle the ad that asks for "salary requirements."

What if the ad asks for your "salary requirements?"

First, you can ignore that part of the ad and accompany your resume with a cover letter that focuses on "selling" you, your abilities, and even some of your philosophy about work or your field. You may include a sentence in your cover letter like this: "I can provide excellent personal and professional references at your request, and I would be delighted to share the private details of my salary history with you in person."

Second, if you feel you must give some kind of number, just state a range in your cover letter that includes your medical, dental, other benefits, and expected bonuses. You might state, for example, "My current compensation, including benefits and bonuses, is in the range of $30,000-$40,000."

Analyze the ad and "tailor" yourself to it.

When you're replying to ads, a finely tailored cover letter is an important tool in getting your resume noticed and read. On the next page is a cover letter which has been "tailored to fit" a specific ad. Notice the "art" used by PREP writers of analyzing the ad's main requirements and then writing the letter so that the person's background, work habits, and interests seem "tailor-made" to the company's needs. Use this cover letter as a model when you prepare your own reply to ads.

Date

To: Search Committee

In response to the urging of someone familiar with your search for a Customer Service Director for the Association of Health Underwriters, I am sending you a resume which summarizes my background. I offer a unique combination of knowledge, experience, and abilities which I believe would ideally suit the requirements of the Association of Health Underwriters.

Health industry expertise
You will see from my resume that I offer expertise related to health insurance and underwriting. In my current job I have sought out and negotiated contracts with major insurance companies to provide insurance for the organization. On a $1 million budget, I have developed insurance programs which generated $2 million in net income based on $32 million in premium. These highly regarded programs which I developed have brought 6,000 new members into the organization.

Proven executive ability
I offer proven executive ability. I have earned a reputation as someone who has not only strategic vision and imagination but also the tenacity and persistence to follow through on the "nitty-gritty" details of implementing new projects, programs, and concepts. I know how to delegate, and I know how to "micro manage," and I am skilled at tailoring my management style to particular circumstances while always shouldering full responsibility and accountability for results. My current job has involved the responsibility of recruiting, training, and continuously developing a national sales force of brokers throughout the U.S. which broke with the tradition of passive mail solicitation and led to dramatic growth in sales and profitability. With a strong "bottom-line" orientation, I have streamlined headquarters staff and reduced central office expenses to save at least half a million dollars while continuously supervising the association's five regional offices in the recruitment and training of more than 1,200 insurance agents nationally.

Extensive association experience
You will also see from my resume that I am accustomed to "getting things done" within the unique environment of a trade/membership association. I am well known for my ability to attract and retain a cohesive and productive staff, and I am also respected for my exceptional skills in relating to, inspiring, and supporting key volunteer members. A skilled communicator, I have made countless appearances and speeches.

I am aware of the requirements defined by the search committee, and I would enjoy the opportunity to discuss this position further with the Executive Committee. I feel certain I could contribute significantly to the growth and financial health of the Association of Health Underwriters as its Customer Service Director. Thank you for your time and consideration.

Sincerely,

Shane Malone

Employers are trying to identify the individual who wants the job they are filling. Don't be afraid to express your enthusiasm in the cover letter!

2. Talk to friends and relatives.

Don't be shy about telling your friends and relatives the kind of job you're looking for. Looking for the job you want involves using your network of contacts, so tell people what you're looking for. They may be able to make introductions and help set up interviews.

About 25% of all interviews are set up through "who you know," so don't ignore this approach.

3. Finally, and most importantly, use the "direct approach."

The "direct approach" is a strategy in which you choose your next employer.

More than 50% of all job interviews are set up by the "direct approach." That means you actually mail, e-mail, or fax a resume and a cover letter to a company you think might be interesting to work for.

To whom do you write?

In general, you should write directly to the *exact name* of the person who would be hiring you: say, the vice-president of marketing or data processing. If you're in doubt about to whom to address the letter, address it to the president by name and he or she will make sure it gets forwarded to the right person within the company who has hiring authority in your area.

How do you find the names of potential employers?

You're not alone if you feel that the biggest problem in your job search is finding the right names at the companies you want to contact. But you can usually figure out the names of companies you want to approach by deciding first if your job hunt is primarily geography-driven or industry-driven.

In a **geography-driven job hunt,** you could select a list of, say, 50 companies you want to contact **by location** from the lists that the U.S. Chambers of Commerce publish yearly of their "major area employers." There are hundreds of local Chambers of Commerce across America, and most of them will have an 800 number which you can find through 1-800-555-1212. If you and your family think Atlanta, Dallas, Ft. Lauderdale, and Virginia Beach might be nice places to live, for example, you could contact the Chamber of Commerce in those cities and ask how you can obtain a copy of their list of major employers. Your nearest library will have the book which lists the addresses of all chambers.

In an **industry-driven job hunt,** and if you are willing to relocate, you will be identifying the companies which you find most attractive in the industry in which you want to work. When you select a list of companies to contact **by industry,** you can find the right person to write and the address of firms by industrial category in *Standard and Poor's, Moody's,* and other excellent books in public libraries. Many Web sites also provide contact information.

Many people feel it's a good investment to actually call the company to either find out or double-check the name of the person to whom they want to send a resume and cover letter. It's important to do as much as you feasibly can to assure that the letter gets to the right person in the company.

On-line research will be the best way for many people to locate organizations to which they wish to send their resume. It is outside the scope of this book to teach Internet research skills, but librarians are often useful in this area.

What's the correct way to follow up on a resume you send?

There is a polite way to be aggressively interested in a company during your job hunt. It is ideal to end the cover letter accompanying your resume by saying, "I hope you'll welcome my call next week when I try to arrange a brief meeting at your convenience to discuss your current and future needs and how I might serve them." Keep it low key, and just ask for a "brief meeting," not an interview. Employers want people who show a determined interest in working with them, so don't be shy about following up on the resume and cover letter you've mailed.

It pays to be aware of the 14 most common pitfalls for job hunters.

STEP THREE: Preparing for Interviews

But a resume and cover letter by themselves can't get you the job you want. You need to "prep" yourself before the interview. Step Three in your job campaign is "Preparing for Interviews." First, let's look at interviewing from the hiring organization's point of view.

What are the biggest "turnoffs" for potential employers?

One of the ways to help yourself perform well at an interview is to look at the main reasons why organizations *don't* hire the people they interview, according to those who do the interviewing.

Notice that "lack of appropriate background" (or lack of experience) is the *last* reason for not being offered the job.

The 14 Most Common Reasons Job Hunters Are Not Offered Jobs *(according to the companies who do the interviewing and hiring):*

1. Low level of accomplishment
2. Poor attitude, lack of self-confidence
3. Lack of goals/objectives
4. Lack of enthusiasm
5. Lack of interest in the company's business
6. Inability to sell or express yourself
7. Unrealistic salary demands
8. Poor appearance
9. Lack of maturity, no leadership potential
10. Lack of extracurricular activities
11. Lack of preparation for the interview, no knowledge about company
12. Objecting to travel
13. Excessive interest in security and benefits
14. Inappropriate background

Department of Labor studies have proven that smart, "prepared" job hunters can increase their beginning salary while getting a job in *half* the time it normally takes. (4½ months is the average national length of a job search.) Here, from PREP, are some questions that can prepare you to find a job faster.

Are you in the "right" frame of mind?

It seems unfair that we have to look for a job just when we're lowest in morale. Don't worry *too* much if you're nervous before interviews. You're supposed to be a little nervous, especially if the job means a lot to you. But the best way to kill unnecessary fears about job hunting is through 1) making sure you have a great resume and 2) preparing yourself for the interview. Here are three main areas you need to think about before each interview.

Do you know what the company does?

Don't walk into an interview giving the impression that, "If this is Tuesday, this must be General Motors."

Find out before the interview what the company's main product or service is. Where is the company heading? Is it in a "growth" or declining industry? (Answers to these questions may influence whether or not you want to work there!)

Information about what the company does is in annual reports, in newspaper and magazine articles, and on the Internet. If you're not yet skilled at Internet research, just visit your nearest library and ask the reference librarian to guide you to printed materials on the company.

Research the company before you go to interviews.

Do you know what you want to do for the company?

Before the interview, try to decide how you see yourself fitting into the company. Remember, "lack of exact background" the company wants is usually the last reason people are not offered jobs.

Understand before you go to each interview that the burden will be on you to "sell" the interviewer on why you're the best person for the job and the company.

How will you answer the critical interview questions?

Put yourself in the interviewer's position and think about the questions you're most likely to be asked. Here are some of the most commonly asked interview questions:

Anticipate the questions you will be asked at the interview, and prepare your responses in advance.

Q: *"What are your greatest strengths?"*
A: Don't say you've never thought about it! Go into an interview knowing the three main impressions you want to leave about yourself, such as "I'm hard-working, loyal, and an imaginative cost-cutter."

Q: *"What are your greatest weaknesses?"*
A: Don't confess that you're lazy or have trouble meeting deadlines! Confessing that you tend to be a "workaholic" or "tend to be a perfectionist and sometimes get frustrated when others don't share my high standards" will make your prospective employer see a "weakness" that he likes. Name a weakness that your interviewer will perceive as a strength.

Q: *"What are your long-range goals?"*
A: If you're interviewing with Microsoft, don't say you want to work for IBM in five years! Say your long-range goal is to be *with* the company, contributing to its goals and success.

Q: *"What motivates you to do your best work?"*
A: Don't get dollar signs in your eyes here! "A challenge" is not a bad answer, but it's a little cliched. Saying something like "troubleshooting" or "solving a tough problem" is more interesting and specific. Give an example if you can.

Q: "What do you know about this organization?"

A: Don't say you never heard of it until they asked you to the interview! Name an interesting, positive thing you learned about the company recently from your research. Remember, company executives can sometimes feel rather "maternal" about the company they serve. Don't get onto a negative area of the company if you can think of positive facts you can bring up. Of course, if you learned in your research that the company's sales seem to be taking a nose-dive, or that the company president is being prosecuted for taking bribes, you might politely ask your interviewer to tell you something that could help you better understand what you've been reading. Those are the kinds of company facts that can help you determine whether or not you want to work there.

Q: "Why should I hire you?"

A: "I'm unemployed and available" is the wrong answer here! Get back to your strengths and say that you believe the organization could benefit by a loyal, hard-working cost-cutter like yourself.

In conclusion, you should decide in advance, before you go to the interview, how you will answer each of these commonly asked questions. Have some practice interviews with a friend to role-play and build your confidence.

> Go to an interview prepared to tell the company why it should hire you.

STEP FOUR: Handling the Interview and Negotiating Salary

Now you're ready for Step Four: actually handling the interview successfully and effectively. Remember, the purpose of an interview is to get a job offer.

> A smile at an interview makes the employer perceive of you as intelligent!

Eight "do's" for the interview

According to leading U.S. companies, there are eight key areas in interviewing success. You can fail at an interview if you mishandle just one area.

1. **Do wear appropriate clothes.**
   You can never go wrong by wearing a suit to an interview.

2. **Do be well groomed.**
   Don't overlook the obvious things like having clean hair, clothes, and fingernails for the interview.

3. **Do give a firm handshake.**
   You'll have to shake hands twice in most interviews: first, before you sit down, and second, when you leave the interview. Limp handshakes turn most people off.

4. **Do smile and show a sense of humor.**
   Interviewers are looking for people who would be nice to work with, so don't be so somber that you don't smile. In fact, research shows that people who smile at interviews are perceived as more intelligent. So, smile!

5. **Do be enthusiastic.**
   Employers say they are "turned off" by lifeless, unenthusiastic job hunters who show no special interest in that company. The best way to show some enthusiasm for the employer's operation is to find out about the business beforehand.

6. Do show you are flexible and adaptable.

An employer is looking for someone who can contribute to his organization in a flexible, adaptable way. No matter what skills and training you have, employers know every new employee must go through initiation and training on the company's turf. Certainly show pride in your past accomplishments in a specific, factual way ("I saved my last employer $50.00 a week by a new cost-cutting measure I developed"). But don't come across as though there's nothing about the job you couldn't easily handle.

7. Do ask intelligent questions about the employer's business.

An employer is hiring someone because of certain business needs. Show interest in those needs. Asking questions to get a better idea of the employer's needs will help you "stand out" from other candidates interviewing for the job.

8. Do "take charge" when the interviewer "falls down" on the job.

Employers are seeking people with good attitudes whom they can train and coach to do things their way.

Go into every interview knowing the three or four points about yourself you want the interviewer to remember. And be prepared to take an active part in leading the discussion if the interviewer's "canned approach" does not permit you to display your "strong suit." You can't always depend on the interviewer's asking you the "right" questions so you can stress your strengths and accomplishments.

An important "don't": Don't ask questions about salary or benefits at the first interview.
Employers don't take warmly to people who look at their organization as just a place to satisfy salary and benefit needs. Don't risk making a negative impression by appearing greedy or self-serving. The place to discuss salary and benefits is normally at the second interview, and the employer will bring it up. Then you can ask questions without appearing excessively interested in what the organization can do for you.

Now...negotiating your salary
Even if an ad requests that you communicate your "salary requirement" or "salary history," you should avoid providing those numbers in your initial cover letter. You can usually say something like this: "I would be delighted to discuss the private details of my salary history with you in person."

Once you're at the interview, you must avoid even appearing *interested* in salary before you are offered the job. Make sure you've "sold" yourself before talking salary. First show you're the "best fit" for the employer and then you'll be in a stronger position from which to negotiate salary. **Never** bring up the subject of salary yourself. Employers say there's no way you can avoid looking greedy if you bring up the issue of salary and benefits before the company has identified you as its "best fit."

Don't appear excessively interested in salary and benefits at the interview.

Interviewers sometimes throw out a salary figure at the first interview to see if you'll accept it. You may not want to commit yourself if you think you will be able to negotiate a better deal later on. Get back to finding out more about the job. This lets the interviewer know you're interested primarily in the job and not the salary.

When the organization brings up salary, it may say something like this: "Well, Mary, we think you'd make a good candidate for this job. What kind of salary are we talking about?" You may not want to name a number here, either. Give the ball back to the interviewer. Act as though you hadn't given the subject of salary much thought and respond something like this: "Ah, Mr. Jones, I wonder if you'd be kind enough to tell me what salary you had in mind when you advertised the job?" Or ... "What is the range you have in mind?"

Don't worry, if the interviewer names a figure that you think is too low, you can say so without turning down the job or locking yourself into a rigid position. The point here is to negotiate for yourself as well as you can. You might reply to a number named by the interviewer that you think is low by saying something like this: "Well, Mr. Lee, the job interests me very much, and I think I'd certainly enjoy working with you. But, frankly, I was thinking of something a little higher than that." That leaves the ball in your interviewer's court again, and you haven't turned down the job either, in case it turns out that the interviewer can't increase the offer and you still want the job.

Salary negotiation can be tricky.

Last, send a follow-up letter.

Mail, e-mail, or fax a letter right after the interview telling your interviewer you enjoyed the meeting and are certain (if you are) that you are the "best fit" for the job. The people interviewing you will probably have an attitude described as either "professionally loyal" to their companies, or "maternal and proprietary" if the interviewer also owns the company. In either case, they are looking for people who want to work for *that* company in particular. The follow-up letter you send might be just the deciding factor in your favor if the employer is trying to choose between you and someone else. You will see an example of a follow-up letter on page 16.

A follow-up letter can help the employer choose between you and another qualified candidate.

A cover letter is an essential part of a job hunt or career change.

Many people are aware of the importance of having a great resume, but most people in a job hunt don't realize just how important a cover letter can be. The purpose of the cover letter, sometimes called a **"letter of interest,"** is to introduce your resume to prospective employers. The cover letter is often the critical ingredient in a job hunt because the cover letter allows you to say a lot of things that just don't "fit" on the resume. For example, you can emphasize your commitment to a new field and stress your related talents. The cover letter also gives you a chance to stress outstanding character and personal values. On the next two pages you will see examples of very effective cover letters.

A cover letter is an essential part of a career change.

Please do not attempt to implement a career change without a cover letter. A cover letter is the first impression of you, and you can influence the way an employer views you by the language and style of your letter.

Special help for those in career change

We want to emphasize again that, especially in a career change, the cover letter is very important and can help you "build a bridge" to a new career. A creative and appealing cover letter can begin the process of encouraging the potential employer to imagine you in an industry other than the one in which you have worked.

As a special help to those in career change, there are resumes and cover letters included in this book which show valuable techniques and tips you should use when changing fields or industries. The resumes and cover letters of career changers are identified in the table of contents as "Career Change" and you will see the "Career Change" label on cover letters in Part Two where the individuals are changing careers.

Date

**Addressing the Cover
Letter:** Get the exact
name of the person to
whom you are writing. This
makes your approach
personal.

Exact Name of Person
Title or Position
Name of Company
Address (no., street)
Address (city, state, zip)

Dear Exact Name of Person: (or Dear Sir or Madam if answering a blind ad.)

With the enclosed resume, I would like to make you aware of my interest in exploring employment opportunities with your organization.

Second Paragraph: You
have a chance to talk
about whatever you feel is
your most distinguishing
feature.

As you will see from my resume, I am currently excelling as Customer Service Director of Habitat for Humanity. My major responsibilities include preparing annual operating budgets, budgets for new projects, and budgets for construction while monitoring funds expensed in multiple simultaneous projects. I supervise three staff persons and assure compliance with regulations, including HUD and VA, related to housing ownership. In addition to determining eligibility of applicants and verifying family income as well as criminal records, I approve payment agreements and audit homeowners' compliance with HUD regulations.

Third Paragraph: You
bring up your next most
distinguishing qualities and
try to
sell yourself.

You will notice that I have excelled in a track record of promotion with Habitat for Humanity. After graduating with a B.S. in Finance from the University of North Carolina at Chapel Hill, I began employment with Habitat as a Project Manager, was promoted to Acting Executive Director and then to Director of Occupancy, and subsequently to Customer Service Director.

Fourth Paragraph: Here
you have another
opportunity to reveal
qualities or achievements
which will impress your
future employer.

I am comfortable operating within the unique financial constraints of a nonprofit organization, and I offer a proven ability to manage financial resources for maximum effectiveness. I am respected as a professional who deals effectively with people at all levels, from the top-level HUD official and sophisticated bankers, to relatively unsophisticated applicants for housing.

Final Paragraph: She
asks the employer to
contact her. Make sure
your reader knows what
the "next step" is.

I hope you will call or write me soon to suggest a time convenient for us to meet to discuss your current and future needs. Thank you in advance for your time.

Sincerely yours,

Cecelia McCormick

**Alternate Final
Paragraph:** It's more
aggressive (but not too
aggressive) to let the
employer know that you
will be calling him or her.
Don't be afraid to be
persistent. Employers are
looking for people who
know what they want to
do.

Alternate last paragraph:
I hope you will welcome my call soon to arrange a brief meeting when we might meet to discuss your needs and goals and how my background might serve them. I can provide outstanding references at the appropriate time.

Date

Exact Name of Person
Exact Title
Exact Name of Company
Address
City, State, Zip

Dear Exact Name of Person (or Dear Sir or Madam if answering a blind ad):

This accomplished professional is responding to an advertisement. She analyzed the job vacancy opening very closely and she has made sure that she has tailored her letter of interest to the areas mentioned in the vacancy announcement.

    With the enclosed resume, I would like to make you aware of my interest in exploring employment opportunities with your organization. I am responding to your recent advertisement for a Patient Services Coordinator.

    As you will see from my resume, I have worked for the Shawnee County Health Department since 1995, and I have excelled in a track record of promotion to my current position as Supervisor of the Women's and Children's Health Program. While working within the county's health department, I have become accustomed to interacting with multiple clinics and multiple programs. In my current position, I hire, train, and manage up to 25 individuals while planning and administering multiple budgets totaling more than $2.5 million. I have earned a reputation as a caring individual who is skilled at building consensus and inspiring others to work toward common goals.

    An outgoing and energetic individual, I take great pride in the multiple accomplishments of the county's health department, and I have played a key role in many important programs. I co-developed the Shawnee County Healthy Living Program which provided preventive health screening services to the county's 2,000 employees. I have also played a key role in the Pregnant Living Program which has reduced the incidence of teen pregnancies. In addition to organizing numerous projects related to breast cancer awareness and other areas, I developed the Childhood Poison Prevention Program and the Heart Control Program.

    While serving the health care needs of the county's indigent population, my main "hobby" has been gaining advanced knowledge through earning additional academic credentials. In addition to earning my L.P.N. and R.N. credentials, I received a Bachelor of Science in Nursing and a Master's in Public Health degree. I am proficient with numerous software programs which I have utilized in my job in order to prepare budgets, track expenditures, and control the funding of multiple programs.

    I can provide outstanding personal and professional references at the appropriate time, but I would ask that you not contact the Shawnee County Health Department until after we have a chance to discuss your needs. Since I am in a key management role, I wish my interest in your organization to remain confidential at this time. Thank you in advance for your consideration and professional courtesies.

Yours sincerely,

Lavina Cleveland

Date

Exact Name of Person
Title or Position
Name of Company
Address (number and street)
Address (city, state, and zip)

Follow-up Letter

Dear Exact Name:

A great follow-up letter
can motivate the
employer
to make the job offer,
and the salary offer may
be influenced by the
style and tone of your
follow-up
letter, too!

     I am writing to express my appreciation for the time you spent with me on December 9, and I want to let you know that I am sincerely interested in the position of Customer Service Manager which we discussed.

     I feel confident that I could skillfully interact with your staff, and I would cheerfully relocate to Tennessee, as we discussed.

     As you described to me what you are looking for in the person who fills this position, I had a sense of "déjà vu" because my current employer was in a similar position when I went to work for the Salvation Army. The general manager needed someone to come in and be his "right arm" and take on an increasing amount of his management responsibilities so that he could be freed up to do other things. I have played a key role in the growth and success of the organization, and my supervisor has come to depend on my sound advice as much as well as my proven ability to "cut through" huge volumes of work efficiently and accurately. Since this is one of the busiest times of the year for the Salvation Army, I feel that I could not leave during that time. I could certainly make myself available by mid-January.

     It would be a pleasure to work for your organization, and I am confident that I could contribute significantly through my strong qualities of loyalty, reliability, and trustworthiness. I am confident that I could quickly learn your style and procedures, and I would welcome being trained to do things your way.

Yours sincerely,

Jacob Evangelisto

In this section, you will find resumes and cover letters of professionals seeking employment, or already employed, in the customer service field. How do these individuals differ from other job hunters? Why should there be a book dedicated to people seeking customer service jobs? Based on more than 25 years of experience in working with job hunters, this editor is convinced that resumes and cover letters which "speak the lingo" of the field you wish to enter will communicate more effectively than language which is not industry-specific. This book is designed to help people (1) who are seeking to prepare their own resumes and (2) who wish to use as models "real" resumes of individuals who have successfully launched careers in customer service. You will see a wide range of experience levels reflected in the resumes in this book. Some of the resumes and cover letters were used by individuals seeking to enter the field; others were used successfully by senior professionals to advance in the field.

Newcomers to an industry sometimes have advantages over more experienced professionals. In a job hunt, junior professionals can have an advantage over their more experienced counterparts. Prospective employers often view the less experienced workers as "more trainable" and "more coachable" than their seniors. This means that the mature professional who has already excelled in a first career can, with credibility, "change careers" and transfer skills to other industries.

Newcomers to the field may have disadvantages compared to their seniors.
Almost by definition, the inexperienced professional—the young person who has recently entered the job market, or the individual who has recently received respected certifications—is less tested and less experienced than senior managers, so the resume and cover letter of the inexperienced professional may often have to "sell" his or her potential to do something he or she has never done before. Lack of experience in the field she wants to enter can be a stumbling block to the junior employee, but remember that many employers believe that someone who has excelled in anything—academics, for example—can excel in many other fields.

Some advice to inexperienced professionals...
If senior professionals could give junior professionals a piece of advice about careers, here's what they would say: Manage your career and don't stumble from job to job in an incoherent pattern. Try to find work that interests you, and then identify prosperous industries which need work performed of the type you want to do. Learn early in your working life that a great resume and cover letter can blow doors open for you and help you maximize your salary.

Manufacturing company

Date

Exact Name of Person
Title or Position
Name of Company
Address
City, State, Zip

ACCOUNT REPRESENTATIVE

Dear Exact Name of Person: (or Dear Sir or Madam if answering a blind ad.)

I would appreciate an opportunity to talk with you soon about how I could contribute to your organization through my proven accounts management, customer service, and public relations skills.

You will see from my resume that I began working with Eckerd when I was 16 years old; I continued my employment with Eckerd while attending college and was promoted to Pharmacy Technician while earning my Bachelor of Business Administration degree. After college graduation, the university where I earned my degree recruited me for a job in its admissions office, and I excelled in handling a wide variety of administrative and public relations tasks.

Most recently I have worked full-time as an Account Representative while going to school at nights and on the weekends to earn my MBA, which I received in May 2005. I was handling key accounts worth more than $2 million annually for my employer and was being groomed for rapid promotion into a higher management position.

I have, however, relocated to Phoenix permanently because I recently married and my husband owns and manages his own business in this area. I am seeking an employer who can use a highly motivated individual with very strong communication, sales, customer service, and public relations skills. Because I earned both my undergraduate and graduate degrees while excelling in demanding professional positions, I have acquired excellent organizational and time management skills which permit me to maximize my own productivity.

If you can use a self-starter who could rapidly become a valuable part of your organization, I hope you will contact me to suggest a time when we might meet to discuss your needs and how I might serve them. I can provide excellent personal and professional references.

Yours sincerely,

Anita Woodward

ANITA WOODWARD

1110½ Hay Street, Fayetteville, NC 28305 • preppub@aol.com • (910) 483-6611

OBJECTIVE   To offer my strong accounts management, sales, marketing, and customer service skills to an organization that would benefit from my strong bottom-line orientation and results-oriented style of developing relationships, establishing trust, and maximizing profitability.

EDUCATION   M.B.A., University of Massachusetts, Boston, MA, May 2005. The School of Business is accredited by The National of Collegiate Schools of Business (NCSB).
B.B.A., University of Massachusetts, Boston, MA, 1997. Received a partial athletic tennis scholarship, and was a valued member of the varsity tennis team.

EXPERIENCE   **ACCOUNT REPRESENTATIVE.** Revere Manufacturing, Inc., Boston, MA (2003-05). For a manufacturing company which produces custom and stock file folders, handled sales and customer service for the company's second largest customer, the Government Printing Office.
- Handled accounts which amounted to a total dollar volume of $2 million in 2004; increased the dollar volume of account sales in 2004 over 2003, and was above my targeted 2005 sales goals when I married and resigned in order to relocate to Phoenix where my husband owns and manages a business.
- Worked full-time in this job while simultaneously completing a rigorous MBA program; became skilled at managing my time for maximum efficiency.
- Serviced federal government accounts from the first phone call to following up on the shipment of orders.
- Performed cost estimating; prepared bids on one-time as well as yearly federal contracts; handled purchasing, invoicing, as well as advertising and sales pertaining to my accounts.
- Became skilled at designing specialty products tailored to unique customer needs; was frequently commended by customers for my excellent communication skills and ability to translate their ideas into practical product designs.
- Was honored by my selection to serve on the corporation's Safety Committee, and contributed many ideas which officials regarded as resourceful and practical.
- Was being groomed for rapid advancement into the management structure of this corporation because of my proven ability to handle multiple priorities in a fast-paced environment which required strict attention to detail, precision, and accuracy.

ADMISSIONS ASSISTANT. University of Massachusetts, Boston, MA (2000-03). In my first job after graduation, was recruited by the university where I earned my degree to work in the admissions process; handled administrative and public relations responsibilities.
- Prepared and evaluated files pertaining to prospective students, freshmen, transfer students, and international students; conducted student tours.
- Generated weekly reports containing valuable statistical data used in analysis and strategic decision making; handled the weekly cash deposits of the admissions office.
- Prepared correspondence and reports including key reports distributed to the president and vice president of the university.

Other experience: Eckerd Drug Store, Boston, MA (1993-99).
Pharmacy Technician. (1997-99). Assisted pharmacists in filling prescriptions, handling short-order drug orders, and responding to customer needs.
Senior Sales Associate. (1993-97). Began working in this position when I was 16 and in high school; was rapidly entrusted with payroll and cash handling responsibilities.

PERSONAL   Can provide outstanding personal and professional references. Energetic self-starter.

Manufacturing company

Date

Exact Name of Person
Title or Position
Name of Company
Address
City, State, Zip

ACCOUNT REPRESENTATIVE and CUSTOMER SERVICE SPECIALIST

Dear Exact Name of Person: (or Dear Sir or Madam if answering a blind ad.)

Can you use a reliable hard worker who offers excellent customer service skills along with an ability to accurately and quickly account for large amounts of cash?

I am interested in exploring employment opportunities with your company. My experience includes employment at Northwestern Manufacturing and Hakoiyo, Inc. In the job with Northwestern Manufacturing, I have handled several of its large retail accounts for bedding products. For the Japanese-owned company which marketed fingerprinting equipment internationally, I was rapidly promoted into an assistant supervisor position overseeing the productivity of 80 employees.

An outgoing individual who enjoys working with the public and providing gracious customer service, I am known for excellent analytical and problem-solving skills. For example, as a proof operator at an Idaho bank, I set a record of 16,000 proofing documents in a single day. I excelled as a Cashier and Layaway Clerk at Wal-Mart and was specially recruited as Store Cashier. It was my responsibility to oversee the accuracy of 20 cashiers and reconcile overall daily store accounts totaling more than $20,000. I took pride in my ability to balance all store accounts to the penny, and I have a proven record of handling large amounts of cash quickly and accurately.

Many past employers have invited me to return, and I can provide outstanding personal and professional references.

If you can use a young professional with proven ability to serve the public and expertly handle complicated financial activities, I hope you will contact me. I look forward to your contacting me to suggest a time when we could meet in person to discuss your needs. Thank you in advance for your time.

Sincerely,

Carol Tottle

CAROL TOTTLE

1110½ Hay Street, Fayetteville, NC 28305 • preppub@aol.com • (910) 483-6611

OBJECTIVE	To contribute to an organization desiring a cheerful and reliable worker with excellent customer service and public relations skills as well as experience in accurately accounting for large amounts of cash.
EXPERIENCE	**ACCOUNT REPRESENTATIVE** and **CUSTOMER SERVICE SPECIALIST.** Northwestern Manufacturing, Co., Boise, ID (2005-present). For a large manufacturer of high-quality bedding, manage large accounts throughout the states of Washington, Idaho, Montana, and Oregon; prepare billing for all accounts.

- Have earned respect from management and customers for my customer service skills in handling accounts each producing quarterly sales of over one million dollars.
- Was specially selected as a member of the Quality Control Panel because of my extensive knowledge of the billing process.
- Contributed several ideas for increasing worker productivity and product quality.
- Commended for my gracious style of dealing with customer dissatisfaction and for my ability to tactfully solve problems.

ASSISTANT SHIFT SUPERVISOR. Hakoiyo, Inc, Boise, ID (2003-04). With this Japanese-owned company which marketed fingerprinting equipment to law enforcement organizations worldwide, began as a data entry clerk, and was promoted after only three months to a position involving management of 80 employees.

- Consistently evaluated in the top 5% of company employees.
- While overseeing the speed and accuracy of employees, practiced "leadership by example" by maintaining high personal productivity standards while working with national and international law enforcement agencies.
- Assisted supervisor in completing end-of-shift documents. Earned respect of all employees and supervisors including senior employees who had initially resented my promotion.

PROOF OPERATOR. National Bank of Idaho, Twin Falls, ID (2000-02). Researched discrepancies in customer account information, proofed data, encoded documents, and utilized a high speed sorter; prepared/filed reports.

- Commended for strong analytical and problem-solving skills frequently demonstrated by identifying discrepancies which others could not. Known as one of the bank's fastest and most accurate workers, once set a record of 16,000 proofing documents in a single business day.

CUSTOMER SERVICE REPRESENTATIVE/STORE CASHIER. Wal-Mart, Twin Falls, ID (1995-99). After excelling in jobs as a Cashier and Layaway Clerk, was selected for the position as Store Cashier, with the responsibility of daily cash reconciliation for the store.

- Verified the work of 20 cashiers daily to prepare the overall store balance. Prided myself on the ability to balance to the cent an average of $20,000 daily.
- Processed payroll for 80 employees, including tallying time cards.

EDUCATION	Maintained a 4.0 GPA while completing nearly two years of college studies. Excelled in numerous professional training courses related to banking, retailing, and manufacturing.
SKILLS	Operate equipment including the proof machine and high speed sorter, decalator, burster, and 10-key calculators at 12,000 strokes per hour. Type 60 wpm; proficient with Word, Excel.
PERSONAL	Dedicated and loyal employee who has been asked to return by most previous employers.

Accounting services

Exact Name of Person
Title or Position
Name of Company
Address
City, State, Zip

**ACCOUNTING
SERVICES MANAGER**

Dear Exact Name of Person: (or Dear Sir or Madam if answering a blind ad.)

 With the enclosed resume, I would like to make you aware of my interest in using my accounting, bookkeeping, and administrative background to benefit your organization.

 As you will see, I was involved in virtually all activities in the accounting cycle while working at Whites Slough & Company. While calculating and processing payrolls for 120 clients, both large and small companies, I played a key role in devising a system to organize accounts receivable for the firm's payroll processing service. I was also involved in financial auditing of banks and nonprofit organizations. On a daily basis, I handled all aspects of bookkeeping for companies in various industries, and I also assisted with corporate end-of-year inventories, financial statements, as well as federal and state tax returns. I worked extensively with clients and was frequently commended for my strong public relations and customer service skills.

 Since 2002 I have worked part-time as a manager for a large restaurant where I have worked "on and off" for 14 years. I decided to work part-time in order to spend more time with my daughter, but I have now set up full-time day care at Southern Baptist Church, and I am ready to return to work full-time for a company that can use my strong accounting and administrative skills.

 With an outstanding personal reputation in the community, I am actively involved in various activities at Huntingdon Presbyterian Church.

 If you can use an experienced customer services professional with excellent written and oral communication skills, I hope you will contact me to suggest a time when we might discuss your needs. I can provide outstanding references from my current employer as well as all previous employers.

Yours sincerely,

Regina McDonald

REGINA McDONALD

1110½ Hay Street, Fayetteville, NC 28305   •   preppub@aol.com   •   (910) 483-6611

OBJECTIVE

I want to contribute to an organization that can make use of an experienced professional with strong accounting, bookkeeping, and administrative skills along with a proven ability to communicate effectively with clients and provide excellent service.

EXPERIENCE

DINING ROOM MANAGER & HOSTESS. Kracker Barrell, Montgomery, AL (2002-present). Have worked "on and off" (on an as-needed basis) for the owners of this 300-seat restaurant for the past 14 years. Currently work 35 hours per week, and provide oversight to 12 employees while assigning sections and handling employee problems. Hire and train employees.

- Although I have become skilled in all aspects of the restaurant business, I am seeking a full-time position outside the restaurant industry which will utilize my accounting and customer relations skills.

ACCOUNTING CLERK, PAYROLL CLERK, & BOOKKEEPER. Whites Slough & Company, Montgomery, AL (1993-2002). Gained extensive expertise in the full accounting cycle using generally accepted accounting principles. Prepared billing for tax services delivered.

- **Payroll:** Calculated and processed payrolls for 120 clients, both large and small companies. Played a key role in developing a system to organize accounts receivable for the payroll processing service.
- **Inventory:** Gained experience in determining and preparing corporate end-of-year inventories.
- **Financial auditing:** Was involved in auditing commercial banks and nonprofit organizations; gained experience in financial auditing.
- **Bookkeeping:** Handled all aspects of 16 monthly bookkeeping accounts; maintained books for restaurants, medical offices, used car dealers, hairdressers, and organizations in other industries. Handled 941 payroll tax liabilities, sales tax liabilities, and payroll tax returns.
- **Tax returns:** Assembled state and federal tax returns for individuals and businesses.
- **Banking:** Prepared bank deposits of up to $190,000 in cash and receipts.
- **Financial statements:** Prepared financial statements, and handled monthly/yearly reconciliations.
- **Accounts payable/receivable:** Prepared accounts receivable/payables for the payroll processing service center.
- **Written and oral communication:** Developed a system to ensure timely mailing of correspondence. Dealt with clients extensively by phone and in person. Handled public relations and client relations.

ACTIVITIES & AFFILIATIONS

Member, Huntingdon Presbyterian Church and Presbyterian Women; Vacation Bible School Teacher; Coordinator of Tuesday Evening "Tuesday Together" Programs; Member of Witness Committee and Christian Education Committee; Member Choir and Praise Choir; Contributed regular weekly article to church newsletter.

EDUCATION

Associate of Applied Science, Business Administration, Faulkner University, Montgomery, AL, 1997. 3.8 GPA. Earned this degree while working full-time.
Completed training programs related to accounting and finance.

COMPUTERS

Experience with software including Excel, Quick Books. Rapidly master new software.

PERSONAL

Highly resourceful problem solver with excellent interpersonal skills. Outstanding reputation.

Flooring company

Date

Exact Name of Person
Title or Position
Name of Company
Address
City, State, Zip

**ADMINISTRATIVE
ASSISTANT and
CUSTOMER SERVICE
REPRESENTATIVE**

Dear Exact Name of Person: (or Dear Sir or Madam if answering a blind ad.)

Can you use an articulate and hard-working young professional who offers well-developed analytical and problem-solving skills along with a strong interest in marketing and business management?

As you will see from my resume, I will be receiving my B.S. in Business Administration with a concentration in Management and a minor in Economics in May. Soon after graduation I plan to move to Colorado and will be available for employment around the end of May.

I am a very self-motivated person who wishes to apply my education, computer skills, and variety of experience to a company in need of someone with my determination and drive to excel.

Having been successful in earning my college degree while financing my education in a variety of jobs, I feel that I possess time management skills and a proven ability to handle pressure.

I am looking forward to your call soon to suggest a time convenient for us to meet to discuss your current and future needs and how I might serve them. Thank you in advance for your time.

Sincerely yours,

Jeanie Creger

JEANIE CREGER

1110½ Hay Street, Fayetteville, NC 28305 • preppub@aol.com • (910) 483-6611

OBJECTIVE	To apply my problem-solving, customer service, and computer skills to an organization that can use my "newly minted" degree in business administration and reputation as a hard-working, dependable young professional.
EDUCATION	**B.S. in Business Administration** with a concentration in **Management** and a minor in **Economics**, West Virginia University, Morgantown, WV, May 2005.
TRAINING	Earned certification in Sign Language, West Virginia University, Morgantown, WV. Was certified in CPR by the American Red Cross, Clarksburg, WV. Received numerous honors at the state Distributive Education Club of America (DECA) convention, May 2002. Won certificates in the areas of Free Enterprise/Economics, Marketing Fundamentals, and Marketing Mathematics.
EXPERIENCE	*Gained practical experience while financing my education and earning a reputation as a very mature and dependable young professional:* **ADMINISTRATIVE ASSISTANT** and **CUSTOMER SERVICE REPRESENTATIVE.** Virginia's Flooring World, Clarksburg, WV (2005-present). Contribute to office operations through my computer and customer service skills while performing internal accounting and data entry, answering phones, taking inventory, and ordering carpet and supplies.

* Handle customer concerns and complaints with maturity which allowed the manager approximately 90% more free time to take care of other matters.
* Gained experience in additional areas including working with customers and other employees while scheduling installations.
* Make bank deposits, run cash registers, and process payments.

RECEPTIONIST and **INSTRUCTOR.** Jenny Craig, Clarksburg, WV (2002-04). Became known for my excellent motivational skills and "upbeat" and positive attitude while working with customers in areas ranging from taking payments, to weighing customers, to filling in as an instructor when needed.

* Applied my attention to detail and knowledge of office operations while preparing bank deposits, controlling inventory, distributing supplies, and preparing daily reports.
* Contributed to customer satisfaction through my "helpful and pleasant" personality.

SALES REPRESENTATIVE. Sears, Clarksburg, WV (2001-02). Became skilled in retail sales while processing transactions and accepting payments.

* Learned to "defuse" upset customers and handle complaints to their satisfaction.

RECEPTIONIST. Geico Insurance, Clarksburg, WV (2000-01). Contributed to the smooth operation of a busy insurance office by answering phones, transferring questions to the proper person, typing forms, and giving price quotes. Gained computer operating skills while learning to manage my time effectively working and attending high school simultaneously.

Highlights of other experience: Learned to work under pressure and within strict time guidelines as an office clerk and assembly line worker.

COMPUTERS	Skilled with Microsoft Word, Excel, PowerPoint. Knowledge of Adobe PageMaker software.
PERSONAL	Possess well-developed analytical and problem-solving skills. Have strong interest in marketing and business management. Am available for relocation.

Real estate firm

Date

Exact Name of Person
Title or Position
Name of Company
Address
City, State, Zip

**APPRAISER and
SALES AGENT**

Dear Exact Name of Person: (or Dear Sir or Madam if answering a blind ad.)

Can you use a mature professional who offers a B.A. in Business Management and experience in real property appraisal as well as a broad background including real estate sales, budgeting, and management?

As you will see from my resume, I am licensed as a Real Estate Salesman in both Idaho and Montana and am presently taking the appraiser course at The University of Montana at Missoula.

In addition to my technical customer support and hardware installation and coordination abilities, I also offer "hands-on" computer operating skills. A fast learner, I am familiar with software including Word, Excel, Access, and software used in the real estate industry.

My base of knowledge related to real estate appraisal, sales, financing and banking is enhanced by my creativity and time management skills. I also offer a proven ability to establish programs and services which increase efficiency and productivity.

I hope you will welcome my call soon to arrange a brief meeting at your convenience to discuss your current and future needs and how I might serve them. Thank you in advance for your time.

Sincerely yours,

Frank Crowley

Alternate last paragraph:
I hope you will call or write soon to suggest a time convenient for us to meet and discuss your current and future needs and how I might serve them. Thank you in advance for your time.

FRANK CROWLEY

1110½ Hay Street, Fayetteville, NC 28305　　•　　preppub@aol.com　　•　　(910) 483-6611

OBJECTIVE　　To contribute to an organization through my attention to detail, problem-solving, customer service, and analytical skills as well as my talent for establishing and reorganizing programs for increased productivity/efficiency.

EDUCATION　　**B.A., Business Management**, The University of Montana, Missoula, MT, 2003.
&　　　　　　　**A.A., Business Management**, The University of Montana, Missoula, MT, 2001.
TRAINING　　Currently attend an appraisal class and have completed course work in banking and finance, The University of Montana, Missoula, MT.
Excelled in numerous company-sponsored training programs in banking and finance, management, computer technology, security, and electronics.

LICENSES　　Licensed in Real Estate Sales by the State of Montana and Idaho.

EXPERIENCE　　**APPRAISER** and **SALES AGENT.** Coldwell Banker and Re/Max Real Estate, Missoula, MT (2004-present). Gained experience in appraising, listing, and selling residential properties with Re/Max and am expanding my experience with Coldwell Banker.

SUPERVISOR, TECHNICAL SUPPORT TEAM. U.S. Logistics Company, Fort Carson, CO (2002-03). For a private contractor, directed a team of specialists locating, removing, inventorying, and preparing classified ammunition supplies being transported to Iraq for use during the War on Terror. Received a special citation for supporting "Operation Iraqi Freedom."

SALES ASSOCIATE. Montana Realty, Missoula, MT (2001-02). Refined my time management skills attending college full time while managing commercial leases, residential real estate sales, and new agent training.
* Increased my knowledge of financing, funding, and purchasing procedures in both commercial and residential transactions. Established a 10-point program covering appraisal training, economic trends, and self-training guidelines.

STUDENT. The University of Montana, Missoula, MT (1998-01). Concentrated my studies in Small Business Management and held leadership roles in campus organizations including Student Council Vice President.
* Received two academic scholarships in Accounting.
* Obtained my Montana Real Estate and "General B" Construction licenses.

PRODUCT SUPPORT ENGINEER. Northwestern Technologies, Missoula, MT (1994-98). Participated in sales presentations, installed and serviced computer systems, and provided training for individuals and corporate users. Organized the redesign and reorganization of a computer site, thereby allowing the company to salvage a major contract.

Highlights of other experience:
* Established a computer service facility and team which is now a profitable full-service operation providing bank in-house/time-sharing support.
* Provided customer service support to computer sites by coordinating PBX switchboard and user terminal connections. Maintained mainframe computers to a 98% "uptime" rate as a Data Systems Technician supervising five people and providing security.
* Gained experience as a Property Manager and Residential Repair Manager.

PERSONAL　　Familiar with software used in the real estate industry. Work well under pressure.

Nonprofit organization

Date

Exact Name of Person
Title or Position
Name of Company
Address
City, State, Zip

Dear Exact Name of Person: (or Dear Sir or Madam if answering a blind ad.)

With the enclosed resume, I would like to make you aware of my interest in the position of Regional Cancer Control Director for the Friends of Cancer Center.

Currently I am excelling as Area Executive Director in Nashville. When I took over this area, community organization had deteriorated to the point that there was no working relationship at all between the Friends of Cancer Center and Nashville Regional Hospital System, one of the largest hospitals in the area. Through revitalization of existing programs, development of new programs, as well as the recruiting, training, and management of volunteers, I was able to restore Nashville Regional Hospital's confidence in the Friends of Cancer Center and we now have a successful partnership. To increase community awareness of the Friends of Cancer Center, I have initiated a number of new programs, including a highly successful **"New Beginning"** program at Nashville, in which 30 program facilitators served the needs of 400 participants in the last year. Through my efforts, revenues from the annual Friends for Life increased from $36,000 in 2003 to $114,000 in 2004. In the rest of Davidson County, the Friends of Cancer Center previously had little presence. I now manage the activities of a team of 30 volunteers whom I recruited and trained to handle fundraising and patient service programs. I established Davidson County's Friends for Life event, raising $40,000 in a county with a population of only 29,000. The **"Road to Recovery"** programs are scheduled to be launched in early 2005.

In addition to my expert knowledge of Friends of Cancer Center programs, I offer the strong management and supervisory skills which this position requires. In a previous management position with a profit-making company subcontracted by municipalities to handle appraisal functions, I handled key management responsibilities and played a significant role in creating, implementing, and executing the company's business plan. A major responsibility of mine involved traveling throughout Tennessee to establish "from scratch" and then manage offices performing the tax appraisals. I hired, trained, and provided oversight for all satellite office employees as I performed liaison with local and state officials.

It is my sincere desire to be of service to the Friends of Cancer Center as Regional Cancer Control Director. Please give me the opportunity to talk with you in person about this position, as I feel certain that I could significantly contribute to the Friends of Cancer Center in this capacity. Thank you in advance for your consideration of my deep desire to serve in a management role.

Sincerely,

Kathleen Williams

KATHLEEN WILLIAMS

1110½ Hay Street, Fayetteville, NC 28305 • preppub@aol.com • (910) 483-6611

OBJECTIVE	To offer my experience in program and project management, my proven leadership and motivational skills, as well as my background in planning and development of Cancer Control programs, fundraising, community organization, and volunteer management.
EDUCATION	**B.S. in Merchandising,** East Tennessee State University, Johnson City, TN, 1995. Through training, have become a Certified Appraiser, Tennessee Department of Revenue.
COMPUTERS	Proficient with Windows XP, HBOC hospital software, and Optika Imaging System.
EXPERIENCE	**AREA EXECUTIVE DIRECTOR.** Friends of Cancer Center, Nashville, TN (2002-present). Took over as Executive Director for this area at a time when many activities and tasks were in disarray; through careful management of programs and services, was able to quickly revitalize and restore confidence in the local Friends of Cancer Center. Direct activities of over 150 volunteers in this three-county area, aggressively directing fundraising efforts and handling staffing for patient services, projects, and events.

- Raised nearly $218,000 in 2004, an increase of almost $80,000 over 2003; increased **Friends for Life** income in Nashville dramatically, from $36,000 in 2003 to $114,000 in 2004; rebuilt the Friends of Cancer Center's relationship with Nashville Regional Hospital System which had broken down completely before I took over.
- Established the Friends of Cancer Center presence in Davidson County, developing relationships with the local health department; recruited, trained, and currently manage 30 volunteers; organized within the community to build a solid, capable team in a county with little previous Friends of Cancer Center representation; through my initiative, contributions skyrocketed to 100 times the previous year's level; raised $40,000 in the county.
- Retrained volunteers and am working to rebuild relationships with Nashville Providence Hospital and the medical community; am finalizing plans to implement the following new programs in Nashville: **Lung Cancer Support Group, Road to Recovery.**
- Strengthened existing patient services programs and implemented new ones.
- Completed "**Make Yours a New Beginning Family**" Facilitator Training, 2004.

PATIENT ACCOUNTS REPRESENTATIVE. Nashville Regional Hospital, Nashville, TN (2002). Performed a variety of financial, administrative, and clerical services for patients at this busy medical center; performed follow-up and collections on all self-pay accounts.
- Handled patient complaints, collected past due accounts, filed insurance claims.

MANAGER & COMPUTER SPECIALIST. Copland Services, Nashville, TN (1997-2001). For a company which was subcontracted by counties and municipalities to perform property appraisals, handled key management responsibilities which involved establishing and managing offices throughout Tennessee to perform subcontracted appraisal functions.
- Hired and trained all office employees and functioned as the liaison with corporate officers, computer programmers, as well as officials from state and local governments.
- Interviewed, hired, trained, and supervised as many as 25 data entry clerks.

AFFILIATIONS	Member of Tennessee Association of Volunteer Administrators, Nashville Chamber of Commerce, Cancer Committee at Tennessee Regional Hospital, and Cancer Campaign Committee of the Davidson County Health Department.
PERSONAL	Excellent personal/professional references available. Known for strong personal initiative.

Nonprofit organization

Date

Exact Name of Person
Title or Position
Name of Company
Address
City, State, Zip

ASSISTANT DIRECTOR OF CUSTOMER SERVICE

Dear Exact Name of Person: (or Dear Sir or Madam if answering a blind ad.)

I would appreciate an opportunity to talk with you soon about how I could apply my managerial and administrative skills refined as a U.S. Air Force officer to benefit your organization.

I offer a reputation as a professional who thrives on challenge. I am especially skilled at motivating employees by making their work challenging, using a "hands-on" approach to inspire their dedication. Offering outstanding analytical, problem-solving, and organizational abilities, I am adept at finding areas needing improvement and creating solutions that work.

As you will see by my resume, I am experienced in working in international settings and have a great deal of experience in coordinating with other military services and government agencies to ensure adequate availability of supplies and equipment, negotiating contracts, and overseeing the design and construction of new facilities and renovation of existing ones.

I hope you will welcome my call soon to arrange a brief meeting at your convenience to discuss your current and future needs and how I might serve them. Thank you in advance for your time.

Sincerely yours,

Kyle Whitney

Alternate last paragraph:
I hope you will call or write soon to suggest a time convenient for us to meet and discuss your current and future needs and how I might serve them. Thank you in advance for your time.

KYLE WHITNEY

1110½ Hay Street, Fayetteville, NC 28305 • preppub@aol.com • (910) 483-6611

OBJECTIVE
To contribute my management skills to an organization that can use an energetic and articulate professional who specializes in advising and leading employees, researching and analyzing problems, and developing workable solutions.

EDUCATION
M.A., Management, Johns Hopkins University, Baltimore, MD, 2005.
* Completed specialized management courses including the following:
  group behavior and processes   organizational behavior and leadership
  developing and managing human resources   facility design management
  ethical and legal issues in management

B.S., Physical Education, Westminster College of Salt Lake City, UT, 1996.
* Coached 30 players over a two-year period as the Assistant Coach for the university's women's varsity basketball team which became the division champion two years.
* Received an Award of Merit and was named to the National Dean's List in 1996.
* Was elected president of the Physical Education Majors Club from 1994-96.

EXPERIENCE
ASSISTANT DIRECTOR OF CUSTOMER SERVICE. U.S. Air Force, Andrews AFB, MD (2005-present). As the "second-in-command" of a support services organization, provided leadership during a period of unusual activity surrounding preparations for closing down the base. Managed 86 employees and three budgets totaling approximately $2.3 million.
* Provided housing, meals, linens, and furniture for the entire military community.
* Contributed quality assurance expertise by evaluating requisition requests, voucher orders, contract disputes, and budget projections/submissions.

CHIEF OF SERVICES DIVISION. U.S. Air Force, Andrews AFB, MD (2004-05). Controlled a $394,000 annual budget and directed 32 employees in an operations services center which supported 850 people with two dining facilities and eight dormitories.
* Managed procurement of all equipment and supplies for an isolated community.
* Developed and implemented the standard operating procedures for the center.

ASSISTANT DIRECTOR OF RECREATION AND HOUSING. U.S. Air Force, Hill AFB, UT (2001-03). Administered a $6.5 million annual budget used to provide 363 military personnel and their family members with 21 separate types of support services; reviewed construction designs.
* Received a prestigious trophy for managing "the Air Force's best food service program."
* Improved procedures and ensured compliance with established government standards.
* Handpicked to take over an officer's club with a reputation for poor service, "turned around" the facility by solving personnel problems and improving physical surroundings.

OPERATIONS SUPPORT MANAGER. U.S. Air Force, Spain (1999-01). As "second-in-command" of a 247-employee company, controlled a $980,000 annual budget as well as recruiting, hiring, and releasing a large work force of civilians.
* Provided quality assurance expertise for a supply exchange program.

FOOD SERVICES MANAGER. U.S. Air Force, Charleston AFB, SC (1997-99). Provided supervision for 75 employees and management of six separate food preparation facilities as well as quality assurance expertise for employee contracts.

PERSONAL
Thrive on challenge. Have a Secret security clearance. Earned recognition for humanitarian service while assisting in rescuing a drowning person in Iceland.

Sales and retailing

Date

Exact Name of Person
Title or Position
Name of Company
Address
City, State, Zip

ASSISTANT MANAGER

Dear Exact Name of Person: (or Dear Sir or Madam if answering a blind ad.)

With the enclosed resume, I would like to make you aware of my interest in exploring employment opportunities with your organization.

As you will see from my enclosed resume, I offer extensive experience in outside sales and sales management. After earning my B.A. degree in history, I became employed with the largest manufacturers of atomizers (spray pumps) in the world, and I served with distinction as Customer Service Representative. While managing an outside sales force, I simultaneously handled most of the company's largest accounts. I consistently produced outstanding results through my ability to resourcefully solve problems, forge strong customer relationships, and assure quality performance.

During my career in sales, I have come to believe that personality is critical to the selling process, and I offer an enthusiastic and outgoing personality that is well suited to sales. With a reputation as an aggressive prospector and cold caller, I once transformed a territory in which there was no name brand recognition of my employer's products into an intensely brand loyal area.

In 2002 I decided to make a lifestyle change and relocated from Hawaii to Maine. In my most recent job I applied my strong management skills in reducing shrinkage, increasing gross profit margin, and boosting weekly sales. My most recent position was outside the sales arena, however, and I missed the challenge and excitement of sales.

I am selectively exploring opportunities with companies that can use a dynamic sales professional with the proven ability to establish new accounts, transform ailing territories into profitable areas, and satisfy customer needs while respecting the company's bottom-line needs. If you can use a proven sales producer, I hope you will contact me to suggest a time when we might meet to discuss your needs.

Yours sincerely,

Stephen Johnston

STEPHEN JOHNSTON

1110½ Hay Street, Fayetteville, NC 28305 • preppub@aol.com • (910) 483-6611

OBJECTIVE

To contribute to an organization that can use an accomplished sales professional who offers a proven ability to establish strong working relationships and cement customer loyalty through my extensive experience in problem solving, customer service, and employee training.

EXPERIENCE

ASSISTANT MANAGER. Market Basket, Bangor, ME (2004-present). Was promoted quickly to Assistant Manager and Acting Department Manager after my superior management results; reduced shrinkage by 20%, increased gross profit margin, and boosted overall weekly sales average of $1,500-$2,000.
- Demonstrated my ability to enter a new industry and rapidly master the techniques required for business success. Earned respect for my strong customer service orientation and quality control emphasis.
- Am resigning from this position because I decided that I wanted to return to a career in sales rather than make my professional home in the grocery industry.

OUTSIDE SALES REPRESENTATIVE. Plastics, Inc., Bangor, ME (2002-04). After deciding to make a lifestyle change that involved relocating to Bangor, ME, was recruited by a distributor of plastic packaging components because of my extensive expertise related to both outside sales and the packaging industry. Increased sales throughout the state while expertly representing plastic bottles, closures, spray pumps, and silk screening.

OUTSIDE SALES REPRESENTATIVE. Rainier Corporation, Wailuku, HI (1999-02). Because of my outstanding reputation in the packaging industry, was recruited by a company which is one of the largest plastic manufacturers/distributors of plastic containers in South Pacific.
- Aggressively opened up new accounts; established more than 50 new accounts.
- Became widely acknowledged as the top customer service professional in the company.
- Because of my skill in cold calls and prospecting, became the company's #1 sales person within two years while producing more than $15 million in sales. Transformed a region which had little knowledge of my employer or its products into an intensely brand loyal area. Handled some of the company's largest accounts; some companies bought ½ million spray pumps every few months, and it took constant attention to the customers' needs to maintain the clients' loyalty in a highly competitive marketplace.

CUSTOMER SERVICE REPRESENTATIVE. Pearson, Ltd., Wailuku, HI (1988-99). Managed an outside sales force of four sales professionals for the largest manufacturer of atomizers (spray pumps) in the world.
- Created friendly relationships with the staff at Mary Kay; cemented intense customer loyalty. Recruited, hired, trained, motivated, and developed sales professionals.
- Managed customer orders through the production phase.
- Continuously solved problems related to production and inventory control levels while personally handling multimillion-dollar accounts of companies.
- Handled eight of the company's top ten accounts, and produced outside bottom-line results through my ability to solve problems, satisfy customers, and tailor corporate resources to customer needs.

EDUCATION

Bachelor of Arts (B.A.) in History, Wailuku Community College, HI, 1988.
Extensive training related to sales, sales management, production operations, quality control.

PERSONAL

Can provide outstanding references on request. Positive, enthusiastic individual.

Recreation services

Date

Exact Name of Person
Title or Position
Name of Company
Address
City, State, Zip

ASSISTANT MANAGER,
RECREATION CENTER

Dear Exact Name of Person: (or Dear Sir or Madam if answering a blind ad.)

With the enclosed resume, I would like to introduce myself and the experience I offer related to project management, operations management, and service operations management.

As you will see from my resume, I have excelled as an Assistant Manager in a nonprofit organization which provides food service and recreational programs as part of an effort to enhance employee morale. With my current employer, I began in an entry-level position and was promoted to handle a variety of management responsibilities. I have been involved in employee hiring, training, and evaluation for a seven-day-a-week snack bar as well as a bowling alley. In addition to controlling inventory, I play a key role in budget preparation and budget management, and I have earned respect for my resourcefulness and bottom-line orientation.

On my own initiative, I have organized a variety of special projects and events which included birthday parties, anniversary celebrations, history celebrations and events, Christmas and Hanukkah parties, and other such projects. The emphasis throughout each project was on careful planning, preparation, and follow through while providing outstanding customer service.

The organization I work for conducts continuous customer evaluations of the services we provide, and I have been singled out by name on numerous evaluations because of my gracious style of interacting with the public. I can provide excellent personal and professional references.

Please be assured that I am ready to travel or work whatever hours your needs require. I hope you will contact me if my considerable skills and talents interest you.

Sincerely,

John O'Sullivan

JOHN O'SULLIVAN

1110½ Hay Street, Fayetteville, NC 28305   •   preppub@aol.com   •   (910) 483-6611

OBJECTIVE   I want to contribute to an organization that can use a skilled operations manager who is known for my attention to detail in inventory control and budgeting as well as for my dedication to the highest standards of quality control, customer service, and profitability.

EDUCATION   Pursuing **Bachelor's degree in Business** in my spare time; have completed courses at Jefferson Community College, Watertown, NY; degree anticipated 2006.
Completed courses sponsored by my employers in these and other areas:

Operations Management	Quality Control	Customer Service
Restaurant Management	Catering	Snack Bar Management

EXPERIENCE   **ASSISTANT MANAGER.** Recreation Center, Fort Drum, NY (2001-present). Manage popular services sponsored by the Department of the Army; act as the Assistant Manager of two key operations and routinely manage them with little to no supervision.

- **Employee training and hiring**: In charge of interviewing, training, and supervising new employees.
- **Operations management**: Manage operations of a bowling alley and a seven-day-a-week snack bar.
- **Financial control:** Provide vital input into budgets for both the bowling alley and the snack bar; play a key role in raising profits, reducing expenses, and establishing new controls for inventory in both service operations.
- **Food service management:** Operate a popular facility which maintains operating hours of 11 am-11 pm; I personally arrive at the facility at 7 am in order to examine inventory, determine which items needed to be ordered, and handle the bookkeeping and other paperwork. The snack bar serves pizzas, burgers, hot dogs, chicken, turkey, and other items to as many as 1,000 customers daily.
- **Bowling center management**: Manage all aspects of a 10-lane bowling alley which is a chief form of entertainment for residents of this 5,000-person military community.
- **Events management:** Organize and manage a wide variety of special projects and events which include:

Birthday parties	Anniversary parties	Black history celebrations
Christmas parties	Hanukkah parties	Native American history events

- **Computer operations:** Utilize a computer to input data and maintain records; use software including Microsoft Word, Excel, and Access.
- **Performance evaluations:** Always receive the highest evaluations of my performance in every measured area. Was commended as a very hard worker who set the standard for others and cited for my strong communication skills and ability to relate effectively to customers, employees, and supervisors. Received many citations and awards for outstanding performance.

Experience in high school:
WAREHOUSEMAN. Commissary, Fort Drum, NY (1999-01). Worked up to 30 hours a week after school and on weekends during my junior and senior year of high school.

- Learned to perform nearly every job in a warehouse, and was the only man who worked in the facility; performed a variety of heavy lifting of products such as televisions.
- Became knowledgeable of the basics of stock control and warehouse management.

PERSONAL   Have a strong work ethic and thrive on helping an activity reach its full potential in terms of customer service and profitability. Am known for my reliability and punctuality. Can provide excellent personal and professional references.

Pawn shop/retail store

Date

Exact Name of Person
Title or Position
Name of Company
Address
City, State, Zip

ASSISTANT MANAGER, SALES ASSOCIATE and LOAN SPECIALIST

Dear Exact Name of Person: (or Dear Sir or Madam if answering a blind ad.)

I would appreciate an opportunity to talk with you soon about how I could contribute to your organization through my education in business management along with the natural leadership skills I have refined as a scholar-athlete experienced in customer service and sales.

While attending Faulkner University in Montgomery, AL, I received numerous honors for both my skills as a baseball player and as a scholar while earning a B.B.A. degree in Business Management. I am proud of being selected as the captain of the baseball team my senior year and feel that I was singled out for this role because of my leadership, maturity, and responsible attitude both in the classroom and on the field. As you will see by my resume, these qualities also resulted in my selection for all-conference and all-region honors as well as for NCAA Division III Academic All-American status.

You would find me to be an intelligent and articulate young professional, known for my maturity and dedication to excellence. I am certain that I am capable of meeting the challenges of assuming managerial roles where I could make important contributions to a company's bottom line and continual high quality customer service. With my enthusiasm, motivational abilities, empathy, and compassion for others I can make valuable contributions to an organization that seeks a professional with these qualities.

I hope you will welcome my call soon to arrange a brief meeting at your convenience to discuss your current and future needs and how I might serve them. Thank you in advance for your time.

Sincerely yours,

Richard Peterson

Alternate last paragraph:
I hope you will call or write me soon to suggest a time convenient for us to meet and discuss your current and future needs and how I might serve them. Thank you in advance for your time.

RICHARD PETERSON

1110½ Hay Street, Fayetteville, NC 28305 • preppub@aol.com • (910) 483-6611

OBJECTIVE

To benefit an organization that can use an intelligent and articulate young professional who offers a background of excellent performance combining practical planning, customer service, and sales experience with a background as an award-winning scholar-athlete.

EDUCATION

B.B.A. in Business Management, Faulkner University, Montgomery, AL, 2004.
- Earned numerous athletic and scholastic honors including:
  was named captain of the varsity men's baseball team, 2003-04
  placed on the all-conference team — two seasons
  was named to the NCAA Division III All-Region team — two seasons
  became a baseball Academic All-American in recognition of my above-average GPA while participating in varsity sports, 2002-03
  was Honorable Mention on the All-American baseball team

A.A. in General Studies, Troy State University, Montgomery, AL, 2002.
- Excelled as a member of the college's varsity baseball team.
- Placed on the Dean's List for my high GPA.

EXPERIENCE

Refined my managerial, sales, and customer service abilities in the following full-time and summer jobs:

ASSISTANT MANAGER, SALES ASSOCIATE and **LOAN SPECIALIST.** Birmingham Pawn, Birmingham, AL (2005-present). In mid-February 2005, was selected for promotion to Assistant Manager, and am now in charge of three people; was groomed for rapid advancement based on my skill in providing excellent customer service which ensured repeat business.
- Achieved the level of top salesman for the month in only my second month with the company — sold more than $7,000 worth of merchandise.
- Learned to accurately judge the value of items brought in and determine how much could be paid for them and still make an accurate profit.
- Was cited as a key player in the 61% profit margin for that month.
- Became skilled in making decisions on what items such as TVs, jewelry, guns, and stereo systems were worth.
- Became familiar with time-saving methods for using computers to track and search for inventory.

WAITER and **CUSTOMER SERVICE SPECIALIST.** Corner Stop Coffee & Deli, Montgomery, AL (2004-05). Gained insight into the value of providing courteous customer service while seating and waiting on people of all ages and social backgrounds in this resort-town restaurant.

WAREHOUSE WORKER and **DRIVER.** Dickinson Supply Parts, Co., Montgomery, AL (2004). Learned the value of planning and using time wisely while pulling orders together and delivering them as quickly as possible.

SHIPPING CLERK. Alabama United School Supply, Co., Montgomery, AL (2003). Earned a reputation as a conscientious worker while coordinating orders and seeing that they were complete and accurate along with ensuring that they went out on time.

PERSONAL

Am a natural leader who is effective at guiding and teaching others. Have excellent time management skills. Will travel. Will relocate.

Banking services

Date

Exact Name of Person
Title or Position
Name of Company
Address
City, State, Zip

ASSISTANT VICE PRESIDENT & BRANCH OPERATIONS MANAGER

Dear Exact Name of Person: (or Dear Sir or Madam if answering a blind ad.)

With the enclosed resume, I would like to make you aware of my interest in the position of Assistant to the City Manager for Customer Focus and also make you aware of my strong background related to this position.

As you will see from my resume, I am currently excelling as an Assistant Vice President and Branch Operations Manager. Banking is an intensely customer-oriented environment and this "customer focus" is the part of my job which I enjoy tremendously. I have trained many individuals in the bank in customer service skills, and I am continuously playing a key role in strengthening the bank's customer focus. Respected for my visionary thinking as well as for my organizational skills and ability to lead others in working together, I was named the bank's Team Leader.

Serving customers and assuring customer satisfaction has been a key responsibility in every job I have held. As a Director of Operations prior to my current job, I was constantly involved in problem solving, and I was instrumental in resolving a payroll tax issue which helped the company win $17,000. In a prior track record of accomplishment with Wells Fargo Bank, I managed a high-profile branch of a $39 million bank holding company in an extremely competitive environment. I motivated staff members to achieve the highest levels of customer service, and I conducted Customer Service seminars for all Western Region offices. I was extensively involved in public relations and community service, and I played a role in numerous community and civic organizations.

I have come to believe that customer service and "customer focus" is an attitude, and I am positive that I have the attitude you are seeking in addition to extensive professional experience in this area. Even in my leisure time, I am constantly trying to make the world a better place for consumers. For example, I along with others in the Seattle community recently founded the Pacific Club of the northwestern region, and I am a charter member and a member of the board of directors of that organization.

I truly feel it would be an honor to assist the city of Seattle in strengthening its customer focus, and I would appreciate an opportunity to talk with you in person about my experience related to this position.

Yours sincerely,

Rochelle Dannon

ROCHELLE DANNON

1110½ Hay Street, Fayetteville, NC 28305 • preppub@aol.com • (910) 483-6611

OBJECTIVE   To contribute my versatile management, marketing and sales, community and public relations, and finance and accounting skills to an organization in need of a talented professional dedicated to excellence.

EDUCATION   **B.S., History and Political Science,** Seattle Pacific University, Seattle, WA. Completed numerous courses in customer relations, human resources, finance, and management.

EXPERIENCE   **ASSISTANT VICE PRESIDENT & BRANCH OPERATIONS MANAGER.** National Bank of Washington, Seattle, WA (2004-present). Began as a Management Assistant and was promoted in March 2005; supervise two Customer Service Representatives and four tellers.
- Am respected for my visionary thinking and problem-solving while working in this environment with a strong customer focus; am highly skilled in all aspects of customer relations and customer problem solving.
- Was selected in 2005 as the bank's Team Leader; was handpicked for this job because of my strong organizational skills and ability to work well with others.

DIRECTOR OF OPERATIONS. Puget & Associates, Seattle, WA (1999-04). Managed the accounting office consisting of the office manager and accounting clerks for an organization which served as an intermediary care facility for the mentally challenged.
- Along with a contracted CPA, prepared budgets, financial records, and reports; facilitated the preparation of the annual on-site audit reviews by state regulators; defended an audit and then recovered $240,000.
- Resolved a payroll tax issue and submitted a well-written appeal to a federal agent which won us a waiver of $17,000 in penalty and interests.
- Prepared internal documentation for the annual submission of state-required cost reports; served as the administrator of the company's health insurance and dental plan, and managed the company's workers compensation program.
- Negotiated agreements, contracts, purchase commitments, and expenditures in accordance with the budget and state Medicaid program.

ASSISTANT VICE PRESIDENT and **BRANCH MANAGER.** Wells Fargo Bank, Seattle, WA (1986-99). Advanced to the position of Assistant Vice President and Branch Manager after excelling as a Customer Liaison, then Branch Officer, and then Customer Service Manager in the Executive Inquiry Unit while refining skills in many areas:
- Managed a high profile branch of a $39 million bank holding company, the largest in Pacific Northwest, in an extremely competitive market.
- Directed branch operations including business development for retail and commercial accounts, staffing, security, and compliance with state/federal regulations.
- Developed strong local ties between the branch office and the business community.
- Actively participated in community-sponsored projects and organizations to maintain high visibility and provide an example of good corporate citizenship.
- Successfully maintained customer confidence and trust during an adverse public relations incident through pro-active communications efforts.
- Motivated staff to achieve high levels of customer service and satisfaction; conducted Customer Service Seminars to all Western Region offices.

PERSONAL   Am a charter member and member of the board of directors of the Pacific Club of the northwestern region. Past member of Rotary and the Chamber of Commerce. Served as Public Relations Director for Seattle Bankers Forum. Outstanding decision maker.

Automobile insurance adjusting

Date

Exact Name of Person
Title or Position
Name of Company
Address
City, State, Zip

**AUTO DAMAGE
ADJUSTER**

Dear Exact Name of Person: (or Dear Sir or Madam if answering a blind ad.)

I would appreciate an opportunity to talk with you soon about how I could contribute to your organization through my expertise as an automobile damage adjuster.

As you will note on my resume, I am working for the Allstate Insurance Company and was instrumental in helping the company develop territories throughout New Jersey prior to being transferred to South Carolina in 2002. As the first adjuster sent into South Carolina, I opened the Florence office, which now includes two drive-in locations as well as a guaranteed repair shop which I monitor while also averaging up to 125 claims monthly as the only Allstate adjuster within a 50-mile area.

In previous assignments with Allstate, I was instrumental in training new adjusters, and I am proud to have played a key role in developing some of the industry's most capable appraisers. I offer a reputation for unquestioned honesty, high productivity, strong negotiating skills, and technical knowledge.

I am highly regarded within the Allstate organization and can offer outstanding personal and professional references not only from Allstate but also from satisfied customers, regulators, and others with whom I have worked. Although my future within Allstate is very secure, I am writing to you because I am aware of your company's fine reputation and believe there might be a good fit between your strategic goals and my extensive expertise.

I hope you will call or write me soon to suggest a time convenient for us to meet and discuss your current and future needs and how I might serve them. Thank you in advance for you time.

Sincerely yours,

Richard C. MacDuff

Alternate last paragraph:
I hope you will welcome my call soon to arrange a brief meeting at your convenience to discuss your current and future needs and how I might serve them. Thank you in advance for your time.

RICHARD C. MacDUFF

1110½ Hay Street, Fayetteville, NC 28305 • preppub@aol.com • (910) 483-6611

OBJECTIVE   To benefit a company that can use an expert automobile appraiser and licensed insurance adjuster who offers a proven commitment to outstanding customer service along with a reputation for unquestioned honesty, strong negotiating skills, and technical knowledge.

LICENSE   Licensed by the state of South Carolina as an Auto Damage Adjuster and Auto Appraiser.
- Was previously licensed in New Jersey as an Automobile Damage Adjuster/Appraiser.
- Hold a valid South Carolina Driver's License with a violation-free record.

EXPERIENCE   **AUTO DAMAGE ADJUSTER.** Allstate Insurance Company, Florence, SC (2002-present) and New Jersey State (2000-01). Began with Allstate as a part-time security guard on weekends, and was offered a chance to train as an adjuster; excelled in all schools and training programs, and have exceeded corporate goals in every job I have held within Allstate.
- *2002-present*: Am the first adjuster sent into South Carolina, and have played a key role in implementing the company's strategic plan to do more business inland selling auto policies; in a highly competitive market, opened the Florence office "from scratch," which now includes two drive-in locations as well as a guaranteed repair shop which I monitor while averaging 100-125 claims monthly as the only adjuster within a 50-mile area.
- *2000-01:* After initial training as an adjuster, worked in Jersey City and Trenton, NJ: averaged five claims per day while helping the company earn a reputation for outstanding customer service.
- Relocated to Newark, where I trained new adjusters.
- Worked in Wainscot County, a huge territory 30 miles wide and 100 miles long, where I made a significant contribution to building the territory; when I left as the only adjuster in Wainscot County, I was replaced with four adjusters in this rapidly expanding territory where I had helped Allstate earn a name for excellent service.
- Built a six-adjuster territory into a 14-adjuster territory in Somerville.

Technical knowledge: Skilled at utilizing Mitchell Estimate Systems and CCC Total Loss Evaluation as well as guidebooks, including NADA and the Red Book; routinely use equipment including a CRT and personal computer.
- Known for my excellent negotiating skills and ability to settle claims quickly and fairly.
- In the Florence area, have improved customer relations and reduced loss ratio 15%.
- Skilled at evaluating total losses, coordinating removal of salvage, and handling motor vehicle titles.

Other experience:
AUTO & FURNITURE UPHOLSTERER. Unique Furniture of Trenton, Trenton, NJ (1990-99). Worked in upholstery of auto seats, vinyl tops, convertible tops, and interior trim while customizing automobile and boat interiors.
NAVAL PETTY OFFICER. (1985-89). After joining the Navy, advanced rapidly through the ranks to E-5 in four years while managing people as well as inventories of ammunition, missiles, and nuclear fuel; was strongly urged to make a career out of the Navy.

EDUCATION & TRAINING   Completed college course work in Business Administration and Management, Mercer County Community College, Trenton, NJ, 1990-92.

Completed technical training in Risk & Insurance and Insurance Law as well as numerous courses conducted by companies such as General Motors and Honda pertaining to refinishing, principles of four-wheel steering, transmission repair, computer operation, and other areas.

PERSONAL   Offer an unusual combination of exceptional organizational and communication skills.

Automotive financing services

Date

Exact Name of Person
Title or Position
Name of Company
Address
City, State, Zip

AUTOMOTIVE BUSINESS MANAGER

The cover letter is designed to be versatile, so that she can explore employment options inside and outside the auto industry.

Dear Exact Name of Person: (or Dear Sir or Madam if answering a blind ad.)

With the enclosed resume, I would like to make you aware of my interest in exploring employment opportunities with your organization. As you will see from my resume, I have worked as a Business Manager for the past five years, and I am held in the highest regard by my current employer. I can provide outstanding references at the appropriate time, but I would ask that you not contact my current employer until after we speak.

I give credit for much of my success as a Business Manager to the outstanding training I received in my first job as an Assistant Business Manager. From there, I was recruited for my first full-time job as a Business Manager, and in that job I negotiated and closed more than 80 contracts monthly while single-handedly managing my employer's finance and insurance business. In my current position, I am one of three full-time Business Managers, and I consistently lead the other managers in the amount of income generated.

I am committed to excellence in all I do, and that is why I worked hard to earn my C.B.I.F. Certification which designates me as a certified member of the Connecticut Board of Insurance and Finance. I am skilled at negotiating the details of loan closings, and I have become skilled in selling extended warranties, life insurance, total loss protection, accident and health protection, and other products. My customers know that my concern for their well-being is genuine, and I derive one of my greatest satisfactions in life from creating happy customers.

I am an outgoing individual who is known for my cheerful disposition as well as my reputation as a congenial coworker. I pride myself on my ability to establish warm working relationships with sales professionals and customers as well as with government agencies and business organizations. I believe my attention to detail and commitment to excellence in all I do are qualities transferable to any industry.

If you are interested in discussing the possibility of joining your organization, I hope you will contact me to suggest a time when we might meet in person.

Yours sincerely,

Miriam Nicholls

MIRIAM NICHOLLS

1110½ Hay Street, Fayetteville, NC 28305 • preppub@aol.com • (910) 483-6611

OBJECTIVE

I want to contribute to an organization that can use an experienced and hard-working young business manager who offers a proven ability to increase profit, satisfy customers, sell and explain financial services, and establish congenial working relationships with others.

EDUCATION

Bachelor of Arts Degree in Communicative Arts and Literature, Eastern Connecticut State University, Willimantic CT, 1999.

CERTIFICATION & TRAINING

C.B.I.F. Certified by the Connecticut Board of Insurance and Finance, 2000.
Certified Notary Public.
Completed numerous training programs related to areas including Marketing Concepts, Business Management, Principles of Loans and Finance, Automobile Financing, Extended Warranty Protection, Life Insurance, Total Loss Protection, and Accident/ Health Insurance.

EXPERIENCE

Have derived great satisfaction in life from establishing strong customer relationships and by helping customers finance and protect one of the largest purchases in their lives:
BUSINESS MANAGER. Ed Vader Cadillac, Inc., Hamden, CT (2005-present). Was recruited for this position because of my strong industry reputation. Have consistently achieved the highest "Sales Per Vehicle" income of the three business managers at this auto dealership.

- Assist customers in obtaining credit approval for vehicle purchases; work closely with loan officers at financial institutions. Determine various rate structures which balance consumer needs and company profit goals.
- At the closing of the loan, I achieve additional profit for the dealership of $45,000-$75,000 monthly by selling "add-on" products such as extended service contracts, warranties, total loss protection, and other services which protect the consumer's investment.
- Complete and turn the Department of Motor Vehicles (DMV) and insurance paperwork.
- Have established an atmosphere of "friendly competition" with the other two business managers which has led to a significant increase in finance and insurance income.

BUSINESS MANAGER. Taylor Toyota Dealers of Hamden, Hamden, CT (2001-04). Was specially recruited to become this established Toyota dealership's first full-time Business Manager; produced a significant increase in finance and insurance income through my ability to close the sale and satisfy customers.

- Established cordial working relationships with the dealership's 6-8 sales representatives.
- Became known for my skill in accurately and quickly completing detailed paperwork for financial institutions, DMV, and other organizations. While working as the dealership's only Business Manager, became skilled in multi-tasking.

ASSISTANT BUSINESS MANAGER. New Haven Chrysler/Dodge, New Haven, CT (1999-01). In my first job in the car business, was trained in every aspect of automobile financing and related insurance sales. Was trained by an outstanding industry professional in the importance of preparing perfect paperwork. I believe my subsequent success as a Business Manager was due to the excellent training I received in this job.

ADVERTISING REPRESENTATIVE. New Trends Enterprises, Willimantic, CT (1996-99). In my first job after graduating from college, created effective advertisements for customers who included middle schools, local hotels, and businesses.

- Was the company's first advertising representative, and boosted sales significantly.

PERSONAL

Outstanding references. Strong computer skills including experience with Word.

Restaurant services

Date

Exact Name of Person
Title or Position
Name of Company
Address
City, State, Zip

Dear Exact Name of Person: (or Dear Sir or Madam if answering a blind ad.)

With the enclosed resume, I would like to express my interest in the position of Customer Service Specialist currently available in the Spokane area.

As you will see from my resume, I have excelled in a track record of promotion within the Safeway organization. I began in a part-time Cashier position and was quickly noticed for my strong customer service and communication skills. I was promoted to Office Assistant in a 100-employee store with a weekly volume of $250,000 to $300,000.

I was then promoted to my current position as sole Bookkeeper in a different store, and I am totally responsible for 30 front-end employees. While functioning as acting Customer Service Manager, I have trained cashiers and baggers in effective customer service and cash handling techniques, and I have become skilled at applying Effective Scheduling (ES) techniques in a low-volume environment. On my own initiative, I have developed procedures and shortcuts approved by management which have boosted efficiency and productivity. On a routine basis, I apply my strong analytical and problem-solving skills in finding and correcting money losses.

I would like to make you aware of the fact that my husband is a Safeway Assistant Manager, and we are particularly interested in transferring to the Spokane area because we have family in that area. I am aware that the position requires frequent travel including overnight and weekend travel, and I would welcome the opportunity to travel as the job requires. I am a versatile, outgoing, and adaptable professional who easily masters new tasks and enjoys training others.

If you can use a customer service professional with a solid understanding of cash, customer service, and front-end procedures within the Safeway environment, I hope you will contact me soon to suggest a time when we might discuss this position. I can provide excellent professional and personal recommendations from Area Supervisor Clifford Moser and other Safeway supervisory personnel who know of my strong personal initiative and resourcefulness. Thank you in advance for your time.

Sincerely,

Veronica Andrews

VERONICA ANDREWS

1110½ Hay Street, Fayetteville, NC 28305 • preppub@aol.com • (910) 483-6611

OBJECTIVE   To benefit the Safeway organization as a Customer Service Specialist in Spokane. I offer strong communication and organizational skills along with a background in the Safeway organization including experience as a Bookkeeper and Acting Customer Service Manager.

EDUCATION   Received high school diploma; Chinook Senior High School and Seattle Community College. Extensive hands-on and formal training in the grocery industry and the Safeway organization related to check-cashing and store-closing operations, customer service, other areas.

EXPERIENCE   *Have been promoted in the following track record of promotion within the Safeway company:*
BOOKKEEPER & ACTING CUSTOMER SERVICE MANAGER. Denny Way store #483, Seattle, WA (2005-present). Manage 30 front-end employees including cashiers and baggers; hire, train, schedule, counsel, and evaluate front-end employees and terminate them as necessary.
- Utilize ISAA and ISC computer on a daily basis.
- As the sole Bookkeeper for a low-volume store with sales of up to $145,000 weekly, have become skilled at finding money losses through my resourcefulness and analytical skills.
- Maintain control of cash flow; apply Safeway's principles of Effective Scheduling (ES) in prudent and resourceful ways. Make bank deposits; verify the accuracy of deposits made by assistants.
- Maintain logs on all front-end employees. Perform test checks; count tills; perform daily store closing.
- Have become skilled at applying ES in this low-volume environment, and on my own initiative have developed procedures and shortcuts approved by management which have boosted efficiency and productivity.
- Have been commended for my tact and poise in training and supervising others while handling the sole responsibility for front-end employees; take pride in the fact that I have trained many front-end employees to refine their customer service skills.

OFFICE ASSISTANT. Elliott Avenue store #6611, Seattle, WA (2004-05). Became known for my outstanding customer service skills in this 100-employee store with a weekly volume of $250,000 to $300,000.
- Supervised the front-end at night; oversaw lunchtime scheduling; maintained the front-end operation and trained cashiers and baggers in cash control and customer service.
- On my own initiative, developed and implemented the concept of safe count sheets and a weekly procedures checklist which led to improved performance of front-end employees.

CASHIER. Elliott Avenue store #6611, Seattle, WA (2004). In this part-time job at which I worked simultaneously with the job below, quickly distinguished myself on the basis of my exemplary attitude and superior customer service techniques. Was offered a full-time position to Office Assistant.
- Became skilled at solving problems quickly as I found missing items and performed operations related to misplaced items; learned how to efficiently block and clean the front end. Was offered exceptionally rapid promotion because of my management ability.

MANAGER TRAINEE. Blockbuster Video, Seattle, WA (2003). Began as an entry-level employee and rapidly became a Manager Trainee; counted tills, made deposits, provided exemplary customer service, and trained new employees.

PERSONAL   Resourceful problem solver. Strong personal initiative. Excellent references.

Automobile claims adjusting

Date

Exact Name of Person
Title or Position
Name of Company
Address
City, State, Zip

Dear Exact Name of Person: (or Dear Sir or Madam if answering a blind ad.)

With the attached resume, I would like to make you aware of my interest in the position as Claims Manager – Field in MD. Nancy Riverdale suggested that I fax this resume to you, and she feels that my expertise and skills would be assets for Aetna in the MD Claims Manager position in Annapolis, MD.

Extensive claims expertise

Shortly after receiving my college degree from Bowie State University, I embarked upon a career as a Claims Representative and I have been promoted to Senior Claims Representative and Office Team Leader within GMAC. While excelling in all aspects of my job, I have contributed significantly to numerous task forces designed to improve the efficiency of claims processing and customer satisfaction. I have trained and mentored numerous junior adjusters, and I have set an example for them to follow in my positive attitude, work ethic, and aggressive pursuit of advanced training and professional development courses. In GMAC's 13-adjuster office, I function as the Litigation Adjuster and have acquired much experience in settling disputes through mediation.

Proven management and communication skills

In addition to the numerous management courses I took while earning my college degree, I have refined my management and communication skills in jobs as an assistant manager for a shoe store, small business manager, and district sales representative. I offer a proven ability to establish effective working relationships, and I enjoy the responsibility of training, coaching, and developing junior employees.

Outstanding track record

I recently completed my annual performance appraisal and received exemplary scores on all performance areas. GMAC has recognized my management abilities: the company offered me a management position in Georgia, and GMAC has also identified me as the individual it wants to build and manage the company's force of adjusters in Montana if business volume grows to a level where field adjusters are justified.

I am well acquainted with Aetna's reputation for excellence, and I would appreciate an opportunity to discuss the MD–Claims Manager position in Annapolis with you. Although I can provide outstanding references from GMAC at the appropriate time, I would appreciate your holding my expression of interest in your company in confidence until we discuss the position. Thank you in advance for your time and professional courtesies.

Yours sincerely,

Edward R. Stickman

EDWARD R. STICKMAN

1110½ Hay Street, Fayetteville, NC 28305 • preppub@aol.com • (910) 483-6611

OBJECTIVE

To benefit an organization that can use a resourceful problem solver with strong analytical, communication, and management skills who has excelled as a claims adjuster in all aspects of automobile and homeowners property/claims settlement including material damage (MD).

EDUCATION

Bachelor of Science in Leisure Science, Bowie State University, Bowie, MD, 2001.
- Played varsity football, 1998-99; was active in intramural sport including softball, basketball, co-ed football, and football.
- Placed on Honor Roll in 1997, Dean's List in 1999, and Athletic Dean's List in 1999.
- Completed numerous courses in management and excelled in internships which tested my ability to plan, program, manage, and evaluate recreational programs and activities.

LICENSE

Maryland Property & Casualty (P&C) license
Licensed as a Notary Public through 2005
Completed AIC 33 designation; planning to pursue further AIC courses

EXPERIENCE

SENIOR CLAIMS REPRESENTATIVE & INSURANCE ADJUSTER. GMAC Insurance, Baltimore, MD (2001-present). Have become respected for my material damage (MD) expertise in an office with 13 adjusters; function as the Litigation Adjuster and have acquired vast experience in settling disputes through mediation.
- Handle daily office claims management responsibilities including the disbursement of claims load to adjusters in Baltimore and Montgomery counties.
- As the Office Team Leader, I examine files, provide direction toward claim settlement, and handle external and internal complaints.
- Assume responsibilities as office supervisor in the office manager's absence.
- Approve authority requests and all extended hours scheduling.
- Have trained many adjusters, and continuously set an example for other adjusters through my positive attitude, work ethic, and aggressive pursuit of advanced training.
- Have played a key role on numerous company task forces designed to streamline claims performance, improve cross-claims coordination, and increase the contact percentage as well as customer satisfaction of loss participants.
- Coordinated the company's local Catastrophe (CAT) Team, and was a quarterly award winner within GMAC for my contributions to the CAT Team.

Prior management and sales experience (mostly summer and part-time jobs while earning my college degree): ASSISTANT MANAGER. Foot Locker, Largo, MD. Was involved in hiring, training, and managing retail associates at this store which employed six people; continuously provided training designed to refine the customer service, communication, and problem solving skills of associates.

TRAINING & CONTINUING EDUCATION

I-Car Certifications, 2001-present:

Advanced Vehicle Systems	Aluminum Repair
Steering and Suspension	Electronics 1 and 2
Electronics 3 and 4	Collision Repair 2000
Plastic Repair	Finish Matching
Finish Matching Combo	Detailing Update
Aluminum Repair, Replacement, and Welding	

PERSONAL

Can provide outstanding references from all employers. Pride myself on my dedication to physical fitness. Offer experience in automobile and homeowners property/claims settlement.

Computer sales and service

Date

Exact Name of Person
Title or Position
Name of Company
Address
City, State, Zip

**CLIENT RELATIONS
SPECIALIST**

Dear Exact Name of Person: (or Dear Sir or Madam if answering a blind ad.)

With the enclosed resume, I would like to make you aware of my interest in exploring employment opportunities with your organization and introduce you to my talents and skills.

As you will see from my enclosed resume, I am recognized as a hard-working young professional who is effective in prioritizing tasks, managing time effectively, and handling multiple simultaneous activities. I am in the process of relocating to Columbia, where I worked previously, so that I can work full time while attending University of South Carolina in my spare time in order to complete my degree.

In early 2004, I relocated from Columbia, SC, to Dallas, TX, where my parents live. I became employed by a newly opened Dell store and have quickly earned a reputation as an efficient and knowledgeable Client Relations Specialist (Customer Service Representative). I am excelling in assisting customers in having their computer systems configured to their particular user needs. Since making Dell aware of my decision to return to Columbia to work and attend college, Dell has offered me employment in a Columbia store. I have decided, however, to explore employment opportunities with other Columbia companies, and I am selectively approaching organizations which could use my customer service, technical support, and administrative background.

I am a hard worker who excels in dealing with people in a gracious and helpful manner while troubleshooting problems and finding solutions. I work well independently or while contributing to the efforts of team. Fluent in Spanish, I have volunteered with Special Olympics as well as military organizations as a translator. I can provide outstanding references.

If you can use a cheerful and adaptable individual who offers a proven ability to work well with others, I hope you will contact me to suggest a time when we might discuss your needs.

Yours sincerely,

Bessie Devons

BESSIE DEVONS

1110½ Hay Street, Fayetteville, NC 28305 • preppub@aol.com • (910) 483-6611

OBJECTIVE

To offer excellent customer relations and communication abilities as well as technical computer skills and knowledge to an organization that can use a self-motivated and enthusiastic young professional who excels whether working independently or as a contributor to team efforts.

EDUCATION & TRAINING

Have completed 30 hours of course work in pursuit of an A.A. degree, Southern Methodist University, Dallas, TX. Demonstrate my ability to prioritize tasks and manage time effectively while attending college in the mornings and working from approximately noon to 9 PM.
- Volunteer with the homeless shelter and as a Translator for Special Olympics events.

Graduated from Freeman High School, Columbia, SC, 2004.
- Selected by Junior ROTC instructors for a leadership role. Junior and Senior Class **President.** Honored as the **Salutatorian** (2nd in class academically) of my graduating class based on my grade point average, was a member of the National Honor Society throughout high school.

Completed a Dell, Inc., technical computer, sales, and customer service course.

Completed customer service training program sponsored by American Services, Inc.

SPECIAL SKILLS

Language: Speak, read, and write Spanish fluently.

Computers: Familiar with software which includes Word, Excel, PowerPoint, and other commonly used programs as well as with hardware and peripheral equipment.

EXPERIENCE

CLIENT RELATIONS SPECIALIST. Dell, Inc., Dallas, TX (2004-present). Have quickly earned recognition for my ability to relate technical applications to a common sense approach while assisting customers in this newly opened store which specializes in configuring computer systems and designing them to meet users' needs and requirements.
- Have been cited as a dedicated young professional with a knack for helping customers through my knowledge of the company's products and system capabilities.
- Patiently yet aggressively resolve client issues when shipments are delayed due to inventory or configuration problems. Work extensively with the ordering system (AS-400) while creating and updating configurations. Was officially rated as excellent.
- Based on my excellent performance in this job, have been offered a position with Dell in Columbia, SC, where I will be attending University of South Carolina in my spare time.

CUSTOMER SERVICE TRAINEE. PWC, Columbia, SC (2004). Was recognized for my patient, professional, courteous style of dealing with callers in a center which processed credit cards. Excelled in this program before resigning to relocate to Dallas, TX.

Other experience while still in high school:
CUSTOMER SERVICE SPECIALIST. American Services, Inc., Columbia, SC (2004). Worked up to 40 hours a week on a 4 PM to 1 AM shift for this company owned by American Airlines: provided Visa card holders with account information concerning their Membership Awards Program benefits. Consistently received 100% evaluations.

ADMINISTRATIVE ASSISTANT. Richland Country School System, Columbia, SC (2003-04). Became familiar with professional office procedures and functions while answering phones, making copies, updating files and transcripts, and assisting with various activities at Columbia Elementary School.

PERSONAL

Offer well-developed decision-making and problem-solving skills. Am a positive, energetic, and enthusiastic individual who can be counted on to get the job done. Outstanding references.

Retail shoe store

Date

Exact Name of Person
Title or Position
Name of Company
Address
City, State, Zip

CLUSTER MANAGER
for Burlington Shoe Store

Dear Exact Name of Person: (or Dear Sir or Madam if answering a blind ad.)

I would appreciate an opportunity to talk with you soon about how I could contribute to your organization through my versatile experience in retailing and product line management, customer service and public relations, as well as sales, inventory control, and financial management.

As you will see from my resume, I am currently enjoying a track record of promotion within the Burlington Shoe Store, which is grooming me for further rapid promotion into store management. Since graduating from the Lansing Community College with a A.A. degree, I have become a valuable asset to Burlington and have been commended for my creativity, resourcefulness, and problem-solving ability.

I have attended numerous seminars and training programs related to managing nearly every area of retail operations. I have also received a Supervision Certificate from Burlington Shoe Store and am currently in their District Manager's Training Program. I credit one of my earlier jobs for gaining management and motivational skills. One aspect that is most beneficial in the retail business is realizing that a positive mental attitude is the key to success in most areas of life.

If we meet in person, I feel confident that you would find me to be an enthusiastic and congenial individual who offers highly refined skills in getting along with people. I believe I have learned how to strike a balance between aggressively pushing sales and profitability while maintaining excellent working relationships with customers, employees, and vendors. I am certain I could make valuable contributions to your organization.

I hope you will welcome my call soon when I try to arrange a brief meeting at your convenience to discuss your current and future needs and how I might serve them. Thank you in advance for you time.

Sincerely yours,

Doreen Louise Masterson

Alternate last paragraph:
I hope you will welcome my call soon to arrange a brief meeting at your convenience to discuss your current and future needs and how I might serve them. Thank you in advance for your time.

DOREEN LOUISE MASTERSON

1110½ Hay Street, Fayetteville, NC 28305 • preppub@aol.com • (910) 483-6611

OBJECTIVE I want to contribute to an organization that can use my management and organizational skills along with my reputation as a resourceful self starter with strong entrepreneurial instincts combined with an aggressive sales attitude.

EDUCATION **A.A. in Business**, Lansing Community College, Lansing MI, 2000.
Received Supervision Certificate, Burlington Shoe Store, 2003; am currently in District Manager's Training Program. Have attended numerous seminars and training programs.

EXPERIENCE **CLUSTER MANAGER.** Burlington Shoe Store, Grand Rapids, MI (2003-present). Have rapidly advanced with this company, and am being groomed for promotion to District Manager.
- Travel with the District Manager or alone to document store visits, oversee special projects, and observe/audit special areas of concern.
- Oversee the operations of three stores in addition to my responsibilities for training managers in 15 different stores; have met or exceeded quarterly sales goals two out of four times and received the "Above and Beyond Duty Award" for the summer of 2004.
- Train and develop managers for placement in stores within 10 weeks; empower managers to successfully operate stores with little supervision. Coordinate training guidelines and follow-on training provided to assure compliance of 15 managers in 15 stores.
- Perform troubleshooting in 26 locations and have excelled in correcting problems related to shrinkage, staffing, and general store operations.
- On my own initiative, designed a Training Recap for the entire district which has greatly facilitated the proper development of staff.

ASSISTANT CO-MANAGER. Lerner, Grand Rapids, MI (2002-03). Recruited, hired, and trained new associates in an extensive three-day program; assigned duties to a 27-person staff while directing the fast pace of sales activities.
- Performed a wide range of administrative duties which included making deposits, preparing weekly and monthly paperwork, administering payroll, conducting performance and salary reviews, controlling inventory, organizing and leading store meetings, overseeing assets, and communicating store policies.
- Received 2003 award for "Best performance in a new position." Beat 2002 sales by 33%.

ASSISTANT MANAGER & COLLECTIONS MANAGER. Circuit City, Grand Rapids, MI (1999-02). Performed light accounting while handling the responsibility of approving or denying credit applications; developed financial contracts, started allotments, checked references and established client applications.
- Prepared and distributed collections letters; ran credit checks and handled all areas of collections including CBI and TRW. Developed numerous new forms and documents which became valuable parts of the company's credit and collections systems.
- Achieved seven days of taking in $18,000; consistently beat the previous year's sales.

SALES PACESETTER. Express, Lansing, MI (1998-99). Began as a Sales Associate and was promoted to Pacesetter and trained for the Assistant Manager Position; set sales pace for this store which became upgraded to a superstore because of its 1999 sales increases.
- Was #4 sales associate in entire nation in sales volume and was #2 in our store's classification volume; was honored with various gifts including a trip to Chicago, IL.

PERSONAL Skilled in using aggressive sales tactics and pride myself on achieving ambitious sales goals. Known for my ability to motivate, train, and develop others. Strategic thinker.

Computer sales

Date

Exact Name of Person
Title or Position
Name of Company
Address
City, State, Zip

COMPUTER PRODUCTS SALES

Dear Exact Name of Person: (or Dear Sir or Madam if answering a blind ad.)

With the enclosed resume, I would like to express my interest in exploring employment opportunities with your organization.

As you will see from my resume, I have excelled in a track record of promotion during more than 15 years with Mayfair Corporation, which led to my present position as Director of Sales in the Santa Fe regional office. I have achieved spectacular results related to product sales and support with this major high-tech telecommunications company providing support to corporate giants including Sprint and Bell Communications.

In my current position since 1998, I direct regional sales and support services while managing 11 consultants involved in product introduction and customer training. I was promoted based on my effectiveness as an Area Sales Manager. I earned the distinction of **"National Sales Manager of the Year"** for achieving an unprecedented 300% of the corporate goal and six new product approvals.

Although I am held in the highest regard by my current employer and can provide an outstanding reference at the appropriate time, I have decided to selectively explore opportunities in companies which can utilize a dynamic high achiever who can produce outstanding bottom-line results. I would appreciate your holding my expression of interest in your company in confidence until after we speak.

If you can use a results-oriented and technologically knowledgeable producer with an astute understanding of sales, marketing, and product introduction, I hope you will contact me soon to suggest a time when we might meet to discuss how I could contribute to your organization. I will provide excellent professional and personal recommendations at the appropriate time. Thank you in advance for your time.

Sincerely,

Edward Grimes III

EDWARD GRIMES III

1110½ Hay Street, Fayetteville, NC 28305   •   preppub@aol.com   •   (910) 483-6611

OBJECTIVE To offer a background of success in managing the full process of product introductions through product approvals while providing quality customer support of cable and electronics equipment to an organization that can benefit from my leadership, team-building, and analytical abilities.

EDUCATION **B.S. in Engineering Technology (BSET),** University of Texas at Houston, 1986.
& TRAINING **A.A.S. in Electronics,** Central Texas Technical College, Houston, TX, 1984.
Completed training programs sponsored by Global Knowledge: Understanding Network Fundamentals (2000) and ATM, Converging Voice, and Data Networks (1999).

HONORS Received the honor of **"National Sales Manager of the Year" for North America** in recognition of achieving the largest sales growth and new product approvals for the Mayfair Telephone digital carrier system.

EXPERIENCE Have advanced in the following track record with the Mayfair Corporation:
DIRECTOR OF SALES. Santa Fe, NM (1998-present). For this company which was formerly the Lightning GTM Division, direct all phases of sales and support services for access electronics to major telecommunications companies.
- Manage the new product approval process, from concept to compliance with company standards.
- Consistently exceed sales goals as products are integrated into customer operations.
- Develop and maintain strong and mutually respectful relations with support staff at the customer telephone companies in order to support continued growth as well as to meet their needs with new products.
- Manage 11 consultants who assist in product introduction and customer training.
- Contribute as an active member of the internal sales and marketing team involved in product development and the rollout of new products.
- Am recognized as a detail-oriented manager who applies excellent written and verbal communication skills while listening to customers and understanding their requirements.

AREA SALES MANAGER. Charlotte, NC and Richmond, VA (1990-98). After 1-1/2 years in Charlotte, was promoted to the Richmond location to direct sales of telephone and cable television products.
- Held direct responsibility for sales to the headquarters of these major customers as well as to independent telephone and broadband companies.
- Acted as liaison between other sales regions and the corporate product development and manufacturing activities.
- As U.S. Account Team Manager, developed and made presentations on new product ideas to headquarters management staff.
- Achieved sales records leading to recognition as "Sales Manager of the Year" in 1996 including an unprecedented 300% of corporate goals and six new product approvals.
- Developed a thorough understanding of the telephone industry and its organization.

APPLICATIONS ENGINEER. Fuquay-Varina, NC (1986-90). In my first assignment at the company headquarters, assisted in development and functional testing of three new product lines. Provided field support for sales and marketing and for customer training aids.
- Quickly earned recognition for my emphasis on quality and customer satisfaction.

PERSONAL Am known for my open mind, willingness to listen to the customer, and manage sales to meet goals and objectives as well as customer needs. Outstanding references on request.

Rent-a-car service

Date

Exact Name of Person
Title or Position
Name of Company
Address
City, State, Zip

CORPORATE ACCOUNT MANAGER

Dear Exact Name of Person: (or Dear Sir or Madam if answering a blind ad.)

I would appreciate an opportunity to talk with you soon about how I could contribute to your organization through my demonstrated skills in sales and sales management as well as my exceptional communication, organizational, and time management abilities.

As you will see from my enclosed resume, I am presently excelling as a Corporate Account Manager with Avis Rent-a-Car. When I assumed responsibility for corporate accounts, monthly sales were an averaging of $45,000. Due to my initiative in developing new accounts and maximizing existing accounts, sales have risen to $160,000 per month, and I have received numerous awards for sales excellence.

Joining this national company three weeks after graduating from college, I quickly mastered all aspects of branch management, customer service, sales, and administration during the management training program. As Assistant Branch Manager, I was the top seller in the Dakotas in both outside and inside sales, and my branch was the top office in the region in Customer Satisfaction scores. In addition, two employees that I trained were promoted through two levels of advancement, to Assistant Branch Manager positions. Since first joining this company in 2003, I have earned a reputation as a talented and articulate sales professional with strong managerial abilities.

Although I am highly respected in my present job and achieving results in all areas of performance, I feel that my abilities would be better utilized in sales and sales management roles than in the administrative positions for which Avis is grooming me.

If you can use an intelligent, enthusiastic, and results-oriented professional, I hope you will contact me to suggest a time when we might meet to discuss your needs. I can assure you in advance that I could rapidly become an asset to your organization.

Sincerely,

Lakota Masters

LAKOTA MASTERS

1110½ Hay Street, Fayetteville, NC 28305   •   preppub@aol.com   •   (910) 483-6611

OBJECTIVE   To contribute to an organization that can use a articulate young sales and management professional with exceptional communication, time management, and organizational skills and a background in multi-unit sales management, corporate sales, and staff development.

EDUCATION   **B.S., Psychology and Business Administration**, Northern State University, Aberdeen, SD, 2002.
- Maintained a cumulative 3.1 GPA while working 30 hours per week and completing this rigorous degree program in three years; completed course work in Speech Communications, University of Sioux Falls, SD, 2001.
- Was elected Dakotas Chairwoman (2001) and Class Vice President (1999), Alpha Kappa Sorority. Played first-string goalie on the NSU women's water polo team (2000-02), participated on the USF women's cross country team (2001), and placed second in a scholarship pageant.

EXPERIENCE   *Am advancing in a track record of promotion with Avis Rent-a-Car (2003-present):*
CORPORATE ACCOUNT MANAGER. Aberdeen, SD (2005-present). Design and sell corporate account programs to business and government clients; increased monthly sales to $160,000 from $45,000 since taking over corporate accounts for this 12-store area.
- Provide government and private industry representatives with information on the advantages of a corporate rental car program in their travel plans.
- Generate business through a combination of client visits and employee referrals.
- Prepare and submit bids used in obtaining federal, state, and local government contracted business from 12 rental car offices throughout northern South Dakota.
- Created and implemented a corporate business training manual; responsible for all corporate training for 52 current employees and new hires.
- Was recognized with the **Employee Excellence Award** in 2005 and 2004; and the **Marketing MVP Award** in 2005 and 2004. Received the **#1 Corporate Class Performance Award** for North Dakota/South Dakota, 2005.

ASSISTANT BRANCH MANAGER. Watertown, SD (2004-05). Set sales records in several areas while also supervising a staff of four full-time and three part-time employees.
- Earned recognition as "Top Seller" in both inside and outside sales for the Dakotas and established the highest number of corporate accounts of any manager in the area.
- Trained and motivated manager trainees in all aspects of daily branch rental business.
- Managed and collected branch receivables and vehicle repossessions.
- Devised a new method for the reservations process which streamlined branch operations and increased productivity. Provided exceptional customer service which enabled the branch to place first in customer satisfaction scores for the region in 2005.

MANAGEMENT TRAINEE. Bismarck, ND, and Rapid City, SD (2003-04). Mastered all aspects of branch office management, customer service, sales, and administration; achieved sales in the top 5% of my training groups.
- Orchestrated a branch delivery service project which involved a staff of 12 and 225 vehicles. Displayed the ability to produce results in a fast-paced environment.

PERSONAL   Affiliations and professional memberships include the Aberdeen Chamber of Commerce, Military Affairs Council, Brown County Business Network, and American Defense Transportation Association. Excellent personal and professional references on request.

Cosmetics sales & retailing

Date

Exact Name of Person
Title or Position
Name of Company
Address
City, State, Zip

Dear Exact Name of Person: (or Dear Sir or Madam if answering a blind ad.)

I am sending my resume in response to the advertisement you recently placed for a Service Merchandiser.

As you will see from my resume, I have skills and abilities that could make me a valuable part of your team. In addition, I feel certain that you would find me to be a hard-working and reliable professional who prides myself on doing any job to the best of my ability.

In a current position as a Cosmetic Sales and Merchandising Specialist, I have increased sales of major cosmetic lines such as Maybelline, Revlon, and Fashion Fair within the Kansas City area. My extensive sales experience expands over a period of ten years. I can provide excellent personal and professional references at the appropriate time.

I hope you will call or write me soon to suggest a time convenient for us to meet to discuss your current and future needs and how I might serve them. Thank you in advance for your time.

Sincerely,

Kamala M. Miradesh

KAMALA M. MIRADESH

1110½ Hay Street, Fayetteville, NC 28305   •   preppub@aol.com   •   (910) 483-6611

OBJECTIVE
To contribute to an organization that can use my experience in sales and merchandising, my specialized knowledge of beauty and health care products, and my reputation as a professional who can work well independently.

EDUCATION & TRAINING
Studied **Business and Accounting**, Kansas City Community College, Kansas City, KS (2001-2002).
Completed numerous Revlon and Elizabeth Arden corporate-sponsored seminars in sales, management, marketing, and beauty advisory skills.

EXPERIENCE
COSMETIC SALES AND MERCHANDISING SPECIALIST. LaFayette Beauty Supply, Kansas City, KS (2003-present). Increase sales of several major cosmetic lines while covering the main retail store plus five other outlets throughout Kansas City.
* Handle sales and merchandising for a multiline corporation which marketed Maybelline, Revlon, and Fashion Fair cosmetics as well as Liz Claiborne fragrances.
* Advanced the Liz Claiborne line with award-winning sales promotions and displays.
* Supervise two employees who gave demonstrations and completed sales.
* Was credited with bringing about impressive increases in the sales of all lines: Maybelline by 11%, Revlon by 28%, Fashion Fair by 9%, and Liz Claiborne by 5%.
* Am skilled in judging correct amounts to stock to avoid running out of items or overstocking.
* Gained experience in ensuring proper stock rotation while servicing the military base's main commissary and 21 outlets.
* Process weekly orders, control a yearly inventory of $120,000, and set up sales promotions.
* Increased sales 17% by applying my product knowledge and sales skills.

REGIONAL SALES/MERCHANDISING MANAGER. VACO, Inc., Kansas City, KS (2001-2003). Supervised four employees and directed the merchandising for 24 accounts at five locations throughout Kansas.
* Became highly knowledgeable of product lines and refined communications skills working closely with clients throughout the region. Developed displays to promote products as well as conducting inventories, ordering, and stocking merchandise.

SALES REPRESENTATIVE. Inline Cosmetics, Kansas City, KS (1998-2001). Was promoted to the regional management team on the basis of my product knowledge, sales abilities, and performance while representing eight accounts. Represented Maybelline and Revlon which included preparing inventory reports, ordering merchandise, and promotions.

BEAUTY ADVISOR/COORDINATOR. Merle Norman, Kansas City, KS (1995-1998). Promoted to oversee a marketing account with $130,000 in annual sales, earned many awards while developing excellent rapport with vendors, management, and retail personnel.
* Performed makeovers, conducted beauty seminars, assisted with the makeup for fashion shows, and set up attractive displays to promote merchandise sales.
* Increased annual sales from approximately $90,000. Scheduled three employees.

Highlights of other experience: DENTAL ASSISTANT. Appel & Appel Dentistry, Kansas City, KS (1992-1995). Displayed my versatility as a dental assistant performing additional tasks in the X-ray and oral surgery departments while also acting as a receptionist.

PERSONAL
Offer language skills including speaking, reading, and writing German and speaking conversational French. Am very effective in situations requiring a self-sufficient professional.

Credit card services

Date

Exact Name of Person
Title or Position
Name of Company
Address
City, State, Zip

CREDIT CARD VICE PRESIDENT

Dear Exact Name of Person: (or Dear Sir or Madam if answering a blind ad.)

With the enclosed resume, I would like to indicate my interest in your organization and my desire to explore employment opportunities.

As you will see from my enclosed resume, in my current job as Vice President of Customer Service and Sales, I have supervised an 800-person workforce and improved customer satisfaction from 79% to 95%. Although I am held in high regard by my current employer, my wife and I have decided to relocate to the east coast to be closer to our aging parents.

If you can use an experienced customer service manager with extensive quality assurance knowledge, I hope you will welcome my call soon to arrange a brief meeting at your convenience to discuss your current and future needs and how I might serve them. Thank you in advance for your time.

Sincerely yours.

Denford Hanby

Alternate last paragraph:
I hope you will call or write me soon to suggest a time convenient for us to meet and discuss your current and future needs and how I might serve them. Thank you in advance for your time.

DENFORD HANBY

1110½ Hay Street, Fayetteville, NC 28305 • preppub@aol.com • (910) 483-6611

OBJECTIVE   To add value to an organization that can use an energetic and innovative executive who offers a dynamic communication style, superior motivational skills, as well as problem-solving and decision-making abilities refined as a corporate executive.

EDUCATION   Completed **Graduate Management Training Program**, MasterCard.
M.B.A., San Diego State University, CA, 1990; Led a team of MBAs to earn honors in a state competition solving profitability problems of real companies.
B.S. in Business Administration, Georgia State University, Atlanta, GA, 1983.
- Received a full athletic scholarship; was captain of the track team.

EXPERIENCE   **VICE PRESIDENT, CUSTOMER SERVICE & SALES.** MasterCard, San Diego, CA (2000-present). Lead and develop strategies for one of three major customer service and sales centers located in the United States; responsible for serving over 20 million cardmembers with exclusive relationship management responsibilities for customers that hold co-branded MasterCard cards like the Travelers Group product while controlling a $36 million annual operating budget.
- Supervise 800-person workforce; improved customer satisfaction from 79% to 95%.
- Achieved best annual employee satisfaction scores in the company's history to date.
- Improved revenue attainment by 6% in customer service "concept test."

REGIONAL SALES DIRECTOR. Sprint, Huntington Beach, CA (1994-00). After excelling as Regional Sales Director in Huntington Beach from 1994-96, was handpicked to manage the consolidation of two offices with a total of more than 300 employees which involved managing sensitive customer relations for Sprint residential customers while controlling a $35 million annual budget.
- Supervised 1,100 employees operating out of two remote customer contact centers.
- Improved revenue attainment 15% and customer satisfaction 10% while meeting a $190 million revenue objective.
- Provided the leadership which allowed the region to achieve first-place honors in tough competition with the seven other regions throughout the country.
- At Huntington Beach, improved revenue attainment 20%, customer satisfaction 5%, and productivity 30% while managing customer service and sales relationships with more than 200,000 small business customers; supervised 200 employees located in a remote business sales center operating on a $9 million budget while working as a key member of a team to achieve a $40 million corporate revenue objective; cut expenses by $300,000.

Previous MasterCard experience: Was promoted in this track record:
1990-94: **RE-ENGINEERING DIRECTOR.** Managed re-engineering project portfolio worth $3 million in savings; redesigned work flows and eliminated activities that did not add value to the process of delivering excellent customer service.
- Aggressively managed re-engineering projects, reaping over $2 million in savings; consulted with retailers on streamlining credit card operations to improve customer service.
- Developed innovative concept for resolving customer inquiries that saved $500,000.

1984-90: **CUSTOMER SERVICE DIRECTOR.** Began as a Customer Service Manager managing 85 employees, settling cardholder-retailer disputes, and controlling a $2 million budget; then was promoted to manage customer relationships with over 400,000 retail merchants nationwide to develop strategies for improving service levels and re-engineering workflows.
- Re-engineered workflows; reduced by 50% the correspondence time for selected retailers.

Office products and business services

Date

Exact Name of Person
Title or Position
Name of Company
Address
City, State, Zip

CUSTOMER SERVICE COORDINATOR & DISPATCHER

Dear Exact Name of Person: (or Dear Sir or Madam if answering a blind ad.)

I am in the process of relocating to your area to be nearer to my family and elderly mother, and I would appreciate an opportunity to talk with you if you feel my strong background in customer service, bookkeeping and accounting, data entry and word processing, and inventory control could be of use to your organization. I can make myself available for an interview at your convenience, and I can provide outstanding references from all previous employers and from my current employer, who is aware of my desire to live closer to my mother.

As you will see from my enclosed resume, I am an adaptable professional who enjoys working with people either as a supervisor or team member. Accustomed to working in hectic, fast-paced environments, I am very detail oriented and skilled at ensuring that bookkeeping, accounting, or any other type of information is accurate and complete. Familiar with Windows, I am proficient in using all standard office equipment from typewriters and computers, to multiline phones, to fax machines and copiers.

From my extensive customer service background, I have learned how to deal with people with tact and courtesy in any type of situation. I am known for my creative ability to find new ways to make office environments more efficient.

I hope you will welcome my call soon to arrange a brief meeting at your convenience to discuss your current and future needs and how I might serve them. Thank you in advance for your time.

Sincerely yours,

Shannon Goodey

Alternate last paragraph:
I hope you will call or write me soon to suggest a time convenient for us to meet and discuss your current and future needs and how I might serve them. Thank you in advance for your time.

SHANNON GOODEY

1110½ Hay Street, Fayetteville, NC 28305 • preppub@aol.com • (910) 483-6611

OBJECTIVE

To offer my office operations and clerical skills to an organization that can use a mature and creative individual who possesses a strong customer service orientation, experience in accounting and bookkeeping, and knowledge of inventory control and sales.

EXPERIENCE

Gained strong background in office operations/bookkeeping, Lincoln, NE:

CUSTOMER SERVICE COORDINATOR & DISPATCHER. Toshiba Business Products (2005-present). Personally respond to approximately 200 to 300 calls a day from customers in a two-state area (NE and KS); ask questions that allow me to determine which of 30 technicians to dispatch to handle copy machine, camera, and image systems repairs.

- Use outstanding communication skills to ensure responses are complete and problems are described in full for the technician's benefit.
- Provide high quality service; sold customers on our business. Handle high volume of business in a hectic, fast-paced environment. Enter information into an in-house dispatching system while also using my clerical skills in typing, filing, and data processing.

WORD PROCESSOR & DATA ENTRY CLERK. Express Personnel Temporary Services (2003-04). Displayed a high level of adaptability in adjusting to short-term assignments including jobs in public relations, data entry, and as a file clerk.

- Earned praise from the head of the Community Relations department of the Lancaster County Public Library for my initiative and creativity in developing attractive and informative public awareness displays used throughout the county's library system.

BOOKKEEPER. Saturn of Lincoln, (1996-02). For a large automobile dealership, handled accounts payable/accounts receivable while balancing daily disbursements and assisting with month-end closings of the books.

- Supported the clerical staff through my data entry skills and my knowledge of payroll, title transfers, reporting, and warranty management. Answered customer inquiries and was called on by staff members to verify procedures and methods of keeping records.

BOOKKEEPER/ACCOUNTING CLERK. Marshall's (1992-95). Performed bookkeeping functions for this retail facility; worked with cashiers on a regular basis by keeping adequate change on hand and preparing daily reports on money collected from each cashier.

- Contributed to the smooth transition to a new shopping complex; assisted in setting up inventory and accounting procedures for the facility.

Highlights of other experience:

- Refined skills in jobs including Bookkeeper for a manufacturing company and Department Manager/Sales Associate for a bookstore.
- In one job as an Administrative Assistant with a concrete company, provided support to the divisional manager while processing correspondence, preparing payroll, reviewing daily delivery receipts, dispatching trucks, developing cost sheets, and making deposits.

EDUCATION

Completed 50 hours of course work in Administrative Technology, Accounting, and Bookkeeping at the community college level.

SKILLS

Type 45 wpm; skilled in data entry, bookkeeping, multiline phones, and filing. Familiar with Windows; utilized in-house software program used for dispatching service technicians.

PERSONAL

Enjoy serving the public and working with others as a supervisor or as a team member.

Retail products and services

Date

Exact Name of Person
Title or Position
Name of Company
Address
City, State, Zip

**CUSTOMER SERVICE
DEPARTMENT
SUPERVISOR**

Dear Exact Name of Person: (or Dear Sir or Madam if answering a blind ad.)

With the enclosed resume, I would like to make you aware of my interest in exploring employment opportunities within your organization. After investigating opportunities within Alaska Railroad Company, I have decided that I would like to embark upon a career as a Hostess, and I am confident that I offer strong customer service skills which could contribute to your success.

As you will see from my resume, I have excelled as a Customer Service Supervisor with the Army and Air Force Exchange Service (AAFES), which has given me numerous awards for my excellent results related to satisfying customers and achieving maximum proficiency. I will be resigning my position as Customer Service Department Supervisor when my husband's current military assignment will take us to Alaska. Although I am held in high regard by the AAFES organization and have been offered a position with the organization in Alaska, I am interested in making a career change into the Alaska Railroad organization. I can provide outstanding references at the appropriate time, but I would appreciate your not contacting my current employer until after we have a chance to talk in detail about the opportunities with Alaska Railroad Company.

You will also notice from my resume that I have excelled in jobs outside the AAFES organization, in both food service and child care. In one job in food service, I was Second-Shift Cafeteria Operations Supervisor in a plant which operated 24 hours a day. I am certain that my background in food service could be useful to Alaska Railroad. I believe my experience as a Teacher in child care environments has also prepared me for a career in customer service with Alaska Railroad, because I have learned how to be patient with the youngest of customers and how to tend to their specific needs.

If you can use an experienced young professional with exceptional customer service and public relations skills along with an ability to relate well to all types of people, I hope you will contact me to suggest the next step I should take in pursuing my goal to become a part of the Alaska Railroad organization. Thank you in advance for your time and for whatever guidance you can provide.

Yours sincerely,

Felicia Davis

FELICIA DAVIS

1110½ Hay Street, Fayetteville, NC 28305 • preppub@aol.com • (910) 483-6611

OBJECTIVE

I want to contribute to an organization that can use my strong customer service skills, background in the hospitality and food service industries, as well as my outgoing personality and desire to assure the highest standards of customer satisfaction.

LANGUAGES

Familiar with German and Spanish

FOREIGN TRAVEL

Became accustomed to dealing with people from other countries and became a skilled traveler myself while visiting countries including Germany, Spain, Holland, Denmark, Italy, France, and other countries.

EDUCATION

Completed one year of college course work towards a computer programming major, Methodist College, Fayetteville, NC, 1992-93.

Completed extensive training and professional development courses related to the art of customer service, quality control, vendor relations, and other areas sponsored by Army and Air Force Exchange Service (AAFES), locations worldwide.

EXPERIENCE

CUSTOMER SERVICE DEPARTMENT SUPERVISOR. Army and Air Force Exchange Service (AAFES), Fort Bragg, NC (1992-present). Train new employees in customer service procedures while working with vendors all over the world in handling the responsibility of placing orders for specialized military clothing for the Fort Bragg community.

- While acting as a Customer Service Representative, handled calls and placed orders through sub-contractors for VIPs including Generals and retired military professionals.
- Utilize a computer on a daily basis to order merchandise, process payments, track inventory, cross reference purchase order numbers with payments, and identify checks; coordinated frequently by phone with computer personnel in Tennessee.
- Coordinated special projects and activities, including weekly dress uniform fittings for up to 100 recruiting school graduates.
- My orientation was always, "Get it right the first time," and "Please the customer."

CAFETERIA OPERATIONS SECOND-SHIFT SUPERVISOR. Food Services Inc., Cheyenne, WY (1990-92). Worked for a large plant of a Fortune 500 company which operated 24 hours a day, supervised the 3-11 P.M. second shift which provided buffet-style cafeteria food to plant workers; assisted with intra-plant catering.

- Maintained dietitian-ordered menus for workers with special dietary restrictions.
- Performed inventory control; ordered and received food merchandise.

CUSTOMER SERVICE REPRESENTATIVE. Wal-Mart, Casper, WY (1988-90). Provided customer service assistance for the lay-a-way department; established credit card accounts. Was commended for my meticulous handling of cash; balanced cash drawer daily.

TEACHER'S AIDE. Kids Korner, Cheyenne, WY (1986-88). Refined my ability to deal with people of all ages in a facility which served 250 children from 6 A.M.-6:30 P.M.

- Supervised up to 15 children; prepared lesson plans for pre-schoolers on a daily basis.

Other experience: SALES ASSOCIATE. Wal-Mart, Casper, WY. As a high school student, worked in the Jewelry Department, excelled in sales and customer service.

PERSONAL

Can provide outstanding personal and professional references and letters of recommendation.

Grocery services

Date

Exact Name of Person
Title or Position
Name of Company
Address
City, State, Zip

CUSTOMER SERVICE MANAGER

Dear Exact Name of Person: (or Dear Sir or Madam if answering a blind ad.)

Can you use a motivated and detail-oriented young professional with a background of excellence in staff development and training, management, and customer service?

As you will see from my enclosed resume, I have been working for the 1,200-store Kroger grocery chain for several years. I started with the organization as a cashier when I was in high school and have progressively moved up the ladder to reach my current position as Customer Service Manager. I supervise as many as 30 employees, interview and hire new staff, provide training, and am known as the top performer in cash handling, speed, and accuracy. I was selected for this position when the store opened at a new location because my high standards were recognized and valued.

I am a versatile individual who can organize for maximum productivity and handle multiple simultaneous projects and responsibilities with ease. I have gained much experience dealing with the public and supervising employees. I am currently working towards my Bachelor of Science degree in Business Administration, which I have found complements my work and assists me in becoming an even more valued asset. I am confident that through my education, experience, and background of success that I offer the drive, skills, and personality that would allow me to be successful in your organization.

I hope you will welcome my call soon to arrange a brief meeting to discuss your current and future needs and how I might serve them. Thank you in advance for your time.

Sincerely,

Tenille D. Jackson

Alternate last paragraph:
I hope you will call or write me soon to suggest a time convenient for us to meet and discuss your current and future needs and how I might serve them. Thank you in advance for your time.

TENILLE D. JACKSON

1110½ Hay Street, Fayetteville, NC 28305 • preppub@aol.com • (910) 483-6611

OBJECTIVE

To benefit an organization that can use a motivated and detail-oriented young professional with exceptional communication, planning, and organizational skills who offers a background of excellence in staff development and training, management, and customer service.

COMPUTERS

Skilled in utilizing grocery bar scanning technology and mainframe computers on a daily basis – operate specialized systems linked to the home office in OH.

EXPERIENCE

Have built a reputation as a dedicated team player and skilled trainer while excelling in the following "track record" with the 1,200-store Kroger grocery chain:
2003-present: **CUSTOMER SERVICE MANAGER.** Manchester, NH. Selected to help open the new location on Village Road to ensure that high standards in training, customer service, and cash controls were met or exceeded from day one; assist the other managers in implementing company programs, policies, and standards.

- Supervise as many as 30 cashiers and baggers; interview and hire new employees.
- Known for my patient, effective training style, provide instruction to new store managers on Kroger office procedures.
- Provide training to newly hired cashiers and customer service personnel, effectively presenting new and existing company programs, policies, and procedures.
- Consistently the top performer in cash handling, register speed, accuracy, and efficiency.

2002-03: **CUSTOMER SERVICE MANAGER.** Manchester, NH. Transferred to the Northpark location to resolve existing problems, rapidly improved cash controls, reducing losses and increasing customer satisfaction by providing friendly and efficient service.

- Provided supervision and training to 20-30 cashiers and baggers; oversee employee performance to ensure high standards of customer service and cash handling.
- Trained new store managers in company procedures related to office operations.

1994-2002: **CUSTOMER SERVICE MANAGER.** Manchester, NH. Promoted to this position in recognition of my exceptional performance as Bookkeeper at the Snyder Street location; supervised and trained more than 25 cashiers, baggers, and office personnel.

- Entrusted with additional responsibility as Front End Trainer for the area, instructing new customer service managers, cashiers, and other customer service personnel.

1993-94: **BOOKKEEPER.** Manchester, NH. After excelling as an Office Assistant, advanced to this position upon graduating from high school; entrusted with handling all office responsibilities, cash controls, and supervision of personnel; interviewed and hired new employees. Supervised as many as 30 cashiers and baggers.

Other experience: OFFICE ASSISTANT. Started with Kroger as a **CASHIER** when I was 16; was rapidly promoted based on my maturity and ability to effectively meet challenges.

EDUCATION

Completed nearly two years of college-level course work towards a Bachelor of Science in Business Administration, New Hampshire College, Manchester, NH.
Finished numerous training courses sponsored by Kroger, including Women in Conference, a Vendor Training class, NGAA Training (new office procedures), and Western Union/Money Order, as well as Kroger Library course.

PERSONAL

Have received many outstanding performance awards. Excellent references upon request.

Home installation services

Exact Name of Person
Title or Position
Name of Company
Address
City, State, Zip

CUSTOMER SERVICE MANAGER

Dear Exact Name of Person: (or Dear Sir or Madam if answering a blind ad.)

With the enclosed resume, I would like to express my interest in exploring employment opportunities with your organization. Although I have succeeded in both management and sales positions, I have decided that I would like to embark on a career in the insurance field, and I am confident that my sales skills and enthusiasm for insurance products would become valuable assets to a leading industry firm.

As you will see from my resume, I was recruited for a management position by Home Depot before the 115,000 sq. ft. superstore opened in Myrtle Beach. After I produced outstanding bottom-results as the manager of a department producing $1.3 in annual sales, I was promoted to my current position managing customer service for installed sales. I am highly valued by the Home Depot organization and can provide strong references at the appropriate time. I previously demonstrated my aptitude for succeeding in commission sales while working at Lowes and pursuing completion of my college degree in my spare time. I have also worked as a Service Station Manager and as a State Trooper—I had dreamed of becoming a State Trooper since I was a child and, although I made that dream come true for myself, I quickly saw that it did not hold sufficient challenge to be a lifelong career for me.

While involved in retail sales, I was particularly successful in selling service contracts, maintenance agreements, and warranties. I personally believe strongly in the value of insurance products, and I am confident that my outgoing personality, ability to establish trust, and proven sales skills would be highly effective in the insurance industry. I have given considerable thought to this career change, and I have determined that the Charlotte area would be fertile soil for insurance sales. Obviously, however, I am flexible and feel that I could become a top producer in any geographical area and with any product line.

If you can use a results-oriented producer with an astute understanding of sales, customer service, and product introduction, I hope you will contact me soon to suggest a time when we might meet to discuss how I could contribute to your organization. I can provide excellent professional and personal references at the appropriate time. Thank you in advance for your time.

Sincerely,

Vincent Jackson

VINCENT JACKSON

1110½ Hay Street, Fayetteville, NC 28305   •   preppub@aol.com   •   (910) 483-6611

OBJECTIVE   To benefit an organization that can use a versatile professional with strong sales and communication skills along with a commitment to exceptionally strong customer service.

EDUCATION   Completing Bachelor of Science degree with 20 hours remaining; completed two years of coursework at East Carolina University, Greenville, NC, and one year of coursework at Methodist College.
Extensive on-the-job sales and customer service training, Home Depot and Lowes.

EXPERIENCE   *Was recruited by Home Depot for a management position before the superstore opened in Myrtle Beach, and excelled in the following "track record" of promotion at Home Depot, Myrtle Beach, SC.*
2005-present: CUSTOMER SERVICE MANAGER, INSTALLED SALES. At this 115,000 sq. ft. store, was promoted to oversee a profit center which produces sales fluctuating from $18,000 to $30,000 weekly, depending on the season; vigorously monitor and maintain a healthy margin of sales.
- Manage up to 20 individuals involved in installing anything sold by Home Depot, such as water heaters, storm doors, fencing, appliances, and other equipment and fixtures.
- Hire and supervise installers and subcontractors; also recruit and train sales personnel.
- Coordinate with customers and provide outstanding customer service; resolve complaints.

2004: DEPARTMENT MANAGER. Supervised five employees in a department specializing in appliance sales; continuously met or exceeded $1.1 million budget in annual sales. Played a key role in helping to set up this superstore in Myrtle Beach. Trained and supervised employees and taught them effective customer relations techniques.

SALES REPRESENTATIVE. Lowes, Myrtle Beach, SC (2000-04). Relocated to Myrtle Beach for family reasons, and then sought out a job which would allow me to continue working toward my college degree in my spare time.
- Sold electronics equipment; was continually identified as one of Lowes' top sales producers.
- Excelled in selling maintenance contracts and service agreements, and developed a strong belief in the usefulness of warranties and service contracts. Learned valuable techniques related to sales and customer service from one of the country's leading retailers.

STATE TROOPER. S.C. Highway Patrol, Columbia, SC (1998-00). Achieved a goal which I had developed as a child—to become a state trooper. Completed the six-month S.C. Highway Patrol Trooper School and then was assigned to Columbia.
- Enforced the law, directed traffic, and apprehended law breakers.
- Worked routinely with insurance companies as I estimated damage resulting from wrecks.
- After becoming a Trooper, I decided that I did not want to make a career out of it, and I decided that my sales personality and management skills would be better suited to the profit-making sector.

STATION MANAGER. 501 Exxon, Myrtle Beach, SC (1994-98). Managed an older-style Exxon station which operated seven days a week and provided full-service auto repair services in addition to retailing tires and operating a wrecker service.

PERSONAL   Offer a proven ability to relate to the general public in sales situations. Experience at Home Depot and Lowes helped me gain experience in working with all types of consumers. Excellent references.

Electronics engineering

Date

Exact Name of Person
Title or Position
Name of Company
Address
City, State, Zip

CUSTOMER SERVICE MANAGER

Dear Exact Name of Person: (or Dear Sir or Madam if answering a blind ad.)

I would appreciate an opportunity to talk with you soon about how I could contribute to your organization through my outstanding technical skills along with my ability to use my knowledge and communication skills to instruct non-technical equipment users as well as other technicians.

As you will see from my enclosed resume, I am currently working as a Customer Service Manager for Walgreens Drug Stores. In my six years with the company I have become recognized as a talented technician who can be counted on to get the job done. After being initially hired for installation projects in the midwest, I was then selected to handle installation of new point-of-sale systems in a five-state region. Once the installations were completed in the existing stores, I was chosen to oversee servicing and any additional installations for stores within an 80-mile radius of St. Louis, MO.

I excel in dealing with people and in being able to work with everyone from the non-technical end users in the stores to other technicians. In addition to the 23 stores I handle on a regular basis, I am often called on to help in troubleshooting and diagnosis of problems experienced by technicians in stores outside of my territory.

I hope you will welcome my call soon to arrange a brief meeting at your convenience to discuss your current and future needs and how I might serve them. Thank you in advance for your time.

Sincerely yours,

Michael White

Alternate last paragraph:
I hope you will call or write me soon to suggest a time convenient for us to meet and discuss your current and future needs and how I might serve them. Thank you in advance for your time.

MICHAEL WHITE

1110½ Hay Street, Fayetteville, NC 28305   •   preppub@aol.com   •   (910) 483-6611

OBJECTIVE To offer my outstanding technical background related to the installation and servicing of a wide range of equipment as well as my skills in training and customer service.

SUMMARY OF QUALIFICATIONS Offer six years of field service experience and have received extensive training, both factory-sponsored and hands-on, in the installation and servicing of IBM point-of-sale equipment including PCs, peripherals, laser printers, asynchronous modems, Netrix networking, telephones, and keyed service units. Possess strong communication skills and am accustomed to working with non-technical users.

EDUCATION Earned an **Associate's degree in Electronic Engineering Technology,** National Education Center, St. Louis, MO, 2003.

EXPERIENCE *Advanced in a track record of accomplishments with a national company, Walgreens Drug Stores, 2003-present:*
2005-present: CUSTOMER SERVICE MANAGER. St. Louis, MO. After a period of time completing point-of-sale equipment installation projects in other areas, was selected to take charge of the installation and servicing of all equipment in 23 stores within an 80-mile radius of St. Louis, MO.
* Earned a reputation as a talented technician and am frequently called on to handle the overflow of service calls for stores in the surrounding areas.
* Travel to stores throughout my service territory to familiarize their personnel with the equipment and train them on its use.
* Apply my troubleshooting skills while helping other technicians diagnose problems.

2003-05: FIELD SERVICE REPRESENTATIVE. Various locations. Initially hired by Walgreens to service stores in Kansas and Oklahoma while based in Tulsa, OK; was selected for a "floating" position to handle installations in the five-state region including Missouri, Iowa, Illinois, Arkansas, and Indiana.

EQUIPMENT KNOWLEDGE Through training and experience, have become highly proficient in installing and servicing a wide range of equipment including the following:
Telephones: Northern Telecom/Meridian M7208 telephone system
    Northcom 1A3 keyed service unit and phones   Panasonic multiline telephones
Registers: Transaction Management, Inc. Model 2100
    IBM point-of-sale terminals models 4683 and 4693
Computers: IBM compatibles
Printers: Hewlett Packard Laser Jet Series II
    IBM laser printer 4019E Okidata Microline 320
    NEC Astra 310VS P6   NEC Astra 220VS P2
Local Area Networks (LANs): Ethernet and Token Ring
Telecommunications: Netrix model 30
    General DataComm modems 596, 296B, 500C/UXR, 500SR, 224+, and ZON JR XL
Secondary equipment: American Express money order machine
    Telxon RFC-30 FM radio data transmission system Telxon 912
    Telxon PTC-750 and hand-held scanner

PERSONAL Constantly seek opportunities to expand my experience in field service. Have the ability to instruct and train others — both those with technical and non-technical backgrounds.

Cable services company

Date

Exact Name of Person
Title or Position
Name of Company
Address
City, State, Zip

Dear Exact Name of Person: (or Dear Sir or Madam if answering a blind ad.)

With the enclosed resume, I would like to make you aware of my interest in exploring employment opportunities with your organization.

You will notice from my resume that I have worked in responsible positions since I was a sophomore in high school. In my first job with a retail store, I advanced rapidly from Sales Representative to Assistant Manager. As a junior in high school, I worked up to 25 hours a week handling accounts receivable and accounts payable for an insurance office, and I accepted an offer of full-time employment and a promotion to Office Manager upon my graduation from high school.

In a subsequent position as a Sales Assistant for a home building business, I earned respect for my "attention to detail" as well as my outgoing personality and public relations skills. I was entrusted with the responsibility of showing new homes in the $120,000-$200,000 range to potential buyers, and I became involved in helping interested buyers submit written offers and complete contracts. When that business relocated more than an hour away (not a reasonable commuting distance for me), I resigned and became a Customer Service Representative for a cablevision company. In addition to serving customers and handling data entry, I used my strong computer and written communication skills to create fliers and brochures which the company used as tools to explain services and procedures.

With very strong computer skills which include proficiency with Excel, Word, and PowerPoint, I possess a proven ability to rapidly master new applications. Known for my initiative and highly motivated nature, I can be counted on to persist in solving stubborn problems. You would find me in person to be a congenial individual with the ability to establish and maintain warm working relationships with others while handling multiple tasks and responsibilities with a high degree of comfort.

If you feel that your company could make use of my versatile skills and talents, I hope you will contact me to suggest a time when we might talk about your needs. I can provide excellent references.

Yours sincerely,

Tonia Jimmie

TONIA JIMMIE

1110½ Hay Street, Fayetteville, NC 28305　•　preppub@aol.com　•　(910) 483-6611

OBJECTIVE

To contribute to an organization that can use a highly motivated young professional with strong sales and public relations skills along with a style of "attention to detail" in all areas.

COMPUTERS

Highly proficient in utilizing computers for business purposes. Very skilled in using Windows operating system with software that includes Word, Excel, and PowerPoint as well as customized software such as Cable Data. Created fliers and brochures for customer information.

EXPERIENCE

CUSTOMER SERVICE REPRESENTATIVE. Time Warner Cable, Greensboro, NC (2005-present). Am involved in a wide range of duties related to customer service, office operation, and sales.

- **Sales:** Am highly effective in upgrading customers to services such as digital cable.
- **Reception & front desk:** Handle the front desk frequently, and is the public's "first impression" of the organization. Take payments, exchange converter boxes, and generally educate the public on the proper method of resolving their financial and service problems.
- **Written communication:** Because of my strong written communication skills and knowledge of correct grammar, became involved in creating fliers and brochures which are printed as tools for explaining business services and procedures.
- **Data entry:** Earned respect as a highly efficient worker performing data entry.

SALES ASSISTANT. High Point Furniture Outlet, Winston-Salem, NC (2004). Worked for this business for eight months; excelled in all activities but voluntarily resigned when the business relocated its office nearly one hour away—not a reasonable commuting distance for me, since the business office frequently closed as late as 9 pm.

- Was told that my outgoing personality and attention to detail were well suited to new home sales; advanced rapidly to handle more complex duties, and was entrusted with the responsibility of showing new homes to potential buyers in the $120,000-$200,000 range.

OFFICE MANAGER. P.R. Stanley Financial Services, Greensboro, NC (2001-03). Began working for P.R. Stanley while I was a junior in high school, and worked up to 25 hours a week until I graduated. Upon high school graduation in 2002, was hired full time.

- Handled accounts receivable and accounts payable. Coordinated with insurance companies since most receivables were from private insurance companies. Prepared payroll for three people.
- Became knowledgeable of insurance products including life, dental, 401k, and IRAs. Met with insurance representatives to discuss insurance products. Communicated with all clients, who included individuals and businesses. Filled out insurance applications.

Other experience (while in high school): ASSISTANT MANAGER. Kay-B-Toys, Greensboro, NC (2000-01). Began working as a sophomore in high school, and advanced rapidly from Sales Representative to Assistant Manager. Scheduled up to seven employees, and became skilled in solving customer problems.

EDUCATION

Graduated from Applewood Senior High School, Greensboro, NC, 2002.
Completed on-the-job training related to the real estate and insurance industries.

PERSONAL

Outgoing individual with exceptional interpersonal skills. Known for my ability to gain the trust of others and establish warm working relationships with others. Experienced in multitasking and handling simultaneous responsibilities. Outstanding professional reputation.

Savings & loan association

Date

Exact Name of Person
Title or Position
Name of Company
Address
City, State, Zip

**CUSTOMER SERVICE
REPRESENTATIVE**

Dear Exact Name of Person: (or Dear Sir or Madam if answering a blind ad.)

With the enclosed resume, I would like to make you aware of my interest in exploring employment opportunities with your organization.

As you will see from my resume, I have excelled in customer service roles in financial institutions. Known for my outgoing personality as well as my ability to train and develop junior employees who are committed to the highest levels of customer satisfaction, I thrive on competing for market share based on outstanding customer service. I am confident that I could profitably impact your company's bottom line and make significant contributions to customer satisfaction.

I hope you will call or write me soon to suggest a time convenient for us to meet to discuss your current and future needs. Thank you in advance for your time.

Sincerely yours,

Maria Joseph

Alternate last paragraph:
I hope you will welcome my call soon to arrange a brief meeting when we might meet to discuss your needs and goals and how my background might serve them. I can provide outstanding references at the appropriate time.

MARIA JOSEPH

1110½ Hay Street, Fayetteville, NC 28305   •   preppub@aol.com   •   (910) 483-6611

OBJECTIVE To benefit an organization that can use an experienced customer service professional who offers excellent planning and organizational skills, a strong "track record" in public relations, as well as the proven ability to perform graciously and accurately under pressure.

EXPERIENCE *Have established a track record of exceptional performance while refining my financial and public relations skills during this company's three major restructurings, from Missouri Savings & Loan, to Missouri Federal Savings & Loan, to its current status as National Bank of Missouri, Kansas City, MO.*

CUSTOMER SERVICE REPRESENTATIVE. (2003-present). During a time of organizational transition, played a key role in retaining customers and selling this company's services in a highly competitive market.

- Performed advanced cash handling procedures, including processing commercial deposits, opening and closing accounts, issuing U.S. savings bonds, and controlling safety deposit box accounts. Learned importance of creating good audit trails for accurate record keeping.
- Became skilled in applying new federal guidelines required by legislation pertaining to banks and savings and loan associations.

CUSTOMER SERVICE REPRESENTATIVE. (1995-03). Trained new employees in all aspects of office operations while selling the full range of banking services.

- Opened and maintained IRA's, acted as brokerage liaison, and processed U.S. savings bonds and travelers checks.
- Provided administrative support including handling nonsufficient funds checks, serving as safety deposit box custodian, updating computer account files, and serving as backup to the Operations Supervisor. Handled all automatic teller machine functions, accounting, and record keeping. Prepared written correspondence between the bank and its customers.

ASSISTANT BRANCH MANAGER. (1991-95). Performed financial transactions while also overseeing branch office operations during Manager's absence. Supervised administrative and operational procedures. Maintained accounts payable and employee health insurance claims. Assisted in implementing new checking account program by attending seminars on the new federal guidelines.

BANK TELLER. (1988-91). Ensured accurate completion and satisfaction of customer needs; posted accounts, withdrawals, loan payments, and deposits; opened and closed accounts; made loans against savings accounts; developed diverse communication skills.

Highlights of other experience:

- Supervised savings transactions of 16 Union National Bank offices located in nine cities, and fine-tuned organizational skills through running an efficient office.
- Worked in a Sears Department Store office processing sales and inventory transactions.

EDUCATION & TRAINING Completed accounting coursework and attended various banking-related seminars, including those on Consumer Rights vs. Banking Laws, Principles of Savings & Loans, Principles of Banking, as well as several computer classes including Microsoft software.

PERSONAL Elected to multiple offices in Kansas City Business and Professional Women's Organization. Excelled in mastering continuously changing procedures and guidelines while staying with the same company through several corporate transitions during a turbulent era in the banking industry. Known for my ability to rapidly become an expert on new procedures.

Cellular wireless services

Date

Exact Name of Person
Title or Position
Name of Company
Address
City, State, Zip

**CUSTOMER SERVICE
REPRESENTATIVE**

Dear Exact Name of Person: (or Dear Sir or Madam if answering a blind ad.)

With the enclosed resume, I would like to express my interest in exploring employment opportunities with your organization.

As you will see from my resume, I excelled in a track record of promotion with the U.S. Army while advancing rapidly to senior management responsibilities. In my final military assignment, I supervised a 10-person information support team which traveled extensively to countries including Cuba, Panama, Puerto Rico, Columbia, and Brazil. I led other individuals in a variety of projects which included training personnel from other countries and implementing the counter drug objectives of embassies throughout Central and South America. I held a Top Secret security clearance with SSBI (TS/SSBI) and I communicated fluently in Spanish. Working with computers was a daily part of my job, and I am proficient with Word and PowerPoint as well as with Access and Excel. I received more than 15 medals and other honors while serving in the military.

After leaving the military, I worked as a Correctional Officer and, more recently, as a Customer Service Representative in Jacksonville, FL. Although I was considered to be "on the fast track" within the Cingular Wireless Services company for which I was working, I am in the process of resigning from my position in Florida in order to relocate to the Northwestern area for family reasons. While working as a Customer Service Representative, I gained extensive experience in solving problems and providing quality customer technical support.

It is my goal to make a long-term commitment and contribution to an organization that can utilize a versatile individual who excels in dealing with the public while applying a wide range of technical skills and knowledge. I can provide outstanding personal and professional references at the appropriate time, and I would appreciate an opportunity to talk with you about your human resources needs.

Sincerely,

Nick O'Grady

NICK O'GRADY

1110½ Hay Street, Fayetteville, NC 28305   •   preppub@aol.com   •   (910) 483-6611

OBJECTIVE	To contribute to an organization that can use a versatile young professional with extensive management and customer service experience along with a background in providing information support services used worldwide to support law enforcement activities.
EDUCATION	Completed three years of coursework towards **Bachelor's degree in Criminal Justice,** University of North Florida, Jacksonville, FL; and Fayetteville Technical Community College, Fayetteville, NC. Named to the **Dean's List** and **Honor Roll.**
	• Working towards completion of my degree in my spare time.
	Completed extensive U.S. Army training related to psychological operations, computer information systems, counter drug analysis, Spanish language, and leadership development. Completed training provided by Cingular Wireless Services related to customer service.
EXPERIENCE	**CUSTOMER SERVICE REPRESENTATIVE.** Cingular Wireless Services, Jacksonville, FL (2005-present). Because of my strong communication skills and problem-solving ability, was promoted after only six months of employment to work in "technical support."
	• Research billing problems; issue credits; resolve a wide range of problems related to equipment, service, and equipment.
	• Was being groomed for further promotion, but in the process of resigning in order to relocate to the Northwest area.
	CORRECTIONAL OFFICER. Florida Department of Corrections, Jacksonville, FL (2005). Supervised 120 inmates within assigned areas in Jacksonville Correctional Hospital.
	SENIOR PSYCHOLOGICAL OPERATIONS MANAGER. U.S. Army, Fort Stewart, GA (2004-05). Supervised a 10-person information support team which traveled extensively to countries including Cuba, Panama, Puerto Rico, Columbia, and Brazil, assisted in planning and implementing counter drug goals of embassies in Central and South America.
	• Proficiently spoke, wrote, and fluently communicated in Spanish.
	• Controlled $500,000 in equipment as well as a $100,000 budget.
	• Implemented counter narcotics hotline in Panama which earned widespread respect.
	TRAINING SUPERVISOR. U.S. Army, Fort Jackson, SC (2003-04). Supervised training activities for a 400-person organization; scheduled training at military schools and other facilities for employees. Maintained the organization's training files. Briefed top executives.
	• Developed and wrote standard operating procedures for schools, language, and training.
	PSYCHOLOGICAL OPERATIONS SPECIALIST. U.S. Army, Fort Lewis and U.S. Army Reserve, Seattle, WA (1997-03). Conducted research and analysis for PSYOP activities in support of U.S. Asian command objectives in Asia; operated as a member of a PSYOP team during Operation Enduring Freedom, Operation Iraqi Freedom, and War on Terror.
LANGUAGE & CLEARANCE	Strong working knowledge of Spanish; gained proficiency in speaking, reading, writing. Held a Top Secret security clearance with SSBI (TS/SSBI).
COMPUTERS	Proficient with Word and PowerPoint; utilize them to prepare reports and give briefings. Skilled in utilizing Excel and Access to develop and maintain databases.
PERSONAL	Highly motivated individual with strong communication and problem-solving skills. Received more than 15 medals and a General's Letter of Commendation in military service.

Video rentals company

Date

Exact Name of Person
Title or Position
Name of Company
Address
City, State, Zip

**CUSTOMER SERVICE
REPRESENTATIVE**

Dear Exact Name of Person: (or Dear Sir or Madam if answering a blind ad.)

I would appreciate an opportunity to talk with you soon about how I could contribute to your organization through my proven abilities related to customer service, sales, management, and finance.

In the process of completing my B.S. degree in Economics with concentrations in Banking and Finance, I worked during the summers and holiday seasons and held part-time jobs throughout the school year. While juggling those part-time jobs with a rigorous academic curriculum, I also found time to become a respected campus leader and was elected Treasurer of my residence hall in my junior year and President in my senior year. Although I am just 21 years old, I have been told often that I am "mature beyond my years." I am known for my responsible and hard-working nature.

In a summer job as an Assistant to a Financial Analyst, I gained exposure to the operations of the stock market and acquired hands-on experience in working with customers of various financial services and financial instruments. I obtained my current job as Customer Service Representative with Hollywood Videos because the company created a position for me in Tempe when I moved from Phoenix, where I had become a valued employee and was a major contributor to achieving the fourth highest holiday sales volume of all stores in the chain. I have been encouraged by both CitiFinancial and Hollywood Videos to seek employment after college graduation, and I feel certain I could become a valued part of your organization within a short period of time, too.

You would find me in person to be an outgoing individual who prides myself on my ability to remain poised in all customer service situations. I can provide outstanding personal and professional references, and I would cheerfully relocate and travel extensively according to your needs.

I hope you will call or write me soon to suggest a time convenient for us to meet and discuss your current and future needs and how I might serve them. Thank you in advance for you time.

Sincerely yours,

Dean Amos

Alternate last paragraph:
I hope you will welcome my call soon to arrange a brief meeting at your convenience to discuss your current and future needs and how I might serve them. Thank you in advance for your time.

DEAN AMOS

1110½ Hay Street, Fayetteville, NC 28305 • preppub@aol.com • (910) 483-6611

OBJECTIVE   To contribute to an organization that can use a hard-working young professional who offers proven leadership ability and management potential along with a congenial personality, outstanding communication skills, and an ability to relate well to anyone.

EDUCATION   **Bachelor of Science (B.S.) degree** with a major in **Economics** and concentrations in **Banking** and **Finance**, Arizona State University, Tempe, AZ, 2005.
- Worked part-time during the school year as well as every summer and holiday season in order to finance my education; became a highly valued employee of every organization in which I worked and can provide outstanding references from all of them.
- Was a popular and respected campus leader; was elected **President** of my residence hall, Bartlett Hall, in my senior year and **Treasurer** of Bartlett Hall in my junior year.
- Was an active member of the Economics/Finance Club and the Modeling Club.

COMPUTERS   Familiar with Word and Excel; knowledgeable of Adobe PageMaker.

EXPERIENCE   **CUSTOMER SERVICE REPRESENTATIVE.** Hollywood Videos, Tempe and Phoenix, AZ (2003-present). Worked in the Phoenix Hollywood Videos Store part-time while going to college and was commended for playing a key role in helping the Phoenix store achieve the fourth highest sales volume in the chain during the 2003 holiday season; when I transferred to ASU to complete my degree in economics, Hollywood Videos persuaded me to stay with the company and found a similar spot for me in Tempe.
- Handle thousands of dollars daily; handle transactions utilizing computer-assisted cash registers. Train new personnel hired by the company.
- Earned a reputation as a gracious individual while assisting dozens of customers. Have been encouraged to enter the company's management trainee program after college.

RESIDENCE MANAGER. Bartlett Hall at Arizona State University, Tempe, AZ (2004-present). In a part-time job simultaneous with the one above, work closely with the dorm director to ensure the efficient administration of this residence hall housing 400 students.
- Supervise the conduct and activities of students living the dorm, and pride myself on setting an example for them in terms of my own morals and actions.
- Solved a wide range of maintenance and administrative problems while also counseling students with financial matters and personal problems ranging from depression and loneliness to poor academic performance and insufficient motivation.

CREDIT ANALYST. Deuce Technology Systems, Tempe, AZ (Holiday Season 2003 and 2004). At this internet company, determined credit ratings for prospective customers and made decisions about whether deposits were required before internet lines were established.

ASSISTANT TO FINANCIAL ANALYST. CitiFinancial Group, Tempe, AZ (Summer 2002). Was the "right arm" of a financial analyst with this worldwide investment company; prepared documents designed to persuade potential clients to transact business with CitiFinancial, and also processed and filed accounts of current customers.
- Gained insight into how selling and customer service occur within a brokerage firm.
- Scored very high on a mock test administered by my supervisor to test my knowledge of stock market issues and facts.

PERSONAL   Am skilled at remaining calm and courteous in all customer service situations. Can provide outstanding personal/professional references. Will relocate according to employer need.

Telecommunications company

Date

Exact Name of Person
Title or Position
Name of Company
Address
City, State, Zip

CUSTOMER SERVICE REPRESENTATIVE & COACH

Dear Exact Name of Person: (or Dear Sir or Madam if answering a blind ad.)

With the enclosed resume, I would like to make you aware of my interest in exploring opportunities with Broadband in the New York area. I would like to relocate to New York for family reasons, and I would very much like to continue my distinguished track record of employment with Broadband.

As you will see from my resume, I have worked for Broadband, LTD, in a call center environment in Pittsburgh, PA, since 2004. I began as a Customer Service Representative and was promoted in 2005 to Customer Service Representative and Coach. In my current position, I handle escalated calls on a daily basis, and I have become known for my tactful and resourceful style of dealing with the public when a customer situation requires the intervention of a manager. I have received three Customer Commendations from customers who have written to voluntarily praise my initiative and effectiveness in resolving their problems. I have also received three Outstanding Sales Awards for excellent performance in sales as well as a "Broadband Excellence" on-the-spot award from my co-workers.

In previous positions prior to joining Broadband, I refined my communication and problem-solving skills working in human services, employment services, and medical insurance services. In those fast-paced environments, I learned to make rapid decisions under tight deadlines, and I refined my ability to work with the public. In one job in a medical insurance organization, I began as a Claims Clerk and Receptionist and was rapidly promoted to Lead Administrative Assistant in charge of five people while we worked as a team to support a 20-person sales staff.

Since joining Broadband, I have excelled in all aspects of working in sales and in a call center environment. I have completed numerous training courses sponsored by Broadband, and I have also completed numerous courses in my spare time in order to strengthen my customer service and management skills.

I hope you will contact me if you can use my experience and expertise in your New York office. I would be delighted to make myself available for a personal interview at your convenience. You may feel free to call me at my work number, which I have provided on my resume along with my home number.

Sincerely,

Amanda Cooper

AMANDA COOPER

1110½ Hay Street, Fayetteville, NC 28305 • preppub@aol.com • (910) 483-6611

OBJECTIVE
To contribute to an organization that can use a highly experienced customer service and sales professional with call center expertise who offers a proven ability to resolve customer problems.

EDUCATION
Completed two years of college course work toward **Bachelor of Science degree in Psychology with minor in Personnel and Organizational Leadership**, Drexel University, Pittsburgh, PA.
* Completing degree in my spare time as my demanding work schedule permits.

TRAINING
Excelled in these and other training programs at Broadband's Education of Excellence:
     Telephone Techniques-Determining Caller Needs
     Telephone Techniques-From Curt to Courteous
     LTD Consumer Features-Phase I & II
     Telephone Techniques-On Incoming Calls
     Telephone Techniques-Five Forbidden Phrases
     Achieving Extraordinary Customer Relations
     Incoming Demand Service Representative-Sales
On my own initiative, have attended seminars to refine my management and communication skills which included: The Organized Employee; Telephone Skills; Non-Violent Crisis Intervention; Diamonds in the Ruff

EXPERIENCE
Have excelled in a track record of promotion with Broadband LTD, Pittsburgh, PA (2004-present).
2005-present: CUSTOMER SERVICE REPRESENTATIVE & COACH. Was promoted to oversee other customer service representatives and to provide a management presence in difficult customer situations.
* Have received three **Customer Commendations** from customers who voluntarily wrote to Broadband describing my initiative and resourcefulness in resolving their problems.
* Assist with training of new hires; provide individual development training requested by managers. Consult on customer account/billing scenarios and handle scheduling.

2004-05: CUSTOMER SERVICE REPRESENTATIVE, SALES. Began with Broadband in this job in which I was the primary contact with customers for new service or for changes in existing service; educated the public as I marketed Local Telephone Division (LTD) products and services, long distance, PCS wireless, and ISP services.
* Consistently achieved 150% of my sales objectives monthly.

Other experience:
CRISIS BEHAVIORAL TECHNICIAN. Allegheny Behavioral Services, Pittsburgh, PA (2002-04). Worked one-on-one with children diagnosed with behavioral problems using positive reinforcement to change behavior; documented patterns and reaction to stimuli.
STAFFING MANAGER. Erie Staffing, Inc., Erie, PA (2000-01). Was responsible for recruitment, advertising, hiring, firing, evaluation, placement, and supervision of 40 staffing specialists on a daily basis. Also handled payroll, inventory, client relations, workers compensation, and the development of utilities for recordkeeping.
LEAD ADMINISTRATIVE ASSISTANT. Lake Erie Physicians Health Plan, Inc., Erie, PA (1996-00). Began as a Claims Clerk; was promoted to Lead Administrative Assistant.

PERSONAL
Single; will relocate. Physically fit. Excellent references available on request.

Communications devices company

Date

Exact Name of Person
Title or Position
Name of Company
Address
City, State, Zip

Dear Exact Name of Person: (or Dear Sir or Madam if answering a blind ad.)

With the enclosed resume, I would like to make you aware of my interest in exploring employment opportunities with your organization. I offer a reputation as a cheerful hard worker and resourceful problem solver, and I can provide outstanding references from all previous employers.

Extensive experience in customer service and problem solving
As you will see from my resume, I offer extensive experience in sales and customer service in worldwide environments. For my current employer, I provide sales, administrative, and customer service support for customer organizations which include police departments, fire departments, and municipalities.

Proven management skills
In my previous position with a leading security firm, I passed a rigorous background investigation, drug tests, and a personality profile in order to gain employment. I quickly advanced into a management position as a Site Supervisor, and I was in charge of security officers working 24 hours a day on three shifts to provide security services for multiple locations of Verizon. I became widely respected for my communication skills and problem-solving ability, and I was named Employee of the Month.

Versatile accounting and communication skills
I am experienced in working with software including Excel spreadsheets while handling accounts payable and receivable, and I have administered payroll for up to 10 people. My employers have always praised my strong personal initiative. For example, in one of my earliest work experiences with a music company in Spain, I organized the corporation's telecommunications bills by department and this led to a substantial cost savings. In my job as a Site Supervisor providing security services for Verizon, I conducted inspections of multiple company locations, authored new security procedures, and trained employees and managerial staff.

Although I am held in the highest regard and can provide outstanding references, I am selectively exploring opportunities in companies which can use a strong problem solver with excellent customer service skills. If you can use a reliable hard worker with excellent communication skills, I hope you will contact me to suggest a time when we might meet to discuss your needs.

Yours sincerely,

Eliza Malone

ELIZA MALONE

1110½ Hay Street, Fayetteville, NC 28305 • preppub@aol.com • (910) 483-6611

OBJECTIVE

I want to contribute to an organization that can use a resourceful problem solver and cheerful hard worker who offers extensive experience in customer service, office administration, and computer operations along with outstanding personal and professional references.

EXPERIENCE

CUSTOMER SERVICE REPRESENTATIVE & SALES/ADMINISTRATIVE ASSISTANT. Eastern Communications, Fargo, ND (2005-present). Provide customer service and administrative support for a company which sells and services two-way communication devices used by municipalities, fire departments, police departments, and other organizations in Trail, Steele, Barnes, Ransom, Richland, and Cass counties.
- **Accounting and administration:** Administer a customer database and utilize an Excel spreadsheet while handling accounts receivable/payables.
- **Sales and customer service:** Sell equipment and accessories; assist customers in coordinating with the service department on programming. Resolve customer problems.

Was promoted in the following track record of promotion by Prairiewood at its Fargo, ND office (2003-05). Passed a rigorous background investigation including a personality profile, lie detector test, and drug test to be considered for employment by this company:
2004-05: SITE SUPERVISOR. Verizon. Was promoted to manage ten security officers overseeing the security of hundreds of Verizon employees and customers at three sites.
- **Communication:** On my own initiative, developed and updated office manuals containing security procedures. Trained Verizon's office personnel in security procedures. Communicated extensively with Sprint managers from Rapid City and Fargo.
- **Accounting:** Administered payroll for ten employees.
- **Inspection:** Inspected all sites routinely to ensure compliance with security procedures.
- **Staffing and supervision:** Was responsible for staffing three shifts of security officers working 24 hours a day; wore a pager and was essentially "on call" 24 hours a day for staffing and security issues.
2003-04: LEAD OFFICER. NDSU Medical Center. Began as an entry-level employee and was rapidly promoted to Lead Officer in 2004 after being named **"Employee of the Month."** At this major medical center, ensured the security of patients, employees, and visitors, and directed administrative procedures at the central controller's base station.

Other experience: ADMINISTRATIVE ASSISTANT & ACCOUNTING TECHNICIAN. Madrid, Spain (2000-02). For an international music and record company with offices in Madrid and Los Angeles, began as a receptionist handling calls on a multi-line switchboard, and advanced to handle customer service. Provided customer service for international visitors; communicated in both English and Spanish, and acted as an interpreter and translator. Authorized purchase orders for products and services, domestic and foreign; consulted with accounts payable personnel.

EDUCATION

Completed college course work at North Dakota State University related to finance and accounting; received a certificate of completion from Bank Teller training, 2002.
Completed extensive technical training sponsored by employers related to security operations, radio communications, sales, and customer service.

PERSONAL

Self-starter with strong personal initiative. Employers have praised me for my "highest work ethic" and absolute reliability. Outstanding references upon request. Fluent in Spanish.

Yellow Pages advertising

Date

Exact Name of Person
Title or Position
Name of Company
Address
City, State, Zip

CUSTOMER SERVICE REPRESENTATIVE & TEAM LEADER

Dear Exact Name of Person: (or Dear Sir or Madam if answering a blind ad.)

With the enclosed resume, I would like to express my interest in exploring employment opportunities with your organization.

Since graduating with my B.S. degree, I have worked for the Yellow Pages company, and I have been recommended for management training because of my strong leadership and communication skills. You will notice from my resume that I gained extensive public speaking and leadership experience during high school and college. I served as Vice President of my fraternity in college, and I was elected President of the Future Leaders of America in 2000-01. I was selected for that honor because of my ability to excel in a strenuous schedule of public speaking and interviewing in competition with 20 highly qualified people all over the state. I was also elected a National Ambassador for the National Council of Leaders Cooperatives, and I served as Chairman for the organization's national convention. I credit those early leadership experiences with giving me a high degree of self-confidence and poise in business situations. While working for Yellow Pages, I have excelled as a Team Leader and have been commended for my tact and courtesy in resolving customers' issues with products and service.

While earning my degree, I worked as an Intern for the Sheriff's Department in Mercer County in the Spring of 2004, and I made contributions to the Drug Abuse Resistance Education Program. I took great pride and pleasure in making a difference in the lives of many troubled and confused teens.

If you can use a resourceful young problem solver with outstanding sales and customer service skills along with a proven ability to work well with others at all organizational levels, I would enjoy an opportunity to meet with you to discuss your needs. I can provide outstanding personal and professional references.

Sincerely,

Jared Fitka

JARED FITKA

1110½ Hay Street, Fayetteville, NC 28305   •   preppub@aol.com   •   (910) 483-6611

OBJECTIVE

I want to contribute to an organization that can use a promising young leader who offers exceptionally strong communication and customer service skills along with a strong desire to utilize my analytical and problem-solving abilities to help others.

EDUCATION & TRAINING

B.S. degree in Human Behavior, Thomas Edison State College, Trenton, NJ, 2005.
Completed two years of studies at Mercer County Community College, Trenton, NJ, 2000-02.

LEADERSHIP EXPERIENCE

Elected **President,** Alpha Kappa Sigma Fraternity, Inc., 2004-05.
* Became a popular role model for younger students as I served as "Chief Executive Officer" of this organization; provided oversight for financial management while developing and implementing programs which encouraged academic excellence and promoted service to the community.

Elected **President,** Future Leaders of America, 2000-01.
* Was elected to this office after waging an effective campaign against 20 qualified peers; excelled in extensive public speaking during the campaign as well as in the numerous interviews conducted of all candidates for this office.

Elected **National Ambassador,** National Council of Leaders Cooperatives, 2000-01.
* Was selected for this honor based on my proven leadership ability.
* Served on the planning committee for the organization's national conference, and served as **Chairman** of the 2001 Convention; gained experience in planning multiple social and educational events attended by hundreds of people.

EXPERIENCE

CUSTOMER SERVICE REPRESENTATIVE & TEAM LEADER. Yellow Pages, Trenton, NJ (2005-present). Have been identified as an individual of executive ability and am being groomed for advancement within the Yellow Pages corporation.
* Achieve and exceed ambitious monthly sales goals while providing outstanding customer service in a highly competitive marketplace.
* Resolved problems with tact and courtesy when customers had issues with products or services.
* Gained experience as a Team Leader, and mentored junior sales associates in effective techniques of sales and customer service. Gained a reputation as a highly effective motivator.

SALES REPRESENTATIVE. Roebling Jewelers, Trenton, NJ (2004-05). For a prominent jewelry corporation, maintained an outstanding sales record while assisting in inventory control.
* Learned effective techniques of customer service related to high-ticket items.

STAFF INTERN. Mercer County Sheriff's Department, Mercer County, NJ (Spring of 2004). As an intern in the Drug Abuse Resistance Education Program, provided a strong example and strong counseling in order to help teenagers avoid drug use.
* Took great pride and pleasure in making a difference in the lives of others; several teens told me that my words and example influenced them to "go straight."
* Became known as an enthusiastic communicator.

PERSONAL

Strong leader and resourceful problem solver. Unlimited personal initiative. Excellent references available on request. Enjoy music and singing in my spare time. Computer enthusiast; proficient with Word and the Windows operating system.

Banking services

Date

Exact Name of Person
Title or Position
Name of Company
Address
City, State, Zip

CUSTOMER SERVICE
REPRESENTATIVE &
TELLER

Dear Exact Name of Person: (or Dear Sir or Madam if answering a blind ad.)

With the enclosed resume, I would like to initiate the process of being considered for employment within your organization. I am in the process of permanently relocating back to Washington state area where I grew up and where my parents live.

As you will see from my resume, after excelling with Wells Fargo I accepted a job with Bank of America, and I have been promoted to increasing responsibilities since 2005. Although I am being groomed for further promotion within the organization, I have decided that I wish to make my permanent home in Washington.

In my current job I rotate among a wide range of positions for which I have been cross-trained. I have won numerous awards and honors, including Employee of the Month and the Teller Referral Award, and I have become skilled in selling the bank's wide range of financial, credit, protection, and savings products. While graciously serving more than 5,000 customers monthly, I train and supervise other tellers, act as Vault Custodian, resolve a wide variety of customer problems, and make decisions on credit applications.

I can provide outstanding personal and professional references at the appropriate time, and I can assure you that you would find me to be a hard-working, congenial individual who prides myself on always doing my best. I have a reputation for reliability, speed and accuracy in daily operations, as well as tact and diplomacy in customer relations.

If you can use a hard worker who could become a valuable part of your organization, I hope you will contact me to suggest a time when I can make myself available for a personal interview at your convenience. Thank you in advance for your time.

Sincerely,

Camille White

CAMILLE WHITE

1110½ Hay Street, Fayetteville, NC 28305   •   preppub@aol.com   •   (910) 483-6611

OBJECTIVE   I want to contribute to an organization that can use a hard worker and fast learner with extensive knowledge of banking operations and activities along with proven skills in sales, customer service, and public relations.

EDUCATION   **College:** Have completed general college courses, Truckee Meadows Community College, Reno, NV, related to computer operations, merchandising, and business management.
Banking: Excelled in technical training sponsored by the Bank of America and Wells Fargo Bank; completed courses including Advanced Teller Training, Deposit Sales and Service, and Consumer Loan Procedures.

SPECIAL   Operate a variety of banking, office, and automated equipment including:
SKILLS
Sharp teller machine	Brandt currency dispensing machine
ATM machines	Brandt currency counters
IBM 4700	Hogan system
coin rolling machine	10-key calculator
coin sorter	cash machines
on-line computer systems	

EXPERIENCE   **CUSTOMER SERVICE REPRESENTATIVE & TELLER.** Bank of America, Reno, NV (2005-present). Graciously serve more than 5,000 customers a month while rotating among several positions for which I have been cross-trained; have won numerous awards including **Employee of the Month** and the **Teller Referral Award.**
- As the "right arm" to the Teller Supervisor, am involved in training and supervising other tellers, and have become skilled in training others to sell the bank's products and services.
- Order money from the Federal Reserve; act as Vault Custodian.
- Process deposits including night deposit bags; balance, maintain, and service 3 ATMs.
- Report large sum transactions to Internal Revenue Service according to banking policy.
- Provide back-up support to Customer Service Branch, and have been cross-trained in all customer service activities.
- Perform research, and assist customers in resolving problems.
- Obtain credit reports; approve or deny credit card applications based on my analysis.
- Have become respected for my excellent consulting skills while demonstrating my understanding of the bank's wide range of financial products and services related to investments, savings, credit, and protection.
- Play an active role in all bank community relations activities: am an active participant in the United Way Campaign, and have also been active as a Walk-A-Thon participant in the March of Dimes Campaign.
- Am being groomed for promotion to increased responsibilities in management and customer service.
- Scored 100% on all "shopping surveys" during surprise audits of my work activities.

TELLER. Wells Fargo Bank, Reno, NV (2004-05). After completing a summer internship, was hired permanently.

Other experience: SALES CLERK. Wal-Mart, Reno, NV (2002-03). Excelled as sales clerk, inventory clerk, stocking merchandiser, and store supervisor while assisting customers.

PERSONAL   Outstanding personal and professional references upon request. Strong work ethic.

Hotel services

Date

Exact Name of Person
Title or Position
Name of Company
Address
City, State, Zip

DIRECTOR OF CATERING

Dear Exact Name of Person: (or Dear Sir or Madam if answering a blind ad.)

With the enclosed resume, I would like to make you aware of my background as a detail-oriented sales and hospitality industry professional with exceptional communication, time management, and customer service skills and experience in account management, direct sales, and public relations.

In my current position as a Director of Catering for Marriott Hospitality at the Sunnydale Marriott in Phoenix, I oversee all aspects of the catering department, including direct sales, planning, and execution of all meetings and conferences for the 6,000 square foot meeting space. I am responsible for generating projected annual sales of $660,000 for the hotel. In addition to supervising one assistant and a Banquet Manager, I prepare catering forecasts, predicting future sales based on current bookings.

In previous positions with The Radisson Bougainvillea in Tallahassee, Florida, I started as a sales assistant and was quickly promoted due to my exemplary job performance and dedication. As Sales and Catering Coordinator, I provided administrative support to two departments. My organizational expertise and detail-oriented approach to problem-solving allowed me to assist the Director of Sales, the Corporate Sales Manager, and the Director of Catering, ensuring that functions were carried out smoothly and to the customer's complete satisfaction. After my promotion to Catering Manager, I assisted the Director of Catering in planning weddings, small meetings, and conferences for this 12,000 square-foot meeting space.

Prior to entering the hospitality industry, I excelled as Legislative Assistant to a member of the California House of Representatives, providing a wide range of clerical and office management services while handling all correspondence from the Representative's constituents.

If you can use a self-motivated, articulate sales and hospitality industry professional with outstanding communication, organizational, and customer service abilities, I look forward to hearing from you soon to arrange a time when we might meet to discuss your needs, and how I might meet them. I can assure you in advance that I have an excellent reputation, and would quickly become a valuable asset to your organization.

Sincerely,

Marissa P. Newsome

MARISSA P. NEWSOME

1110½ Hay Street, Fayetteville, NC 28305   •   preppub@aol.com   •   (910) 483-6611

OBJECTIVE   To benefit an organization that can use a detail-oriented sales and hospitality industry professional with exceptional communication, time management, and customer service skills as well as a background in account management, direct sales, public relations, and catering.

EXPERIENCE   **DIRECTOR OF CATERING.** Marriott Hospitality, Inc., Sunnydale Marriott, Phoenix, AZ (2002-present). Oversee all operational aspects of the catering department in this busy hotel; responsible for direct sales, planning, and execution of all meetings and conferences for this 6,000 square foot meeting space.
- Supervise one assistant and a Banquet Manager; plan food and beverage/catering needs for all small meetings and conferences.
- Service existing accounts and develop new business, selling meeting space and catering services to associations, corporations, and military accounts.
- Prepare catering forecasts, determining future business based on current bookings.
- Work closely with the sales department to coordinate event planning and ensure that all details are handled smoothly and carried out to the satisfaction of the customer.

CATERING MANAGER. The Radisson Bougainvillea, Tallahassee, FL (2000-01). Promoted to Catering Manager; planned all small meetings, weddings, and small conferences for the catering department; earned respect for my attention to detail in catering all types of functions for a meeting space over 12,000 square feet.
- Led the hotel to earn a reputation as "the best meeting place in town."
- Worked closely with the Director of Catering as Catering Manager.

SALES AND CATERING COORDINATOR. The Radisson Bougainvillea, Tallahassee, FL (1998-2000). Became thoroughly knowledgeable of the hospitality industry in this job requiring a versatile and adaptable professional; provided administrative support to two departments — sales and catering — which work closely and share some of the same personnel and areas of operation.
- Provided the Director of Sales, the Corporate Sales Manager, and the Director of Catering with my expertise in coordinating details so that functions were carried out smoothly and to the customer's satisfaction.
- Worked closely with clients to plan small meetings and a variety of events for the hotel's banquet and conference facilities.
- Excelled in handling multiple simultaneous responsibilities under tight deadlines.
- Assisted the General Manager when his regular assistant was unavailable.
- Was promoted to this position after six months as a Sales Assistant.

LEGISLATIVE ASSISTANT. The California House of Representatives, Sacramento, CA (1984-97). Provided a wide range of secretarial and office management activities for an elected representative including handling problems and concerns from constituents in a three-county area which was the largest geographical district in the state.
- Worked closely with the representative to ensure that all direct, written, or telephone inquiries were responded to promptly and to the constituent's satisfaction.

TRAINING   Proficient in using Breeze Systems and software including Microsoft Word.
Completed business coursework, California State University extension.

PERSONAL   Have a real knack for putting people at ease, defusing difficult situations, and getting along with others. Enjoy fast-paced environments and meeting challenges. Excellent references.

Youth services

Exact Name of Person
Title or Position
Name of Company
Address
City, State, Zip

**DIRECTOR OF
YOUTH SERVICES**

Dear Exact Name of Person: (or Dear Sir or Madam if answering a blind ad.)

I would appreciate an opportunity to talk with you soon about how I could contribute to your organization through my experience in customer service and sales, as well as through my proven skills in building effective working relationships.

My history, as you will see from my enclosed resume, includes a solid background in sales and customer service. In my current position as Director of Youth Services for a church, I am refining my customer service abilities in an environment which requires creativity in developing and implementing new programs. In a previous job, I worked with Zipp Laboratories as a Professional Sales and Services Representative, and I provided medical professionals with high-quality services. Within three months of joining that firm I had built 20 accounts into more than 75 through my sales abilities, communication skills, dedication to quality, and enthusiasm.

I hope you will welcome my call soon to arrange a brief meeting at your convenience to discuss the current and future needs of Extensive Home Health Care and how I might serve them. Thank you in advance for your time.

Sincerely yours,

Moses Frezel

MOSES FREZEL

1110½ Hay Street, Fayetteville, NC 28305 • preppub@aol.com • (910) 483-6611

OBJECTIVE

To apply customer service, sales, and public relations skills to an organization that can use a hard-working professional who offers strong communication and interpersonal abilities.

EXPERIENCE

DIRECTOR OF YOUTH. Euclid Church, Pierre, SD (2005-present). Spearheaded the youth program for this newly chartered church. Provide leadership for all youth ministries, developing weekly and yearly agendas to achieve goals and creating and maintaining spiritual growth among young people.

- Provide counseling for young adults while also conducting hospital and new-member visitations and teaching adult and youth home Bible studies on a regular basis.
- Created and implemented a variety of community service activities targeted at youth.
- Evaluate and select curriculum for all levels of the youth ministry.
- Lead weekly youth meetings and church services in the absence of the senior pastor.
- Develop and conduct special-interest seminars for the church and the community.
- Prior to accepting this position, was handpicked to teach two seminars at the 2005 South Dakota State Conference on Christian Education and Youth Ministry.

PROFESSIONAL SALES AND SERVICES REPRESENTATIVE. Zipp Biomedical Laboratories, Sioux Falls, SD (2001-04). Provided more than 75 accounts including private physician's offices, comprehensive medical centers, and veterinary hospitals with services as the liaison between these local accounts and the laboratory.

- Nearly quadrupled my customer base in under three months: started working part time with 20 accounts and built to servicing more than 75.
- Worked closely with professionals including doctors and medical office managers to guarantee a high quality of support services.
- Handled operational areas including: mediating problems, managing account-laboratory relations, and conducting technical in-service training. Became proficient in data entry and managing administrative details including preparing documentation and keeping detailed updated records.
- Liaised between clients and the lab, transporting diagnostic specimens and test results.
- Was nominated for the honor of "2004 Employee of the Year."

RETAIL SALES ASSOCIATE. Authentic Jewelers, Sioux Falls, SD (2000-01). Exceeded sales quotas every month of my employment and provided customers of this fine jeweler with outstanding service.

- Refined my phone communication skills calling on existing customers to "sell" them on the idea of purchasing jewelry for special occasion gifts. Learned the importance of taking proper security precautions when working with high-value merchandise.

Other experience: As a **SALES ASSOCIATE**, became skilled in controlling inventory, making and closing sales providing service to customers, developing promotional material, and telemarketing (summers/holidays, 1997-00).

EDUCATION

Completed 80 credit hours in **Christian Education/Administration**, South Dakota State University, Brookings, SD.

Earned certification with two years in Christian Education/Administration, South Dakota State University, Brookings, SD, 2000. Was named to the Dean's List every semester.

- Named to the board of directors of a national consulting firm providing support for youth.

PERSONAL

Am a quick learner who works well under pressure. Will relocate.

Retail sales and service

Exact Name of Person
Title or Position
Name of Company
Address
City, State, Zip

DIVISIONAL
MERCHANDISE
MANAGER

Dear Exact Name of Person: (or Dear Sir or Madam if answering a blind ad.)

   With the enclosed resume, I would like to make you aware of my desire to become a Divisional Merchandising Manager of the Shoe Division.

   As you will see from my resume, I offer a track record of achievements with Sears and Roebuck Department Stores, where I began working after high school. While excelling in numerous professional development and executive training programs, I feel as though I have earned my "Ph.D. in retailing" in my more than 20 years of experience with Sears.

   I am proud of the significant contributions I have made to the organization's bottom line over the years, and I am known for my strong financial control and meticulous attention to detail. I am also respected for my aggressive emphasis on team building and relationship building among the buying team, between the buyers and stores, and with vendors. Through the years, I have acquired the know-how which enables me to foster a results-oriented environment while providing the kind of supervision which buyers thrive on. I have come to believe that buyers are very unusual individuals, and I excel in mentoring, coaching, interacting with, motivating, supervising, and inspiring buyers of different experience levels.

   You will see from my resume that I have utilized my personal initiative and expert knowledge of the shoe business to produce valuable bottom-line results. I am a youthful, energetic, and highly computer-proficient manager who could certainly continue to produce valuable bottom-line results as a Divisional Merchandise Manager, and I would cheerfully relocate as your needs require. I believe in the intrinsic vitality of the Sears and Roebuck organization, and I want to continue to "make it happen" in shoes.

   Sincerely,

   Cyrus Lafferty

CYRUS M. LAFFERTY

1110½ Hay Street, Fayetteville, NC 28305　　•　　preppub@aol.com　　•　　(910) 483-6611

OBJECTIVE　　To continue contributing to the profitability and growth of the Sears and Roebuck Department Stores as a Divisional Merchandise Manager or in a key management role which could utilize my skills in team building, shoe merchandising, financial control, and strategic planning.

EXPERIENCE　　*Have excelled in this "track record" of advancement with Sears and Roebuck:*
2002-present: DIVISIONAL MERCHANDISE MANAGER, SHOE DIVISION. Pittsburgh, PA. In addition to my responsibilities as Divisional Merchandise Manager, handle buying for Kids' shoes for 22 stores for more than two years.
- In a division with a total volume in 2004 of $18.6 million, increased merchandise margin dollars by $280,000 through my prudent decisions related to the merchandise mix of athletic and brown shoes; increased markup by 1.5%.
- Supervise two buyers and an associate buyer; pride myself on the "esprit de corps" and spirit of teamwork I create as I challenge buyers to plan strategically and focus on store needs.
- On my own initiative, established a "non-returnable-to-vendor" credit program which generated $25,000 in bottom-line credits.
- Am highly skilled in utilizing software to improve management decision making; proficient with software including Microsoft Word, Access, and Excel; skilled with merchandise systems POM, Markdown, IMS, Store SKU Database, MPO, and SAR.

2000-2002: DIVISIONAL MERCHANDISE MANAGER, SHOE DIVISION. Pittsburgh, PA. For 27 stores, provided merchandising leadership while undertaking several new initiatives which improved profitability; developed and managed three buyers.
- On my own initiative, developed a process to identify and eliminate aging inventory; this improved stock rotation by ensuring the "first in, first out" stock rotation method.
- Created a seasonal Buying Guide for 27 stores which enabled us to remain within our "open to buy" and stay rigorously within our budget.
- Produced a Standards and Information Guide to assist with the merger of 27 stores.

1997-2000: DIVISIONAL MERCHANDISING MANAGER, SHOE DIVISION, LADIES ACCESSORIES & INTIMATE APPAREL. Supervised five buyers and a merchandise secretary for 11 stores.
1996-1997: DIVISIONAL MERCHANDISE MANAGER, SHOE DIVISION. Supervised three buyers while providing merchandising leadership for 11 stores.
1994-1996: GROUP BUYER, SHOES. Excelled as Group Buyer for 11 stores.
1992-1994: GROUP BUYER, SHOES. Group Buyer for 13 stores in Pittsburgh, Easton.
1984-1991: BUYER/MANAGER. York, PA. Buyer/Manager for Kids and Intimate Apparel.
1982-1984: BUYER/MANAGER. Easton, PA. Buyer/Manager of Men's/Boys Apparel, Men's/Kids Shoes, and the Home Store.

EDUCATION　　**B. S. in Business Administration,** University of Pittsburgh, Pittsburgh, PA, 1997.

AFFILIATIONS　　Deacon, Joshua Baptist Church; am a member of the Children's Ministry Committee, past member of the finance committee, and other church activity involvement.

HONOR　　Named "Best Seller" Divisional Merchandise Manager, 1999.

PERSONAL　　Outstanding reputation. Truly thrive on the fast pace of the retail environment. Am known for my ability to react quickly and decisively to emerging trends. Have an ability to anticipate consumer desires.

Nonprofit organization

Date

Exact Name of Person
Title or Position
Name of Company
Address
City, State, Zip

EMERGENCY ASSISTANCE COORDINATOR, Phoenix Community Center, is responding to an internal opening within the organization for which she works

Dear Exact Name of Person: (or Dear Sir or Madam if answering a blind ad.)

With the enclosed resume, I would like to formally request that you consider me for another position with the Phoenix Community Services Agency. I am responding to your recent ad for a Social Worker for the Senior Citizens Case Assistance Program.

As you are aware, I have served the Phoenix Community Center as its Emergency Assistance Coordinator. I truly enjoy working with the aging population, and I have developed an excellent reputation within the human services community. After reading the ad you placed, I am certain that I have all the qualifications you are seeking. In addition, I offer the advantage of thoroughly understanding the internal operations of the Phoenix Community Services Agency as a proud member of its team.

You may not be aware that, prior to becoming your Emergency Assistance Coordinator, I worked with the elderly as Activities Director of the Canyon Retirement Home. I realized from that job that I had "found my calling" in working with senior citizens, and I truly thrived on bringing laughter and structure to their lives through the creative activities I planned and implemented.

With a reputation as a highly competent and conscientious individual, you will also see that I previously excelled in a track record of promotion with two convenience store chains, where I was promoted to District Manager over nine stores and then to Regional Sales Manager over 76 stores. Although I excelled as a manager in profit-making organizations, I have found that my take-charge, "make-it-happen" personality is well suited to the complex environment of nonprofit services organizations. As Emergency Assistance Coordinator, I have enjoyed the satisfaction of being able to make a difference in people's lives, and I am confident that I could continue to serve with distinction in this new position.

Please give me every consideration for this position, and also please give me the opportunity to formally interview for the position so that I demonstrate that I am the person you are seeking.

Yours sincerely,

Kate Easton

KATE EASTON

1110½ Hay Street, Fayetteville, NC 28305   •   preppub@aol.com   •   (910) 483-6611

OBJECTIVE

To benefit the Phoenix Community Services Agency through my love and admiration for senior citizens, my outstanding reputation within the human services community, and my indepth knowledge of community resources and services suited to this population.

AFFILIATION

Was named "Woman of the Year" in 2004 by the Arizona Business and Professional Women's Organization. Served as President, 2003 and 2004.
Served on the Board of Directors of Rape Crisis in Phoenix, 1998-03.

EXPERIENCE

EMERGENCY ASSISTANCE COORDINATOR. Phoenix Community Services Agency, Phoenix, AZ (2002-present). Continuously interface with the aging population while handling casework for those seeking emergency assistance through the Center; work closely with the executive director and casework committee in developing guidelines for the quantity and quality of assistance provided to clients.

- Work closely with Department of Social Services social workers and maintain cooperative relationships with organizations providing essential human services; have earned respect for my professionalism and compassionate style.
- Had input into the creation of the center's database in my department, and maintain files.
- Inform people including senior citizens about programs and services which could be of assistance to them; provide referral, follow-up, and advocacy activities on behalf of older adults and others.
- Personally approach the service delivery system on the client's behalf, especially in the case of the frail or aging, when the inquirer is unable to investigate the resources available.
- Increase community awareness of information and case assistance services.
- Provide training for other staff who perform casework.
- Established an extensive network of contacts involved in providing emergency assistance within the community; develop and maintain a notebook for staff on resources and key contact individuals within professional helping organizations and volunteer operations.

ACTIVITIES DIRECTOR. Canyon Retirement Home, Phoenix, AZ (2000-01). Excelled in working with the elderly and enjoyed the process of bringing laughter and structure to the lives of senior citizens.

Other experience (1984-00): Excelled in a track record of promotion with Circle K and Convenience Food Marts, Inc.; earned a reputation as an excellent manager.

- Began as a Cashier-Clerk with Convenience Food Marts, Inc., then was promoted to Assistant Manager and Store Manager, then to District Manager.
- Was recruited by Circle K to be District Manager of nine stores in Tucson; promoted to Regional Sales Manager over 76 stores.

EDUCATION

Arizona State University, Tempe, AZ. Completed courses in archaeology, Bible, business education, and computer science.
University of Phoenix, Phoenix, AZ. A.S. degree in Nursery Crops Technology, 1985.

PERSONAL

Am a high energy, take-charge individual who enjoys the challenge of solving problems and finding solutions to human resources dilemmas. Outstanding references. Solid speaking, writing, and computer skills.

Social services organization

Exact Name of Person
Title or Position
Name of Company
Address
City, State, Zip

FAMILY ADVOCACY SPECIALIST,
United Methodist Church

Dear Exact Name of Person: (or Dear Sir or Madam if answering a blind ad.)

I am responding to your advertisement in the newspaper for a Program Coordinator. I was quite excited when I read the ad in the newspaper because I offer all the skills and abilities you seek. Fluent in Spanish, I have counseled clients in Spanish while providing case management services to individuals with a wide range of problems and impairments.

In my most recent job as a Family Advocacy Specialist, I served as the "subject matter expert" on family advocacy issues for the United Methodist Church. Utilizing programming and fundraising techniques which have been hailed as "ingenious" and "unique," I led a small staff in developing the Foster Care & Shelter Programs now used in 23 states. It has been one of the biggest thrills of my life to be involved in designing and implementing programs which I know will positively impact the lives of young children for many years to come.

What my resume does not reveal is my affable nature and warm personality that is well suited to the social services field, which I truly enjoy. Although my chosen profession is one in which case workers encounter tragic and sad human realities on a daily basis, I am confident of my ability, refined through experience, to help anyone improve his or her situation. I also offer highly refined skills in budget planning and administration.

I am an experienced social services professional who would enjoy contributing to your needs and goals, and I hope you will favorably review my application and call me to set up an interview at your convenience. Thank you in advance for your time.

Sincerely yours,

Stephanie Taylor

STEPHANIE TAYLOR

1110½ Hay Street, Fayetteville, NC 28305 • preppub@aol.com • (910) 483-6611

OBJECTIVE

To contribute to an organization that can use a skilled social worker who offers experience in handling problems related to child abuse, mental illness, and family violence as well as problems associated with poverty, illiteracy, and joblessness.

LANGUAGE

Fluent in Spanish

EXPERIENCE

FAMILY ADVOCACY SPECIALIST. United Methodist Church Family Support Center, New York, NY (2003-present). Play a key role in implementing and coordinating the Family Advocacy Program throughout the US for this major Christian church.
- Conduct surveys to identify deficiencies in services for abused spouses or children.
- Implemented an innovative community education program which included training programs for individuals; publicized information describing the grounds for reporting suspected abuse.
- Train social services representatives, youth services staff, and social services volunteers as well as personnel in other organizations and agencies in the procedures for identifying and referring suspected child abuse.
- Serve as the "subject matter expert" on family advocacy issues as a member of the Family Advocacy Case Team. Developed the Foster Care & Shelter Programs now used in 23 states.

CHILD DEVELOPMENT EDUCATION SPECIALIST. The State of Florida, Miami, FL (2000-03). Worked as Training Coordinator in the Child Development Services Branch; advised and trained those providing day care to preschoolers on age-appropriate activities, and assured that centers/homes were arranged to enhance the physical, emotional, social, and cognitive development of children.
- Completed extensive assessments on each home or center module regularly.
- Planned training modules which were used as instructional guides for caregivers. Completed assessments of children identified as having problems such as developmental delay or behavioral difficulty. Gained insight into the factors that cause stress in caregiving, and counseled workers about how to anticipate and cope with such problems.
- Provided both individual training as well as group sessions.
- Became skilled in improving the day care provided in small homes and large centers.

SOCIAL PROGRAMS COORDINATOR. United Methodist Church, Charlotte, NC (1992-99). Worked with nearly every kind of social services problem while counseling individuals and families; dealt with problems associated with unhappy marriages, unwed parenthood, and financial difficulties as well as problems related to caring for the ill and handicapped.
- Developed programs appropriate for mentally challenged and Downs Syndrome children.
- Created educational materials and provided instruction related to First Aid, sex education, nutrition, home management and home economics, and other areas.
- Became extensively involved in delinquency prevention; counseled juveniles.

EDUCATION

Bachelor of Science (B.S.) degree in Social Services Administration, Thomas Edison State College, Trenton, NJ, 1992.
Completed extensive professional training related to family advocacy, parent effectiveness, substance abuse, children's services, and services for the mentally and physically challenged.

PERSONAL

Am considered an experienced public speaker. Have completed extensive training related to preparing and delivering briefings. Truly enjoy the social services field.

Social services organization

Date

Exact Name of Person
Title or Position
Name of Company
Address
City, State, Zip

FAMILY SERVICES PROGRAM COORDINATOR

Dear Exact Name of Person: (or Dear Sir or Madam if answering a blind ad.)

With the enclosed resume, I would like to make you aware of my interest in exploring employment opportunities with your organization.

As you will see from my resume, after obtaining my M.S. degree in Guidance and Counseling/Psychological Counseling, I gained years of experience as a Social Worker and Counselor for several organizations. Currently as Family Services Program Coordinator at a military community, I supervise eight individuals while directing a wide range of human services and outreach programs provided to military professionals and their families. I am considered as the country's leading technical expert in establishing Family Support Groups. I wrote the Family Support Handbook for Ft. Drum which is being adopted for use at all military bases.

My responsibilities include managing programs providing legal and financial advice as well as crisis counseling to individuals experiencing personal problems ranging from marital distress to suicidal feelings. Continuously involved in developing and implementing programs which facilitate people's involvement in life-enriching activities, I have trained hundreds of managers in effective counseling techniques.

You would find me to be a public relations professional who is skilled at coordinating and implementing large-scale events, authoring and publishing materials ranging from handbooks to policy manuals, as well as training and managing teams of dedicated specialists.

I hope you will call or write me soon to suggest a time convenient for us to meet to discuss your current and future needs. Thank you in advance for your time.

Sincerely yours,

Eileen Lincoln

Alternate last paragraph:
I hope you will welcome my call soon to arrange a brief meeting when we might meet to discuss your needs and goals and how my background might serve them. I can provide outstanding references at the appropriate time.

EILEEN LINCOLN

1110½ Hay Street, Fayetteville, NC 28305 • preppub@aol.com • (910) 483-6611

OBJECTIVE

To contribute to an organization that can use a public relations professional skilled at coordinating large-scale events, authoring and publishing materials ranging from handbooks to policy manuals, as well as training and managing teams of dedicated specialists.

EDUCATION

Master of Science in Guidance and Counseling/Psychological Counseling, Jefferson Community College, Watertown, NY, 1987.

Bachelor of Science, majors in Sociology and Political Science and minor in Psychology, Duke University, Durham, NC, 1982.

Completed executive development programs related to human services administration, service program development and management, crisis intervention program management, and outreach program coordination.

EXPERIENCE

PROGRAM COORDINATOR. Community and Family Services, Ft. Drum, NY (2000-present). At the military community, supervise eight individuals while directing a wide range of human services and outreach programs provided to military professionals and their families.

- Am considered the country's leading technical expert in establishing Family Support Groups; wrote the Family Support Handbook for Ft. Drum and have trained hundreds of managers and supervisors.
- Manage programs providing legal and financial advice as well as crisis counseling to individuals experiencing personal problems ranging from marital distress to suicidal feelings; develop and implement programs which facilitated people's involvement in life-enriching activities.
- Supervise a 7-day-a-week Welcome Center; manage a wide range of programs designed to assist individuals and families traumatized by relocation, transition, and other matters. Train hundreds of managers and professional supervisors in effective counseling techniques.
- Plan and implement this military community's annual Family Symposium and train all facilitators; by aggressive promotion, increased participation from 572 in 2003 to 1,811 in 2004.
- Have excelled in recruiting, training, and managing dozens of volunteers, many of whom give up to 40 hours a week to the Outreach Programs which I plan and coordinate.
- Handle extensive public speaking responsibilities; conduct briefings for 2,000 people monthly.

FAMILY SUPPORT SPECIALIST. Family Support Center, Ft. Drum, NY (1997-99). Taught numerous classes including Parent Effectiveness Classes, Employment Workshops, and courses in Communication Skills while working at one of the nation's airlift centers.

- Created a new service directory for this community after developing the fact sheets and other data collection tools used in obtaining and compiling information.
- Interviewed and counseled individuals and referred them to social services agencies.

GUIDANCE COUNSELOR. Army Education Center, Ft. Knox, KY (1993-96). Handled extensive administrative duties including preparing quarterly reports, financial reports, and class projections while enrolling individuals in programs including Headstart, High School Completion Program, language programs, job skills training courses, and other courses; was Test Control Officer, Property Book Officer, and Contracting Officer.

PERSONAL

Offer highly refined public speaking skills. Am known as an outstanding communicator.

Hotel services

Date

Exact Name of Person
Title or Position
Name of Company
Address
City, State, Zip

**FRONT DESK
SUPERVISOR**

Dear Exact Name of Person: (or Dear Sir or Madam if answering a blind ad.)

    With the enclosed resume, I would like to make you aware of my desire to explore employment opportunities with your hotel.

    As you will see from my resume, I have excelled in all aspects of front desk management at hotels in Massachusetts and Maryland. At two Best Western hotels in Salem and Gloucester, MA, I was extensively trained in auditing and office while learning to handle the customer service responsibilities which go into effective front desk management.

    In my current job as Front Desk Supervisor, I ensure outstanding customer service and am totally committed to the hotel's goals of achieving the highest standards of customer satisfaction. I also perform the audit every Sunday which requires me to balance all hotel accounts.

    Held in high regard by my current employer, I can provide outstanding personal and professional references at the appropriate time. If you can use an astute and experienced hospitality industry professional with the proven ability to impact your bottom line in profitable ways, I hope you will contact me to suggest a time when we might meet to discuss your needs. Thank you in advance for whatever time and professional courtesies you can extend.

Sincerely,

Vanessa Morris

VANESSA MORRIS

1110½ Hay Street, Fayetteville, NC 28305   •   preppub@aol.com   •   (910) 483-6611

OBJECTIVE
To contribute to an organization that can use an experienced hospitality industry professional with a proven ability to solve problems and maximize customer satisfaction.

EDUCATION
B.S. in Computer Technology, N.C. A&T, Boston University, Boston, MA, 1998; excelled academically and graduated cum laude with a 3.8 GPA.
A.A. in Hotel Hospitality, Boston University, Boston, MA, 2005.
A.A. in Office Technology, Salem State College, Salem, MA, 2001.
A.A. in Business Management, Bunker Hill Community College, Boston, MA, 1998.

EXPERIENCE
FRONT DESK SUPERVISOR. Marriott Hotel, Baltimore, MD (2005-present). For this 368-room hotel, am excelling at all aspects of this job which involves extensive responsibilities related to customer service for large accounts and individuals, accounting and auditing, billing, as well as training new front desk clerks.
- Currently begin work at 7 AM and handle the heavy volume of customer complaints and questions which occur between 7 AM and 10 AM.
- Work routinely with large accounts to book blocks of rooms and coordinate special events; provide customer service in the booking process and provide liaison regarding any special banquets and events which are set up.
- Handle a wide range of responsibilities related to billing, accounting, and auditing; for two months acted at the hotel's auditor until the position was filled, and am continuing to perform the audit every Sunday which requires me to balance all hotel accounts.
- Handle the billing, and deal with coupons; prepare the ledger.
- Am totally committed to the hotel's policy of assuring customer satisfaction, no matter what, and routinely solve problems to assure guest satisfaction and repeat business.
- Book up to 150 rooms monthly while providing courteous and friendly customer service.
- Have received numerous letters of appreciation because of my professionalism and dedication to the highest standards of customer support and assistance.

STORE MANAGER. Dunkin Donuts, Baltimore, MD (2004-05). After relocating from Massachusetts to Maryland, accepted a job as a store manager with Dunkin Donuts and managed a staff of 12. Emphasized adherence to the highest standards of cleanliness and sanitation, and led the store to receive an O.S.H.A. award for food service and management.

FRONT DESK REPRESENTATIVE. Best Western Hotel, Salem, MA (2001-03). For this 176-room Best Western, helped the hotel earn the Gold Star for customer service.

Other experience:
FRONT DESK RECEPTIONIST. Best Western Hotel, Gloucester, MA (2000-01). For this 125-room hotel, was trained in auditing and office while becoming skilled in reservations and customer service.
GUEST REPRESENTATIVE. Guest House, Fort Bragg, NC (1998-00). Provided customer service at this hotel which housed the families and visitors of military soldiers.
TRAVEL & TOURISM PHONE OPERATOR. MA Travel & Tourism, Boston, MA (1996-98). In this summer job, underwent an intensive training program which made me an expert on the state of Massachusetts; became very knowledgeable of state facts, history, and trivia.

PERSONAL
Highly computer proficient; can operate, design, and build computers. Am a highly self-motivated individual known for my professional attitude. In my spare time, enjoy classical music and the study of religions.

Automobile sales

Exact Name of Person
Title or Position
Name of Company
Address
City State, Zip

GENERAL MANAGER   Dear Exact Name of Person: (or Dear Sir or Madam if answering a blind ad.)

I am writing to express my strong interest in exploring the option of becoming a Toyota dealer. I would appreciate the opportunity to talk with you at your convenience regarding franchise opportunities with Toyota.

With the enclosed resume, I would like to make you aware of the contributions I could make to your organization through my considerable management experience as well as my proven motivational, sales, and organizational skills.

I began my career in the automobile industry as a salesperson with GMAC-Pontiac-Oldsmobile in McLean, VA, applying the exceptional negotiation skills, sales ability, and bottom-line orientation I developed while owning and operating a successful commercial painting business in Virginia. After moving to Reston Nissan in 1996, and rapidly began advancing to positions of increasing responsibility, from Sales Manager, to Business Manager, and finally to General Manager.

Since attending the National Automobile Dealer Association's University of Dealership Management, I have excelled as the General Manager of Reston Ford-Lincoln-Mercury in Reston, VA. Known as an articulate communicator and skilled manager, I have built a reputation for excellence in customer service while increasing sales volume, gross sales, F & I income, and bottom-line profitability. My exceptional training and motivational skills have resulted in increased lease penetration, and the dealership is averaging sales of $15 million over the last two years.

I feel certain that my experience and skills would make me an excellent candidate for a Toyota dealership, and I would enjoy the opportunity to talk with you in person about your needs and how I might serve them. Several letters of recommendation are attached, and I can assure you that I am a dynamic individual with an outstanding reputation within the industry along with an aggressive bottom-line orientation and a results-oriented style of interacting with others. Thank you in advance for your time.

Sincerely,

Jason Lynch

JASON LYNCH

1110½ Hay Street, Fayetteville, NC 28305 • preppub@aol.com • (910) 483-6611

OBJECTIVE

To benefit an organization that can benefit from a proven automotive industry professional and hands-on general manager with exceptional motivational and communication skills who offers a track record of excellence in the management of sales, operations, and finance.

**EDUCATION &
PROFESSIONAL
DEVELOPMENT
PROGRAMS**

Earned a **Business degree** from the National Automobile Dealer Association's University of Dealership Management, McLean, VA, 2003.
Studied Business Administration and Accounting, Marymount University, Arlington, VA.
Completed extensive customer service training programs.

**PROFESSIONAL
AFFILIATIONS
& HONORS**

Was recognized in the 2003 edition of **"Who's Who of Business Professionals."**
Achieved membership in the **"Million Dollar Sales Club"** for 2000, 1999, and 1998.
Earned the **"Ford Customer Service Excellence Award"** in 2002 for a combination of effectiveness in sales, customer satisfaction, and superior performance.
Received **"Silver Level Certification"** from the Nissan Customer Relations Society, 2000.

EXPERIENCE

GENERAL MANAGER. Reston Ford-Lincoln-Mercury, Reston, VA (2003-present). Supervise a staff of 25 employees, directing the sales team to apply effective sales and follow-up techniques which lead to increases in vehicle sales and bottom-line profit.
- Provide oversight for all operational functions of a dealership which currently has a $2 million new car and $1 million used car inventory.
- Responsible for ensuring the dealership maintains the highest possible customer service index while increasing sales volume, gross profit, F & I income, and bottom-line profitability.
- An articulate communicator and skilled trainer, am adept at leading people by motivating them to achieve their goals, rather than through intimidation.
- Through my leadership, have driven the company to achieve exceptional sales, averaging more than $15 million annually for 2003 and 2004.
- Have increased lease penetration through training efforts which ensure that the sales force strongly presents the benefits and protections offered through new car leasing.

SALES MANAGER, BUSINESS MANAGER, and **GENERAL MANAGER.** Reston Nissan, Reston, VA (1996-03). Developed expert abilities as a negotiator as well as in recruiting and training effective sales staff while advancing in a track record of promotion with this new and used car dealership.
- Originally hired as a Salesperson in 1996, was promoted to Business Manager in 2000, then to Sales Manager in 2001, and to General Manager in 2002.

SALESPERSON. GMAC Pontiac-Oldsmobile, McLean, VA (1995-96). In my first job with an automobile dealership, built on business, sales, and customer service skills developed as a small business owner to become highly effective in satisfying customers.

Highlights of earlier experience: OWNER and **GENERAL MANAGER.** Arlington Interior Painting Company, Arlington, VA. Built a successful small business which provided interior and exterior painting and wallpapering services to primarily commercial customers.
- Managed contracts with area churches and schools as well as with the U.S. Army and major corporations such as Sears and Johnson & Johnson.

PERSONAL

Familiar with ADP systems using PC computers with Microsoft Word and Excel. Am a hands-on general manager known for my integrity and work ethic. Excellent references.

Accounting services

Exact Name of Person
Title or Position
Name of Company
Address
City, State, Zip

GENERAL MANAGER   Dear Exact Name of Person: (or Dear Sir or Madam if answering a blind ad.)

Mr. Curtis Peterson, with whom I worked at Financial Services, urged me to submit a resume for the position of Senior Operations Analyst.

I would appreciate an opportunity to talk with you soon about how I could contribute to your organization through my background in accounting, credit administration, operations management, and personnel supervision.

As you will see from my resume, I offer a Bachelor of Science degree in Accounting and a reputation as a knowledgeable professional who can be counted on to produce results. In my most recent position as General Manager for a retail division with $2 million in annual sales, I improved virtually every aspect of operations including employee morale, productivity, standard operating procedures, and increased receivables.

I offer expertise in areas such as financial reporting, the establishment and use of computerized accounting systems, auditing, loss prevention, cash flow analysis, accounts receivable and payable, and all aspects of credit management and debt recovery.

With my education and experience, I know that I could make significant contributions to your organization. I adapt easily to new situations and enjoy the challenge of finding ways to increase bottom-line results through my well-developed analytical and problem-solving abilities.

I hope you will call or write me soon to suggest a time convenient for us to meet and discuss your current and future needs and how I might serve them. Thank you in advance for your time.

Sincerely yours,

Gregory Fletch

GREGORY FLETCH

1110½ Hay Street, Fayetteville, NC 28305 • preppub@aol.com • (910) 483-6611

OBJECTIVE

To benefit an organization seeking a versatile, results-oriented accounting and management professional with a reputation for integrity, specialized knowledge of auditing and financial and general ledger accounting, and experience in designing and using computerized accounting systems, reducing costs, effecting loss containment, and negotiating contracts.

EDUCATION & TRAINING

Bachelor of Science degree in Accounting, Friends University, Wichita, KS, 1999. Completed corporate-sponsored workshops/seminars on management techniques, problem solving, internal communication, inventory control, and total quality management.

EXPERIENCE

GENERAL MANAGER. Wichita Cleaners, Wichita, KS (2005-present). Excelled in finding methods of reducing costs and improving productivity while overseeing fiscal and physical operations for a retail division of Heckman Properties with annual sales of approximately $2 million.

- Established standard operating procedures (SOPs) for nearly every aspect of operations from employee relations, to accounts payable/receivable, to credit applications, to sales.
- Reduced inventory levels $100,000 by implementing a computerized just-in-time (JIT) purchasing system which also resulted in lowering costs 12%. Made additional improvements which significantly reduced the level of back orders and increased the collection of receivables by 20%.
- Redesigned the invoice system which made processes smoother and easier.
- Tightened procedures for repossessing products, setting credit limits, and filing bankruptcy claims thereby reducing losses in accounts receivable.
- Built better relations among service and delivery personnel through incentive programs.
- Prepared the year-end financial statements for presentation to corporate CPA's.

COST ACCOUNTING MANAGER. Financial Services, Inc., Emporia, KS (2004). Supervised cost gathering activities including accounts payable and receivable, payroll, purchasing, and capital expenditures for a manufacturing division of an international company with annual sales of approximately $466 million.

STAFF ACCOUNTANT/AUDITOR. Scott & Scott, PA, CPA, Emporia, KS (2004). Earned recognition from company executives for my attention to detail, pride in my accomplishments, and enthusiastic attitude toward my work while involved in audits, tax preparation, and the review of work papers for independent quality review. Became knowledgeable of the techniques involved in in-depth nonprofit auditing and also became adept at using audit software.

ASSISTANT CONTROLLER. Webber Bros., Emporia, KS (2003). Handled a project to convert all accounting data and records to an IBM system and was involved in the installation of these new systems; oversaw the maintenance of standard cost systems for multiple manufacturing facilities. Became familiar with processes for automating accounting systems.

BRANCH ACCOUNTANT and **ASSISTANT CONTROLLER.** McDowell Construction Company, Emporia, KS (1999-03). Developed knowledge in a variety of areas including supervising general accounting, preparing monthly closings, preparing consolidated financial statements to be presented to corporate executives, and handling payments to subcontractors.

- Established standard operating procedures and spreadsheets used for production tracking and cost analysis for seven manufacturing plants.

PERSONAL

Knowledge of software, including Word, Excel, PowerPoint. Excellent analytical skills.

Hospitality industry

Date

Exact Name of Person
Title or Position
Name of Company
Address
City, State, Zip

**GUEST SERVICES
SUPERVISOR**

for a hotel.
After years of experience in
the hospitality industry,
this professional has
decided to make a change
and become a travel agent
with an airline. Notice how
the resume stresses
experience which is
relevant to aviation.

Dear Exact Name of Person: (or Dear Sir or Madam if answering a blind ad.)

With the enclosed resume, I would like to express my strong desire to become a Flight Attendant with Continental Airlines and make you aware of my background which is ideally suited to your needs.

Throughout my working career, I have excelled in the hospitality industry. I am currently working at Winchester Inn (a local hotel chain) as a Guest Services Supervisor. I started with the chain as a Guest Services Agent and have moved up the promotional ladder. I supervise desk clerks, hire and train new employees, book bus tours, and deal with the hotel guest relations on all levels.

Through graciously and effectively resolving all guest complaints, I have gained invaluable experience that I am certain would be well suited to the needs of Continental Airlines. I hope you will be in touch with me soon to set up a time when we might meet and further discuss my qualifications. I can provide excellent personal and professional references. Thank you in advance for your time.

Yours sincerely,

Kathleen M. Olson

KATHLEEN M. OLSON

1110½ Hay Street, Fayetteville, NC 28305   •   preppub@aol.com   •   (910) 483-6611

OBJECTIVE   To obtain a position as a flight attendant with Continental Airlines.

EXPERIENCE   *With Dalton Hospitality, Inc., a regional holding company that owns a number of chain hotels, advanced in a "track record" of increasing responsibilities:*
2003-present: **GUEST SERVICES SUPERVISOR.** Winchester Inn, Tulsa, OK.
Was promoted to this position from Guest Services Agent; perform a variety of supervisory, administrative, and customer service tasks for this busy branch of a local hotel chain.

- Supervise five front desk clerks, directing their activities to guarantee maximum guest satisfaction.
- Participate in interviewing, hiring, training, development, and evaluation of Guest Services employees.
- Train new Guest Services associates in all front desk procedures as well as in the handling of guests' questions, problems, etc.; continually provide feedback and guidance to staff.
- Prepare weekly work schedules for Guest Services employees, controlling labor hours to minimize overtime and ensure optimum front desk coverage.
- Provide documentation to justify overtime hours to the General Manager; maintain records of staff attendance and tardiness.
- Perform direct sales of hotel services to organizations, such as booking bus tours into the facility.
- Verify accuracy of cash drawer at start of shift and supervise end-of-shift closeout of register and cash receipts; ensure timely and accurate completion of paperwork.
- Listen to, analyze, and resolve all guest complaints in accordance with policies and procedures of the hotel.
- Notify upper-level management if unusual incidents or emergencies arise or if a customer service issue cannot be resolved without higher approval.

2000-03: **GUEST SERVICES AGENT.** Winchester Inn, Benning, OK. Provided a number of customer relations, clerical, and administrative tasks to guests during their stay at this branch of a local hotel chain.

- Checked guests into and out of the hotel; scheduled and canceled guest reservations.
- Answered multiline telephone and operated a switchboard, directing guests' calls to the correct extension and taking messages when guests were not available.
- Performed clerical and secretarial functions, including typing, filing, photocopying, and operating a variety of office equipment.
- Provided assistance to guests, addressing and resolving questions and complaints when possible or directing them to the Guest Services Supervisor when necessary.
- Operated a guest reservation terminal, cash register, credit card terminal, and ten-key calculator.

Other experience:
CASHIER. Friendly's, Tulsa, OK. Provided customer service, unloaded shipments of ice cream and supplies, ran the cash register, and took customer orders for ice cream cakes.
CREW MEMBER. Rally's Hamburgers, Tulsa, OK. Served customers, prepared food, opened and closed the store, and performed cash handling duties.

PERSONAL   Excellent personal and professional references are available upon request.

Call center customer service

Date

Exact Name of Person
Title or Position
Name of Company
Address
City, State, Zip

**INBOUND CUSTOMER
SERVICE
REPRESENTATIVE**

Dear Exact Name of Person: (or Dear Sir or Madam if answering a blind ad.)

   With the enclosed resume, I would like to make you aware of my experience in customer service and call center environments.

   As you will see from my resume, I have worked since 2002 in a call center environment as an Inbound Customer Service Representative. As a "go-between" for agents and supervisors, I monitored quality assurance on inbound calls and was groomed for increasing supervisory responsibilities. While managing a team of up to 30 people, I worked with management to implement new procedures such as Visa application procedures, and I adapted to numerous changes in customer care procedures on a daily basis. I have become skilled at evaluating employees and providing feedback to enhance the effectiveness of sales agents and customer service representatives.

   In prior work experience, I refined my customer service skills in environments which included loan processing and commercial printing. I have become known for my strong problem-solving skills and for my ability to react quickly and make prudent decisions in situations which require immediate decision making.

   If you can use an experienced customer service professional with extensive experience in resolving problems, implementing new programs and procedures, and providing quality assurance, I hope you will contact me to suggest a time when we might meet to discuss your needs.

Sincerely,

Kelly Samson

KELLY SAMSON

1110½ Hay Street, Fayetteville, NC 28305   •   preppub@aol.com   •   (910) 483-6611

OBJECTIVE   To benefit an organization that can use an experienced call center professional with exceptional customer skills along with supervisory experience.

EXPERIENCE   **INBOUND CUSTOMER SERVICE REPRESENTATIVE.** Creighton Industries, Omaha, NE (2002-present). As a "go-between" for agents and supervisors, monitored quality assurance on inbound calls and was being groomed for supervisory responsibilities while meeting or exceeding my personal sales goals.
- Manage a team of up to 30 people.
- Work with management to implement new procedures such as Visa applications.
- Play a key role in implementing a new program related to new hires.
- Evaluate employees and provide feedback to enhance the effectiveness of sales agents and customer service representatives.
- Prioritize customer service in cost management, sales performance, and customer case with quality assurance.
- On a daily basis, adapt to numerous changes in customer care procedures.
- Work as part of a team in coordinating and completing customers' orders within Creighton's policy.

CUSTOMER SERVICE REPRESENTATIVE and **BOOKKEEPER.** Fashion Nails, Omaha, NE (1998-02). Under the supervision of Alyse Mary handled a variety of office operations in this part-time position involving:

customer service	operations management
accounts receivable	sales
cashier	cleaning/general maintenance
bookkeeping	data processing/entry

MAJOR SALES REPRESENTATIVE. Kinko's, Omaha, NE (1996-97). Under the supervision of Gregory McKenzie, excelled in telemarketing, recordkeeping, mailing, sales, production control, job estimation, creating new accounts, providing customer service, and operating computers.

LOAN PROCESSOR TRAINEE. Cornhusker Mortgage, Omaha, NE (1995-96). Handled loan process verifications, data process/entry, filing, and customer service; gained valuable experience checking/verifying clients' credit history.

CUSTOMER SERVICE REPRESENTATIVE. Miracle Hill, Omaha, NE (1991-94). In addition to handling customer service, sales, phone orders, and responding to customer complaints, also performed inventory control and processed customer orders; maintained bookkeeping procedures under the supervision of Chick Adams.

COMPUTERS   *Computers:* Working knowledge of computer software used for word processing, spreadsheets, and recordkeeping.
Office Equipment: Operate a variety of equipment used in office operations including typewriters, calculators, multiline phones, and fax machines.

PERSONAL   Am a home owner and permanent resident who has lived in Omaha since 1980. Enjoy sewing, sports, church activities, reading, and camping. Have a knack for providing top-quality customer-service and enjoy helping customers.

Interior design services

Exact Name of Person
Title or Position
Name of Company
Address
City, State, Zip

INTERIOR DESIGNER   Dear Exact Name of Person: (or Dear Sir or Madam if answering a blind ad.)

I would appreciate an opportunity to talk with you soon about how I could contribute to your organization through my sales and communication skills, interior design expertise, as well as my initiative and ability to work independently.

As you will see from my resume, I have been working since I was 16 years old, and I financed 80% of my college education through summer and part-time jobs. A highly motivated self-starter, I was nominated for numerous honors at Maryville University because of the leadership I provided on campus, to my sorority, and in the community. I am especially proud of the fact that, as my sorority's elected president, I transformed a poorly performing organization with serious financial problems into a respected entity which won the "most improved chapter" award.

I have found that my leadership is a valuable asset in business, too. I have a knack for motivating people, and I am respected for my ability to troubleshoot difficult problems and satisfy even the fussiest customers. You would certainly find me to be a hard worker who would enjoy contributing to your goals, and I would be delighted to provide outstanding personal and professional references at the appropriate time.

I hope you will welcome my call soon to arrange a brief meeting at your convenience to discuss your current and future needs and how I might serve them. Thank you in advance for your time.

Sincerely yours,

Joy Ann Honour

Alternate last paragraph:
I hope you will call or write me soon to suggest a time convenient for us to meet and discuss your current and future needs and how I might serve them. Thank you in advance for your time.

JOY ANN HONOUR

1110½ Hay Street, Fayetteville, NC 28305   •   preppub@aol.com   •   (910) 483-6611

OBJECTIVE

To contribute to an organization that can use a creative and dynamic young professional with expertise related to interior, commercial, and residential design who offers very strong leadership, motivational, communication, and sales skills.

EDUCATION

Bachelor of Science (B.S.) degree in Human Environmental Sciences, Maryville University, Maryville, SC, 1995.
- As elected president of my sorority, Delta Zeta, transformed a disorganized operation into the "most improved chapter in NC and SC"; was personally named "Outstanding President for NC and SC" and inducted into the Greek Hall of Fame.
- Was elected Student Legislator, Student Government Association; was elected Secretary of the legislature's Rules and Judiciary Committee.
- Was nominated for several prestigious awards for campus, community, and sorority leadership; received the respected Artemis Award.
- Personally financed 80% of my college education through part-time and summer jobs.

MEMBERSHIP

Member, American Society of Interior Designers since 1989; presently an Allied Practitioner.

EXPERIENCE

INTERIOR DESIGNER. The Decorator Store, Charleston, SC (1998-present). With this family-owned business, have become an expert in all aspects of residential interior design in a shop that is well known for its creation of quality window treatments.
- Hired and supervised other employees.
- Am known for my skill in working with "fussy" clients in this very custom business.
- Applied my leadership skills by helping this store to expand from its solid niche in window treatments into interior design consultation services.
- Have become skilled in figuring the actual fabrication of window treatments.
- Used my sales and organizational skills to improve customer relations/service.
- Because of my strong communication and motivational skills, am the interior designer who troubleshoots stubborn problems when they arise.

INTERIOR DESIGN INTERN. U.S. Government, Directorate of Engineering and Housing — Design Branch, Ft. Bragg, NC (May - August 1997). Received a letter of praise and appreciation and was complimented for my initiative and independence while excelling in an internship which required me to design an entire building; specified carpets, tile, and paints; performed some architectural sketching; redesigned a map.
- Worked on interior design recommendations for the new medical center at Ft. Bragg.
- Studied the design of local churches.
- Received an "A" for my internship; invited to participate in meetings on the new hospital.

COMPUTER OPERATOR. Maryville Technical Community College, Maryville, SC (June -August 1996). Processed information for a tire recycling project using the Apple computer; data processed the results of others research, and inputted mailing lists.

TYPIST. World Travel, Maryville, SC (June 1996). Typed letters, delivered tickets, and set up displays of travel brochures; took pride in doing very small jobs to the best of my ability.

PERSONAL

Believe my leadership qualities are very valuable as they help me sell and motivate people. Am interested in gaining expertise in every aspect of interior design.

Loan closing services

Date

Exact Name of Person
Title or Position
Name of Company
Address
City, State, Zip

LOAN CLOSING
SPECIALIST &
LEGAL ASSISTANT
for a private
real estate practice

Dear Exact Name of Person: (or Dear Sir or Madam if answering a blind ad.)

I would appreciate an opportunity to talk with you soon about how I could contribute to your organization through my training as a Loan Closing Specialist/Legal Assistant.

Currently employed as a Loan Closing Specialist/Legal Assistant for Kevin H. Fuller, a well-known Attorney in Springfield with a private real estate practice, I assist in preparing loan packages and closings while preparing legal documents, conducting title searches, and providing customer service. In a previous position as a Loan Processing Clerk for the Springfield Federal Reserve Bank, I became skilled in all aspects of loan processing while handling mortgage banking and loan processing within a budget of over one million dollars. I submitted loans, coordinated appraisals, prepared legal documents, and compiled loan packages as well as interviewed loan applicants and prepared applications. I also coordinated with a wide range of real estate attorneys, appraisers, residential and commercial sales professionals, and VA/FHA officials.

While earning a Bachelor of Arts degree in English from the Chaminade University of Honolulu, Hawaii, I completed courses in Public Speaking, Business Writing, and English Literature. I am also skilled in utilizing various accounting and banking programs being proficient with Windows XP, Microsoft Word, Excel and PowerPoint.

I hope you will welcome my call soon to arrange a brief meeting at your convenience to discuss your needs and goals and how I might serve them. Thank you in advance for your time.

Yours sincerely,

Tina M. Shaver

Alternate last paragraph:
I hope you will call or write soon to suggest a time convenient for us to meet and discuss your current and future needs and how I might serve them. Thank you in advance for your time.

TINA M. SHAVER

1110½ Hay Street, Fayetteville, NC 28305 • preppub@aol.com • (910) 483-6611

OBJECTIVE   To benefit an organization that can use a hard-working professional experienced in office operations with specialized knowledge of loan closing procedures, accounting/bookkeeping, and marketing/publicity.

EDUCATION   Earned **B.A. in English**, Chaminade University of Honolulu, Honolulu, HI, 1999.
In my spare time, am completing courses toward a B.S. degree, University of Illinois, Springfield, Illinois.

COMPUTERS   Skilled in utilizing various accounting and banking programs; proficient with Windows XP, Microsoft Office, and MLS.

EXPERIENCE   **LOAN CLOSING SPECIALIST & LEGAL ASSISTANT.** Kevin H. Fuller, Attorney-at-Law, Springfield, IL (2004-present). For a private real estate practice, assist in preparing loan packages and closings while also preparing legal documents, conduct title searches, and provide customer service.
* Use Windows operating system with specialized software.

LOAN PROCESSING CLERK. Springfield Federal Reserve Bank, Springfield, IL (2002-03). Became skilled in all aspects of loan processing while handling mortgage banking and loan processing within a budget of over one million dollars.
* Submitted loans, coordinated appraisals, prepared legal documents, and compiled loan packages.
* Interviewed loan applicants and prepared applications; provided customer service.
* Coordinated with a wide range of real estate attorneys, appraisers, residential and commercial sales professionals, and VA/FHA officials.

ACCOUNTING SPECIALIST. Morrison Business Services, Honolulu, HI (1997-02). Played a key role in the substantial growth of this small business which provided accounting services for small businesses.
* On my own initiative, developed and implemented aggressive marketing programs which coordinated telemarketing and direct mail activities with persistent follow-up.
* Provided all accounting support for small businesses: prepared P&Ls, payroll, general ledgers, and journals.
* Trained small businesses in recordkeeping procedures and performance reporting activities.

MARKETING COORDINATOR. Felder-Marcum, Inc., Honolulu, HI (1995-97). Developed and implemented national and local marketing programs for restaurants in Honolulu, Kahului & Laie.

MARKETING REPRESENTATIVE. Hampton Golf Club, Springfield, IL (1993-95). Excelled in a key position in marketing and public relations and worked closely with Hampton's founder and Springfield native Michael Bradford.
* Was instrumental in the development of the company's first marketing manual.
* Designed and published a golf course magazine; coordinated national tournaments and reporting results.

PERSONAL   Excellent references. Possess excellent written and verbal communication skills and work well with people at all ages. Congenial personality.

Office products

Date

Exact Name of Person
Title or Position
Name of Company
Address
City, State, Zip

**MAJOR ACCOUNTS
MANAGER & SALES
REPRESENTATIVE**

Dear Exact Name of Person: (or Dear Sir or Madam if answering a blind ad.)

With the enclosed resume, I would like to make you aware of my interest in exploring sales opportunities within your company. Although I am excelling in my current position and am held in the highest regard, I am selectively exploring other options.

A graduate of University of Dayton, I am highly skilled in utilizing all Microsoft applications, and I am adept at creating PowerPoint presentations on a laptop computer. After graduating from University of Dayton with a degree in History, I went to work in sales for a company in Columbus, and I quickly discovered that my strong communication and problem-solving skills were highly effective in sales and marketing situations. As a Territory Manager and Sales Associate, I established the company's largest-ever national account which generated business for the company in 48 states. I was awarded numerous honors because of my success in exceeding sales quotas.

I was recruited for my current job in 2004 as a Major Accounts Manager and Sales Representative, and in less than a year I have transformed an unproductive territory in what was considered a "secondary market" into one of the top territories in the nation. I am currently ranked #5 among 1,000 sales representatives in the U.S. and I have won numerous awards in 2005, including a trip to Florida which was awarded to only 10 people in the company. I was named Company Sales Representative of the Month in January, March, and May 2005 for achieving the highest sales among my sales peers.

In my current job I call on major accounts including hospitals, and I have established a strong network of contacts. I am skilled at utilizing every type of sales tool and technique including cold calling, networking through friends and referrals, and developing superior written proposals. I am a highly self-motivated individual who is satisfied with producing no less than the highest-quality results in any project I take on. I have thoroughly enjoyed applying my intellect and intelligence in the process of serving customers, because I have discovered that sales is all about solving problems for people and companies.

If you can use a polished go-getter who would thrive on whatever challenge you place in my path, I hope you will welcome my call soon when I try to arrange a brief meeting to discuss your goals and how my background might serve your needs. I can provide outstanding references at the appropriate time.

Sincerely,

Alois Tinker

ALOIS TINKER

1110½ Hay Street, Fayetteville, NC 28305 • preppub@aol.com • (910) 483-6611

OBJECTIVE

To benefit an organization that can use an aggressive young sales professional and highly effective communicator with the proven ability to exceed ambitious goals while maximizing profitability and assuring the highest level of customer service, support, and satisfaction.

EDUCATION

Bachelor of Arts in History, University of Dayton, OH, 2001.
- Concentration was in Conversational Germany.
- Studied abroad through the University of Dayton program in Germany, 1999-00.

Have excelled in extensive professional development courses related to sales including Solution Selling I and II, Advance System Selling, and numerous other courses.

COMPUTERS

Highly computer proficient with all Microsoft applications; am skilled in creating PowerPoint presentations for customers on a laptop computer. Work with Microsoft and Novell Computer Networks in the process of installing new products and add-ons to computer networks.

EXPERIENCE

MAJOR ACCOUNTS MANAGER & SALES REPRESENTATIVE. National Business Office & Solutions, Dayton, OH (2004-present). Took an unproductive territory in what is considered a "secondary market" and have transformed it into one of the top territories in the nation in only one year.
- Am **ranked #5 among nearly 1,000 U.S. corporate sales representatives**, and am currently the top sales producer in my area after only one year with the company.
- Have exceeded year-to-date quota by 155% of which $393,000 (or 98%) was new business.
- Have already won the **National Sales Award** for 2005, a trip to Florida awarded to only 10 people nationwide; previously won a trip to California, and was one of only 15 reps to win that trip based on second quarter sales.
- After only nine months with the company, received the prestigious **Century Gold Level Award**, an award recognizing $200,000 in sales which normally takes an individual 1 ½ years to achieve.
- Named **Company Sales Representative of the Month** in January, March, and May 2005, for producing the highest monthly sales of all reps.
- Call on hospitals and other institutional buyers as well as businesses of all sizes while prospecting for new business and establishing highly profitable new accounts; have established a network of contacts within the medical community and hospitals.
- Call on large companies in 18 counties in western OH; have increased market share dramatically and have significantly grown the customer base while consistently exceeding my sales quota of $33,333/month.

TERRITORY MANAGER & SALES ASSOCIATE. Teletronics Information Systems, Inc., Columbus, OH (2001-04). Prospected for new customers in eight zip code areas while servicing 400 existing accounts; became skilled in utilizing every sales tool and technique including cold calling, writing proposals, and networking through friends and referrals.
- Established the company's largest-ever national account—a Nikon national account for 48 states. Exceeded year-to-date sales goals by $178,000 (218% of quota).
- Was the recipient of the **Century Club Award** for exceeding $100,000 in sales, May 2004; was awarded the President's Club Vacation for excellence in work performance, March 2004; was named a member of the **President's Club** in 2002, 2003, and 2004; received the **Nifty Award** for exceeding $50,000 in sales for May, April, and January 2004 as well as October and April, 2003.

PERSONAL

Thrive on the challenge of solving customer problems. Highly motivated self starter.

Medical and optical services

Date

Exact Name of Person
Title or Position
Name of Company
Address
City, State, Zip

MANAGER   Dear Exact Name of Person: (or Sir or Madam if answering a blind ad.)

With the enclosed resume, I would like to make you aware of my interest in exploring employment opportunities with your organization. I offer a track record of outstanding bottom-line results based on my strong personal initiative, sales ability, and management skills, and I can provide outstanding references at the appropriate time.

As you will see from my resume, after completing two years of college I became a Sales Representative in the optical industry and rapidly distinguished myself because of my strong customer service skills.

In 1999 I was recruited to become a Sales Representative for a company which was pursuing an ambitious strategic growth strategy. After distinguishing myself in sales, I was promoted to a newly created position as Field Operations Coordinator and Trainer. Although I was considered quite young to handle the senior management responsibilities involved in that job, I quickly excelled and was instrumental in establishing "from scratch" seven new optometric practices which are still ongoing and which have contributed significantly to the company's bottom line. For those seven practices I played the major role in establishing them from the construction phase through the staff training and recruiting phase, and I spent up to three months at each practice to get it firmly established and operating in a sound manner. Frequent travel was involved in that job, and my success depended on my excellent organizational and time management skills. I have proved my ability to work in very demanding positions with little or no supervision.

After excelling as a Field Operations Coordinator, I was promoted to Manager in 2002, and I have succeeded in all aspects of sales, customer service, and personnel management. While managing seven employees, I motivated those employees to achieve bonus-level results for 33 out of 36 months. I have become very skilled at working with doctors' offices, and as a Manager I have worked with various companies and employers in establishing vision benefit programs for their employees. I am experienced in negotiating the details of business agreements.

If you can use a proven performer with unlimited personal initiative and an ability to deliver exceptional bottom-line results, I hope you will contact me to suggest a time when we might meet to discuss your needs. Thank you in advance for your time and professional courtesies.

Sincerely,

Melanie Bowers

MELANIE BOWERS

1110½ Hay Street, Fayetteville, NC 28305   •   preppub@aol.com   •   (910) 483-6611

OBJECTIVE

To contribute to an organization that can use a dedicated young professional who offers a proven ability to achieve excellent bottom-line line results while also applying my strong customer service, sales, and management skills.

EDUCATION

Completed two years of college course work, University of Carolina at Chapel Hill, NC, 1995-99. Completed numerous sales and customer service seminars sponsored by my employer. Graduated from Tar Heel High School, Chapel Hill, NC, 1995.

EXPERIENCE

Have worked for the same employer since 1999, and made significant contributions to the bottom line while excelling in the following track record of advancement with Carolinas Eye Care Center, various locations in NC and SC:

2002-present: MANAGER. Chapel Hill, NC. Was promoted to a key position which involved recruiting, training, and supervised seven individuals.

- In an essentially entrepreneurial role, took the initiative to establish "from scratch" vision programs with local companies and employers which contributed greatly to the growth and revenue of the company.
- Received the **Dedicated Service Award** in 2004 for five years of dedicated service.
- Worked closely with doctors in following up on patient referrals.
- Am responsible for payroll, insurance filing and billing, optical store sales, supervising staff and patient scheduling, coordinating with vendors for purchasing and inventory purposes, reconciling expense registers, and conducting inventory audits every six months. Meet routinely with the President and Operations Manager of the company to discuss office budget, advertising, and expenses.
- Work daily on a computer, and became proficient in utilizing RLI Optical software; assisted in the lab as needed with fabrication of new lenses.
- Motivate the seven people I managed to achieve the office bonus level for 33 out of 36 months; the bonus is calculated on revenue figures and customer goals.
- Became known for my exceptional emphasis on customer service, and trained the people I managed to provide the finest level of customer service in the industry.

2000-02: TRAINER & FIELD OPERATIONS COORDINATOR. SC Region. Worked in the corporate office of the company and traveled extensively in this job.

- Played a major role in the success of seven optometric practices in SC; all practices are now extremely successful and profitable; was instrumental in opening the new facilities, hiring and training staff, and then worked in each office for 2-3 months to assure proper implementation of all policies and procedures.
- Trained employees in sales, customer service, office procedures, computer operations.
- Performed extensive liaison with doctors, and was called in to troubleshoot the most difficult customer service and operational problems.

1999-00: SALES REPRESENTATIVE. Chapel Hill, NC. Became skilled in all aspects of sales as I assisted patients in frame selection, fitted and dispensed new glasses, educated patients on lens options, wrote up sales orders, and relayed sales orders to the lab.

- Because of superior performance, was promoted by the company to manage its field operation during an ambitious time in the company's history.

Other experience: SALES REPRESENTATIVE. Spectacle Opticians, Raleigh, NC (1997).

PERSONAL

Can provide outstanding references. Skilled in working with computer software and hardware.

Nonprofit organization

Date

MEMBERSHIP SERVICES
DIRECTOR,
National Home Builders
Association

To: Search Committee

In response to the urging of someone familiar with your search for a Customer Service Director for the Association of Health Underwriters, I am sending you a resume which summarizes my background. I offer a unique combination of knowledge, experience, and abilities which I believe would ideally suit the requirements of the Association of Health Underwriters.

Health industry expertise

You will see from my resume that I offer expertise related to health insurance and underwriting. In my current job I have sought out and negotiated contracts with major insurance companies to provide insurance for the organization. On a $1 million budget, I have developed insurance programs which generated $2 million in net income based on $32 million in premium. These highly regarded programs which I developed have brought 6,000 new members into the organization.

Proven executive ability

I offer proven executive ability. I have earned a reputation as someone who has not only strategic vision and imagination but also the tenacity and persistence to follow through on the "nitty-gritty" details of implementing new projects, programs, and concepts. I know how to delegate, and I know how to "micro manage," and I am skilled at tailoring my management style to particular circumstances while always shouldering full responsibility and accountability for results. My current job has involved the responsibility of recruiting, training, and continuously developing a national sales force of brokers throughout the U.S. which broke with the tradition of passive mail solicitation and led to dramatic growth in sales and profitability. With a strong "bottom-line" orientation, I have streamlined headquarters staff and reduced central office expenses to save at least half a million dollars while continuously supervising the association's five regional offices in the recruitment and training of more than 1,200 insurance agents nationally.

Extensive association experience

You will also see from my resume that I am accustomed to "getting things done" within the unique environment of a trade/membership association. I am well known for my ability to attract and retain a cohesive and productive staff, and I am also respected for my exceptional skills in relating to, inspiring, and supporting key volunteer members. A skilled communicator, I have made countless appearances and speeches.

I am aware of the requirements defined by the search committee, and I would enjoy the opportunity to discuss this position further with the Executive Committee. I feel certain I could contribute significantly to the growth and financial health of the Association of Health Underwriters as its Customer Service Director. Thank you for your time and consideration.

Sincerely,

Shane Malone

SHANE MALONE

1110½ Hay Street, Fayetteville, NC 28305 • preppub@aol.com • (910) 483-6611

OBJECTIVE To contribute to the growth and financial health of an organization that needs a savvy, creative executive with expert knowledge of the health insurance/underwriting industry along with a proven ability to innovate, manage, motivate, coordinate, communicate, and troubleshoot within the unique environment of a membership association.

EXPERIENCE **DIRECTOR, MEMBERS INSURANCE.** National Home Builders Association, Washington, DC (2003-present). Have excelled in originating insurance programs for the members of NHBA: developed highly regarded insurance programs which brought 6,000 new members into the organization while producing millions of dollars in net income.

- Sought out and negotiated contracts with major insurance companies to provide insurance for the organization.
- On a $1 million operating budget, developed insurance programs which generated $2 million in net income based on $32 million in premium.
- Recruited, trained, and continuously developed a national sales force of NHBA brokers throughout the U.S. which first, arrested declining sales that were the result of passive mail solicitations and second, dramatically boosted sales and profitability.
- Streamlined headquarters staff and reduced central office expenses, resulting in a $500,000 savings; developed annual programs of work and budgets.
- Supervise five regional offices in the recruitment and training of more than 1,200 insurance agents nationally.
- Closely monitor government affairs related to health insurance; maintain excellent relationships with governmental regulatory bodies and state departments of insurance.
- Maintain liaison with association personnel in charge of operations, legislation, education, public relations, and communications as well as with the executive committee.
- Am known for my extraordinary ability to attract, develop, and retain a cohesive and productive staff and for my talent in motivating and inspiring key volunteer leadership.

Other experience:
NATIONAL MEMBERSHIP FIELD DIRECTOR. National Home Builders Association, Washington, DC. Was promoted to this position after excelling as **Membership Director for Mideastern and Eastern U.S.**; formulated and implemented national membership programs and campaigns that led to the development of new units in the U.S.

VICE PRESIDENT OF MARKETING. Schultz & Co., Newark, DE. Developed marketing programs for the manufacturing and marketing companies owned by this conglomerate.

LIFE AND HEALTH INSURANCE BROKER. American Insurance Agency, Newark, DE. Was a property and casualty underwriter as well as a life and health insurance broker.

EDUCATION & TRAINING Hold a **Bachelor of Arts (B.A.) degree,** Delaware State University, Dover, DE.
Complete annually 15 hours of continuing education to maintain Life and Health Insurance Broker's license.
Took numerous courses to comply with life and health insurance industry requirements.

PERSONAL Have given numerous speeches and made hundreds of personal appearances. Am known for my ability to ensure optimum utilization of personnel. Offer a reputation for integrity.

Product sales & distribution

Date

Exact Name of Person
Title or Position
Name of Company
Address
City, State, Zip

OFFICE ASSISTANT   Dear Exact Name of Person: (or Dear Sir or Madam if answering a blind ad.)

With the enclosed resume, I would like to make you aware of my interest in exploring employment opportunities with your organization.

You will see from my resume that I am skilled at providing administrative and technical support for busy operations. In my first full-time job after high school graduation, I became the first female member of a respected sales force, and I rapidly increased sales in my territory by 40% while becoming respected for outstanding customer service. After my success in sales, I was cross trained in all office duties and administrative support activities, and I became the Executive Assistant for the company president. In that role I scheduled appointments, coordinated meetings, maintained files and records, and played a key role in maintaining payroll, accounting, and inventory records. I am proficient in the use of numerous popular software programs including MS Word and have completed advanced course work in Excel.

In my current position with a local company, I am a member of the office staff which handles collections, provides customer service, performs data entry, and maintains databases. Although I am held in high regard in my current position and can provide an excellent reference, the office is very slow paced, and I am seeking an environment which will fully utilize my versatile skills and multiple talents. I am accustomed to working in fast-paced environments where working accurately under tight deadlines is vital.

If you can use a resourceful young individual with a reputation as a intelligent hard worker, I hope you will contact me. I can provide outstanding personal and professional references.

Yours sincerely,

Donna Elliott

DONNA ELLIOTT

1110½ Hay Street, Fayetteville, NC 28305 • preppub@aol.com • (910) 483-6611

OBJECTIVE

To contribute to an organization that can use an outgoing young professional who offers considerable sales skills and proven management potential along with a desire to serve the public and work with others in achieving top-quality results.

EDUCATION

Completing **Bachelor of Arts (B.A.) degree in Business Administration**, Lewiston-Auburn College, Lewiston, ME; degree to be awarded December 2005.

Previously completed course work at University of Vermont, Burlington, VT, and Keene State College, Keene, NH.

Graduated from high school at Northeast High School, Keene, NH.

- Played varsity soccer (stopper) in high school, played on a traveling team in Europe for two months, and then played soccer for the Keene State College.
- Was elected Vice President of the student council; was a member of various organizations including Students Against Drunk Driving (SADD).

COMPUTERS

Proficient with Windows operating system and Microsoft Word; completed coursework related to Excel.

EXPERIENCE

OFFICE ASSISTANT. Denise Roy's, Bridgeton, ME (2004-present). In a full-time job, work in the central office of a store being integrated into the Denise Roy's corporation. Prepare morning reports; handle collection of delinquent accounts; provide customer service.

COLLEGE STUDENT. University of Vermont, Burlington, VT, and Lewiston-Auburn College, Lewiston, ME (2002-04). Pursued my Bachelor's degree full time.

MANAGER. Dunkin Donuts, Portland, ME (2001-02). Began in an entry-level job and was quickly offered a full-time management position; was responsible for hiring and training new employees, terminating them when necessary, and assuring that the company's standards in every area were achieved or exceeded.

- Prepared extensive weekly reports; ordered all food for the store.
- Was commended on my ability to create a happy and efficient operation.
- Became known for my reliability and initiative while working seven days a week.

SALES REPRESENTATIVE & EXECUTIVE ASSISTANT. New England Corporation, Keene, NH (1998-01). Began in a part-time job during my senior year in high school, and was offered full-time employment upon graduation; excelled as the youngest and the only female member of the sales force for a company which functioned as a sales-and-distribution center for numerous products.

- Learned how to effectively introduce and merchandise new products; increased sales in my territory by 40%.
- Earned the trust and respect of numerous small "mom and pop" stores throughout Keene, NH, because I provided superior customer service.
- After being cross trained in office duties including collections and data entry, was specially selected by the company president to act as his Executive Assistant; scheduled appointments, prepared correspondence for executive signature, maintained payroll records, and monitored inventory.
- Learned how to work efficiently in a fast-paced environment.

PERSONAL

My husband and I own a home in Bridgeton and consider ourselves permanent residents. Am a creative and resourceful individual known for my strong personal initiative.

Hospital admissions services

Date

Exact Name of Person
Title or Position
Name of Company
Address
City, State, Zip

**PATIENT REGISTRATION
SPECIALIST**

Dear Exact Name of Person: (or Dear Sir or Madam if answering a blind ad.)

With the enclosed resume, I would like to make you aware of my background in medical, insurance, customer service, and sales environments. I am interested in exploring employment opportunities with your organization and offer exceptional communication and organizational skills which I could put to work for you.

As you will see from my resume, I am currently excelling as a Patient Registration Specialist for an emergency room. I tactfully deal with patients from diverse backgrounds in a fast-paced work environment in order to obtain vital information and provide outstanding customer service. Although I am highly regarded by my present employer and can provide excellent references at the appropriate time, I am interested in exploring career opportunities with other companies that can use a dedicated hard worker.

Throughout my experience in customer service and sales, I have built a reputation as an articulate communicator who is adept at handling difficult customer service situations. A persuasive and effective salesperson, I quickly develop a rapport by focusing on the customer's concerns and emphasizing my desire to see their needs met.

If you can use an enthusiastic young customer service professional with a background in challenging medical, insurance, and sales environments, then I hope you will contact me to suggest a time when we might meet to discuss your goals and how my background might serve your needs. Thank you in advance for your time.

Sincerely,

Yvonne Peterson

YVONNE PETERSON

1110½ Hay Street, Fayetteville, NC 28305 • preppub@aol.com • (910) 483-6611

OBJECTIVE   To benefit an organization that can use an enthusiastic young professional with strong communication and organizational skills who offers a background of excellent performance in medical, insurance, customer service, and sales environments.

EXPERIENCE   **PATIENT REGISTRATION SPECIALIST.** Metropolitan Bordeaux Hospital, Nashville, TN (2005-present). Provide exceptional customer service while interviewing patients in a fast-paced environment to obtain registration information.
- Determine the reason for the patient's visit in order to facilitate prioritizing cases according to the severity of each individual's condition.
- Admit patients into the hospital, entering patient information into the Meditech system and editing or updating information for follow-up or repeat visitors.
- Register orders for laboratory testing, perform complete breakdown of patient charts, and discharge patients from Emergency Room care.

CUSTOMER SERVICE REPRESENTATIVE. Blue Cross-Blue Shield of Tennessee, Nashville, TN (2003-05). Processed a heavy volume of inquiries from customers, medical offices, and other service providers concerning verification of benefits and resolution of claims.
- Verified benefits and coverage for hospitals and doctors' offices in order to ensure that customers were approved for treatment.
- Effectively responded to a variety of questions and complaints from customers who were calling to correct or determine the status of their medical claims. Processed medical claims for doctors and hospitals seeking reimbursement for service provided to customers.

SALES REPRESENTATIVE. Express, Knoxville, TN (2002-03). Became known for my highly developed customer service skills while assisting store patrons in the selection and purchase of fine clothing, accessories, and related merchandise.
- Created effective, eye-catching displays; stocked, straightened, and merchandised my assigned area of the store. Operated a cash register and took credit card, check, and cash payments.

SALES REPRESENTATIVE. Best Buy, Knoxville, TN (2002). Provided customer service, presented information on the cameras, videocassette recorders, and related merchandise that the store sold, and closed the sale. My strong product knowledge and natural sales ability allowed me to effectively persuade customers and develop rapport with individuals.

Other experience:
- In my spare time, utilize my exceptional customer service and sales abilities as a highly effective **SALES REPRESENTATIVE** for the Avon line of cosmetics.
- While attending college, exercised my strong written communication skills as a **REPORTER**, authoring articles on student life, sports, and academic affairs for the school's newspaper, *"The Cool School News."*

EDUCATION   Completed nearly two years of college-level course work in Telecommunications and Medical Assistant programs, Pellissippi State Technical Community College, Knoxville, TN, and East Tennessee State University, Johnson City, TN.
Graduated from Central High School, Knoxville, TN, 2000.
- Was active for four years in ROTC, and was a Captain at graduation.
- Was a member of the varsity track team.

PERSONAL   Have a working knowledge of the Spanish language. Excellent references available.

Cable services

Date

Exact Name of Person
Title or Position
Name of Company
Address
City, State, Zip

Dear Exact Name of Person: (or Dear Sir or Madam if answering a blind ad.)

   With the enclosed resume, I would like to make you aware of my versatile background while emphasizing my strong technical orientation and ability to quickly and easily learn and grasp new equipment, procedures, and techniques.

   As you will see from my resume, I have an open contract with ACS Cable Services, as a Project Supervisor. In this capacity I have traveled throughout the midwest and southeastern areas of the country overseeing fiber optics upgrades and ensuring customer satisfaction with the company's services. Originally hired by the company vice president, promoted to a supervisory role, and asked to continue accepting contracting work, I have recently made the decision to reduce the time I spend traveling and find permanent employment within a reasonable commuting distance.

   Throughout my employment with ACS Cable, I have been the subject of numerous letters of appreciation from customers who singled me out for my customer service orientation and willingness to take the time to do whatever was needed to resolve their problems.

   In one earlier job with Alaska Native Crafts, I was involved in customer service. This company is known for native crafts which are widely recognized as authentic. I took orders, entered data into an automated system, and personally went into the warehouse to ensure proper filling of orders.

   If you can use a results-oriented young professional with strong technical skills who enjoys meeting challenges head on, I hope write or call me soon to suggest a time when we might meet to discuss your goals and how my background might serve your needs. I can provide outstanding references at the appropriate time.

                                        Sincerely,

                                        Charlotte Charles

CHARLOTTE CHARLES

1110½ Hay Street, Fayetteville, NC 28305　　•　preppub@aol.com　　•　　(910) 483-6611

OBJECTIVE
To offer diverse skills and knowledge to an organization that can use a self-motivated young professional with experience in supervision, office administration, and customer service as well as a strong technical orientation and hands-on style.

TRAINING
Am a fast learner who has received on-the-job training and been commended for my ability to easily learn and master new equipment, procedures, and techniques.

SPECIAL SKILLS
Offer a strong background in using automated systems and general office systems:
Computers: operate computers with both DOS and Windows operating systems.
Office equipment: operate most standard office machines including multiline phones, pager systems, copy machines, fax machines, computers, and typewriters
Office operations: offer supervisory skills and am experienced in filing, customer service, resolving complaints, and in finding ways to assure smooth efficient operations

EXPERIENCE
PROJECT SUPERVISOR and **CUSTOMER SERVICE SPECIALIST.** ACS Cable Services, Inc., Fairbanks, AK (2005-present). Handle a wide range of office administrative and support services with an emphasis on providing quality customer service for a cable company while traveling throughout Alaska to oversee upgrade projects and resolve problems.
- Supervise a staff of up to seven people providing support for areas including payroll preparation, invoicing, and filing.
- Place work orders and provide quality control for all office activities.
- Have become familiar with digital upgrades of fiber optics systems while providing technical support during the company's CFT2200 upgrade project.
- Supervise technicians making box swaps for customers as well as during the set up of cable boxes, TVs, and VCRs including cable splicing and fitting.
- Schedule installation calls and route work orders; prepare a variety of daily reports.
- Audit sales and service needs in order to uncover illegal cable theft.
- Have received numerous letters of appreciation from customers who have cited my high personal standards and ability to tactfully resolve complaints and ensure high quality service for customers.

DATA ENTRY CLERK. Alaska Native Crafts, Anchorage, AK (2004-05). Refined multiple skills in data entry and office operations for an industry selling authentic native crafts.
- Provided support services which included answering multiline phones, paging employees, faxing, making copies, filing, and printing materials. Entered sales orders into an automated system and ensured they were filled accurately and quickly.

PATIENT SERVICES ASSISTANT and **ENVIRONMENTAL SERVICES AIDE.** Providence Hospital, Anchorage, AK (1999-03). Handled multiple duties in two functional areas:
Patient Services Assistant: Provided assistance for daily care including help with bathing, dental care, dressing, feeding, and other aspects of personal care and hygiene.
Environmental Services Aide: Cleaned and sanitized patient rooms as well as operating rooms, the Intensive Care Unit, Recovery Room, the doctor's lounges, and the nurse's station.
- Became known as an adaptable young professional while dealing with people including other health care professionals, patients, and family members.

PERSONAL
Outstanding personal and professional references available on request. Offer exceptional customer service skills. Enjoy working with my hands and applying technical knowledge.

Call center services

Date

Exact Name of Person
Title or Position
Name of Company
Address
City, State, Zip

**QUALITY SPECIALIST
& PROJECT TEAM
LEADER**

Dear Exact Name of Person: (or Dear Sir or Madam if answering a blind ad.)

With the enclosed resume, I would like to make you aware of my interest in exploring employment opportunities with your organization and introduce you to my extensive customer service and quality assurance experience.

My customer service training began very early in my life, when I worked as a Client Relations Specialist for Hewlett-Packard in a newly opened store. Based on my outstanding performance, I was offered a job with HP when I relocated back to my hometown of Columbia, SC.

Instead of continuing with Hewlett-Packard, however, I accepted a position with Omaha Mutual as a Bilingual Customer Service Specialist, and I excelled in all aspects of my job while providing customer service support in English and Spanish. In 2003, Omaha Mutual promoted me to the position of Quality Specialist & Project Team Leader in a call center recognized by J.D. Powers and Associates for "call center operation customer satisfaction excellence." As one of only five Quality Specialists overseeing a 427-person call center, I play a key role in assuring the highest level of customer service for Omaha Mutual's 30 million customers. I have excelled in numerous professional development and executive training programs, and I have completed examinations in a variety of areas ranging from customer service to insurance company operations.

What I have discovered in my customer service experience is that the highest level of customer satisfaction is achieved through teamwork and through the creative application of outstanding communication and problem-solving skills. While solving problems and identifying opportunities, I utilize a variety of analytical tools and software including Excel spreadsheets, Access databases, written reports, graphs, and presentation software. I offer a proven ability to work well independently, as a team member, or in a leadership role. In addition to my strong and genuine commitment to customer satisfaction, I possess outstanding written and oral communication skills.

I am now relocating to your area and am selectively approaching organizations who are committed to the highest levels of customer satisfaction and quality assurance

If you can use a cheerful and insightful individual who offers a proven ability to work well with others, I hope you will contact me to suggest a time when we might discuss your needs. I can provide outstanding personal and professional references at the appropriate time. Thank you in advance for your time and professional courtesies!

Yours sincerely,

Lorena Santiago

LORENA SANTIAGO

1110½ Hay Street, Fayetteville, NC 28305 · preppub@aol.com · (910) 483-6611

OBJECTIVE To offer my customer service and quality assurance experience, along with strong computer skills, to a company that can use a skilled communicator and problem solver who offers the ability to profitably impact a company's bottom line through my ability to ensure high levels of customer satisfaction.

LANGUAGE Fluently speak, read, and write **Spanish;** volunteered as a Translator for Special Olympics events and with the U.S. Army, Fort Jackson, SC.

COMPUTERS Proficient with Microsoft XP (Word, Excel, PowerPoint, Visio, Outlook, Access) and Intranet.

EDUCATION Completing **B.S. degree in Chemistry,** University of South Carolina, Columbia, SC. Am pursuing this degree in my spare time while excelling my demanding full-time position.
Previously completed **30 hours of course work pursuing A.A. degree,** Jefferson Community College, Watertown, NY. Attended college in the mornings and worked from noon to 9 p.m.
Graduated from Columbia High School, Columbia, SC, 1999.
- Selected by Junior ROTC instructors for a leadership role. Junior and Senior Class **President.** Honored as **Salutatorian** (2nd academically) of my graduating class; Honor Society member.
Completed computer, sales, and customer service training sponsored by Hewlett-Packard.

EXPERIENCE *Excelled in this promotion to increasing responsibilities with Omaha Mutual Fund, Columbia, SC.*
2003-present: QUALITY SPECIALIST & PROJECT TEAM LEADER. Was promoted to a critical quality position in a call center recognized by the J.D. Powers and Associates Certified Call Center Program (SM) for "call center operation customer satisfaction excellence."
- Have been commended for my strong analytical skills, superior verbal and written communication skills, and in-depth call monitoring experience while continually demonstrating my commitment to providing an outstanding customer service experience for Omaha Mutual's 30 million customers.
- In this 427-person call center, review procedures and processes and recommend enhancements to improve efficiency. Consult with management to develop and formulate long-term strategic plans to ensure Omaha Mutual's leadership in the area of providing the highest quality customer service. Evaluate processes, analyze data, perform root cause analysis, and establish quality control procedures which conducting internal reviews and analyzing quality initiatives.
2001-2003: BILINGUAL CUSTOMER SERVICE SPECIALIST. Excelled in all aspects of my job while providing customer service support in both English and Spanish.

CLIENT RELATIONS SPECIALIST. Hewlett-Packard, Inc., Watertown, NY (1999-2001). Earned recognition for my ability to apply technical training in a common sense approach while assisting customers in a newly opened store specializing in configuring computer systems to users' needs. Was officially rated as excellent in all areas of performance with special attention given to my ability to follow through and solve client issues.

PERSONAL Offer well-developed decision-making and problem-solving skills. Am a positive, energetic, and enthusiastic individual who can be counted on to get the job done. Outstanding references.

Real estate sales

Date

Exact Name of Person
Title or Position
Name of Company
Address
City, State, Zip

REAL ESTATE BROKER   Dear Exact Name of Person: (or Dear Sir or Madam if answering a blind ad.)

Can you use an enthusiastic, results-oriented sales professional who offers outstanding communication skills, a talent for reading people, and a reputation for determination and persistence in reaching goals?

With a proven background of success in sales, I have displayed my versatility while selling and marketing a wide variety of products and services including residential real estate and land, new and used automobiles, and financial products/investment services. In one job I trained and supervised a successful team of mutual fund and insurance sales agents. Most recently as an Independent Real Estate Broker with a Pond Realty office in Langley, VA, I achieved the $3 million mark in sales for 2002 While excelling in all aspects of the business, I have used my experience and knowledge to create marketing strategies and tools which reached large audiences and generated much business.

Earlier experience gave me an opportunity to refine my sales and communication abilities as well as gain familiarity with business management including finance and collections, inventory control, personnel administration, and customer service. Prior to owning and managing a business which bought, reconditioned, and marketed automobiles, I was one of Edwards Buick's most successful sales professionals, earning the distinction of being "Salesman of the Month" for 13 consecutive months and "Salesman of the Year."

If you can use a seasoned professional with the ability to solve tough business problems, maximize profitability, and increase market share under highly competitive conditions, I would enjoy an opportunity to meet with you to discuss your needs and how I might serve them. Known for my resourcefulness, I can provide outstanding personal and professional references.

I hope you will welcome my call soon to arrange a brief meeting at your convenience. Thank you in advance for your time.

Sincerely,

Dirk N. Aetna

DIRK N. AETNA

1110½ Hay Street, Fayetteville, NC 28305 • preppub@aol.com • (910) 483-6611

OBJECTIVE

To offer a track record of success in sales and managerial roles where outstanding communication skills and the ability to close the sale were key factors in building a reputation as a highly motivated professional oriented toward achieving maximum bottom-line results.

EXPERIENCE

INDEPENDENT REAL ESTATE BROKER. Pond Realty, Langley, VA (2000-present). Reached the $3 million personal sales level for 2002 while providing a range of experience which has played a key role in boosting overall sales and profitability of a thriving agency in this highly competitive market.

- Have become known for my strong interpersonal and communication skills while coordinating with potential buyers, lending institutions, construction professionals, sellers, and others.
- Negotiate all aspects of financial transactions; deal with mortgage company representatives to arrange financing and with attorneys to handle real estate closings.
- Utilize my expert marketing abilities; create sales strategies and preparing direct mail materials to capture the interest of prospective clients and generate new business.
- Have become skilled in all aspects of property evaluation and am skilled in comparing newly available homes with those having comparable features.
- Handle the details of researching information and completing paperwork for sales of new and existing homes as well as land.

SALES AND MARKETING REPRESENTATIVE. Self-employed, Langley, VA (1992-99). Trained and then supervised the efforts of as many as 12 agents while also personally marketing and selling mutual funds and insurance.

- Refined my abilities in a competitive field and excelled in developing sales and marketing techniques which resulted in increased sales.

Highlights of earlier experience: Gained versatile experience in sales, inventory control, and customer service in jobs including the following:
FINANCE AND OPERATIONS MANAGE. Became highly effective in handling finances, marketing, and sales as the owner of a business with six sales professionals, a title clerk, a bookkeeper, and 12 employees in the body shop (Genie Auto Shop, Richmond, VA).

- Created marketing and advertising plans and products which were highly effective.

SALES REPRESENTATIVE. For a major automobile dealer, consistently placed in the top three of 22 sales professionals (Edwards Buick, Richmond, VA).

- "Salesman of the Month" for 13 consecutive months and once as "Salesman of the Year."

FIELD SALES MANAGER. Became the youngest person in the company's history to hold this position after only a year (Fuller Brush Company, Plattsburgh, NY, and Phoenix, AZ).

- Became skilled in earning the confidence of potential customers and achieved a highly successful rate of positive responses from four out of each five people I approached.

TRAINING

Completed corporate training programs in areas such as real estate law, brokerage, finance, and securities as well as life, accident, and health insurance.
Am licensed as a real estate salesman, broker, and life/accident/health insurance agent.

PERSONAL

Am known for my ability to see "the big picture" while managing the details. Offer a proven ability to develop strategic plans that maximize profitability and market share in competitive environments. Am a results-oriented, persistent individual.

Utility locating services

Date

Exact Name of Person
Title or Position
Name of Company
Address
City, State, Zip

**REGIONAL CLAIMS
MANAGER**

Dear Exact Name of Person: (or Dear Sir or Madam if answering a blind ad.)

With the enclosed resume, I would like to make you aware of my interest in exploring employment opportunities with your organization. Although I can provide outstanding references at the appropriate time, I would appreciate your holding in confidence my expression of interest in your company until after we talk in person.

You will see from my resume that I am currently excelling as a Regional Claims Manager with Pacific Company Services, Ltd. I saved my employer $958,000 in 2005 through my skillful negotiation of claims, and I have become known for my strong communication and interpersonal skills while dealing with companies and municipalities throughout four states. In my previous position as a Senior Claims Specialist, I oversaw other claims specialist and trained them in effective techniques of investigating utility damage claims and reaching prudent conclusions. I personally responded to high profile damages and delegated field investigations on other claims.

In prior industry experience, I worked as a Field Supervisor and Field Locator for a subsidiary of American Western Services. As a Field Locator in Reno, NV, I became known as an outstanding utility locator technician, and I have excelled in subsequent management positions because I possess expert knowledge of the utility locating business. I also offer exceptionally strong analytical, negotiating, and communication skills.

I am being quite selective in the companies I am approaching. If you feel that your company could make use of my versatile skills and talents, I hope you will contact me to suggest a time when we might talk about your needs. I can make myself available for an interview at your convenience.

Yours sincerely,

Jeremy Corvalis

JEREMY CORVALIS

1110½ Hay Street, Fayetteville, NC 28305   •   preppub@aol.com   •   (910) 483-6611

OBJECTIVE

To contribute to an organization that can use a highly effective problem solver and negotiator who offers expert knowledge of the utility locating business.

EXPERIENCE

Have excelled in a track record of promotion with companies in the utility locating industry, Pacific Company Services, Ltd.:

2004-present: REGIONAL CLAIMS MANAGER. San Francisco, CA. Was promoted to this position which encompasses CA, OR, WA, and NV to handle court litigations and negotiate settlements.

- Saved the company $958,000 in 2005 through intelligent and effective negotiation of claims. Work with companies who include Sprint and other cable companies, Western Pacific Energy and other electric companies, various municipalities, as well as AT&T, and other telephone companies.

2004: SENIOR CLAIMS SPECIALIST. San Francisco, CA. Was promoted to oversee other claims specialists and train them in effective techniques of investigating utility damage claims and reaching prudent recommendations; also personally investigated underground damages and made recommendations while handling third party damages. Negotiated settlements.

American Western Services – AWS was bought by Pacific Company Services in 2003, and I continued to advance into senior management roles with the acquiring company.

2002-03: FIELD SUPERVISOR. San Francisco, CA. Supervised 50 people who were utility locators and lead locators while traveling to cities including Sacramento, San Diego, Los Angeles, San Jose, and Fresno, and others to assess utility locating matters. Evaluated personnel performance and provided managers with detailed recommendations concerning training and damage prevention issues.

2000-02: REGIONAL TRAINING COORDINATOR. CA, OR, WA, and NV. Evaluated personnel performance and provided managers with detailed recommendations concerning training and damage prevention issues. Responsible for assisting managers and supervisors on issues of personnel performance and continued education for utility locators.

1995-00: FIELD LOCATOR. Reno, NV. Performed with distinction as a highly skilled Utility Locator Technician. Searched for underground plants, properly marked the location, completed necessary paperwork, and photographed each location. Read maps/blueprints and used laptops; acquired knowledge of telephone microfiche plats and electric paper prints.

Other experience:
ASSISTANT DISTRICT MANAGER. Avis Car Rental, Salem, OR (1990-94). Coordinated and managed all phases of the rental car business which included hiring and training staff; administered all cash flow including contracts, billing, and bank deposits.
ASSISTANT MANAGER. Hertz Car Rental, Salem, OR (1988-90). Managed contracts, billing, car preparation, pickup, and delivery. Hired and trained staff.

EDUCATION

Completed two years of college studies, Golden Gate University, San Francisco, CA.

PERSONAL

Excellent communicator with exceptional analytical skills. Known for my ability to establish warm working relationships with others. Experienced in multi-tasking.

Telephone services

Date

Exact Name of Person
Title or Position
Name of Company
Address
City, State, Zip

SALES ASSOCIATE   Dear Exact Name of Person: (or Dear Sir or Madam if answering a blind ad.)

With the enclosed resume, I would like to make you aware of my interest in exploring employment opportunities with your company.

As you will see from my resume, I have excelled in every job I have ever taken on. In my current position with Sprint, I have worked as a Sales Associate, and I have numerous awards recognizing my strong personal initiative and customer service skills. Although I am highly regarded by the Sprint organization and can provide excellent references at the appropriate time, I am selectively exploring the possibility of employment with other companies that can make use of a strong performer with exceptional customer service and sales abilities.

In my experience prior to Sprint, I worked in management positions in retail store environments and in the insurance industry. I am skilled at all aspects of public relations, complaint handling, collections, problem solving, and negotiation.

If you can use a hard-working individual who offer a proven ability to set and achieve ambitious goals for productivity and profitability, I hope you will contact me to suggest a time when we might meet to discuss your needs and goals. I would appreciate your holding my expression of interest in your company in confidence until after we talk. Thank you in advance for your time.

Sincerely,

Monica John

MONICA JOHN

1110½ Hay Street, Fayetteville, NC 28305   •   preppub@aol.com   •   (910) 483-6611

OBJECTIVE   To benefit an organization that can use a talented professional dedicated to providing top quality service and with exceptional skills in sales, office management, and human resources.

EDUCATION   **A.A. degree, Business Administration**, University of Wisconsin, Madison, WI.
Completed dBase, Windows, MS-DOS, and Applied System computer courses
Hold a Property & Casualty License, Madison Area Technical College, WI.
Successfully completed courses in Life and Accident.
Studied computer technology and word processing.

EXPERIENCE   **SALES ASSOCIATE.** Sprint, Madison, WI and Chicago, IL (2003-present). Have excelled with this major company during a time of growth and mergers; visit new accounts and implement promotions while also training the customer's staff; after relocating back to Madison from Chicago, have opened 17 new accounts in 1 ½ months.
- Currently manage seven national accounts and 25 local accounts; previously managed up to 45 retail locations, including training in-store sales associates to sell the DCS phone, accounting for inventories of materials and sales, and setting up displays; prepared marketing reports. Opened/maintained accounts; closed old and discontinued accounts.
- For four months in 2005, worked for Sprint as a Sales Associate in Illinois.
- **Awards and honors:** Received the Certificate of Excellence Award in 2005 and the Circle of Excellent Award in 2002; received the "Fast Start" Award in 2005, 2004, 2003.

OFFICE MANAGER. Erie Insurance, Inc., Madison, WI (2002). Directed operations of this busy insurance office; wrote policies, handled bookkeeping and financial matters, and supervised agents' activities; earned Errors and Mission certification.

STORE MANAGER TRAINEE. Shoe Carnival, Madison, WI (2001-02). Developed highly refined customer relations skills while in training to manage this high-volume retail shoe chain while also displaying versatility and flexibility working late nights and weekends.
- Processed/received shipments and displayed merchandise.

CUSTOMER SERVICE REPRESENTATIVE and **AGENT.** ZYX Corporation, Madison, WI (2001). Handled administrative functions and customer service for this company serving customers with various insurance needs and specializing in home owners insurance; served as liaison for numerous underwriters.
- Input policy information and transmitted data for the accounting division using Applied Systems, Rating System, and Windows software programs.
- Passed claims on to adjusters and paid off claims up to a certain level; administered quotes, wrote up policies, conducted direct billings, verified figures, and performed collections under a direct billing system.

OFFICE MANAGER and **INSURANCE AGENT.** All-State Insurance Agency, Madison, WI (1994-01). As the owner's "right arm," managed branch office operations while handling market property, Casualty and Life and Health Insurance policies; quoted and wrote policies; verified that client information conformed to requirements. Prepared bank deposits and receipts. Performed public relations, complaint management, and problem resolution.

PERSONAL   Creative professional with exceptional oral and written communication skills. Have a knack for dealing with people and am a resourceful problem solver and trouble shooter.

Retail services

Exact Name of Person
Title or Position
Name of Company
Address
City, State, Zip

SALES ASSOCIATE

Dear Exact Name of Person: (or Dear Sir or Madam if answering a blind ad.)

With the enclosed resume, I would like to make you aware of my interest in exploring employment opportunities with your organization. I am in the process of permanently relocating to the Columbus area, where my extended family lives, and I am confident that my strong customer service background could benefit your organization.

Background in customer service

As you will see from my resume, I offer an extensive background in customer service. While married to a U.S. Army military professional, I traveled frequently due to my husband's career but I am proud of my ability to quickly gain employment in any new market I entered. I can provide outstanding references from all employers, all of whom encouraged me to enter their management trainee program. Because of my husband's obligation to move frequently, however, I was unable to pursue those management trainee opportunities. Nevertheless, I was frequently placed in charge of training other employers in customer service, and you can see that I have been rehired several times by the same employer because of my outstanding work record.

Strong problem-solving skills

In all the jobs I have held, I have rapidly gained the respect of customers because of my sincere interest in them as well as my ability to resolve problems with tact and good will. During my years in retail, I developed a strong belief that good customer relations is the number one priority of employees. I have become known for my tact and outstanding "listening skills" in difficult customer situations, and I am highly experienced in resolving customer issues so that customer loyalty and the employer's "bottom line" are preserved.

If my background and skills interest you, I hope you will contact me to suggest a time when we could meet in person to discuss your needs. I would enjoy an opportunity to show you in person that I could contribute to your organization through my enthusiasm, communication skills, and creativity. Now that I am no longer obligated to travel frequently because of U.S. military requirements, I would like to make a permanent commitment to an employer that can use my extensive background in customer service and business problem solving.

Yours sincerely,

Selena Malone

SELENA MALONE

1110½ Hay Street, Fayetteville, NC 28305　　•　　preppub@aol.com　　•　　(910) 483-6611

OBJECTIVE　　To benefit an organization that can use an enthusiastic, dynamic, poised, and well-groomed professional with strong communication and organizational skills along with experience in sales, customer service, business problem solving, financial management, and promotion.

SUMMARY OF EXPERIENCE　　I demonstrated my adaptability as well as my highly energetic and self-motivated nature by quickly finding employment in the cities to which I relocated with my husband, a military professional, over a 7 ½-year period. I am now able to settle permanently into a career and can travel/relocate with my job as needed since I have no further obligations to the Army.

EXPERIENCE　　**SALES ASSOCIATE.** Old Navy. Watertown, NY (2005-present). At a community near Fort Drum, one of the world's busiest military bases, work as a member of an enthusiastic team presenting trend-setting clothing.

- Because of my outstanding work record, I was offered a transfer from the Burrs Mills store to the Watertown store when I relocated to Watertown, NY. Other sales associates look to me for guidance related to sales, customer service, and fashion.

SALES ASSOCIATE & KEY HOLDER. Limited. Fayetteville, NC (2004). In a community near Fort Bragg, NC, I was quickly placed in charge of training and managing other cashiers; was aggressively recruited to enter Limited's management training program.

- Managed key accounts, opened new accounts, and performed cashier functions with the designation of **Lead Cashier.** Was entrusted with supervisory responsibilities as **Key Holder.**
- Was entrusted with numerous financial and auditing responsibilities; performed transaction audits and short audits designed to detect reasons for shortfalls.
- Trained cashiers in store policies; was the "go-to" person in charge of resolving difficult customer problems when the utmost tact was required. Was often commended for my "listening skills" by customers whose problems I resolved.
- Utilized my merchandising skills in the role of **Promotion Coordinator** for the store. Promoted various contests

SALES ASSOCIATE. Old Navy. Tulsa, OK (2002-03). While my husband was deployed to Iraq, I lived in Oklahoma; I produced outstanding sales and customer service results while also processing shipments, processing exchanges, and re-ticketing merchandise as appropriate.

- Played a role in store audits.

SALES ASSOCIATE. Payless Shoes and 5-7-9. Tulsa, OK (1999-01). Worked in two jobs simultaneously. At 5-7-9, refined my sales skills. A large number of customers routinely requested me by name to assist them because of my fashion sense.

- At Payless Shoes, excelled in sales and learned to work on commission.

SALES ASSOCIATE. Gap. Tulsa, OK (1998-99). Excelled in sales and customer service.

EDUCATION　　Completed nearly three years of college coursework with a concentration in Business Administration and Management from colleges which included University of Tulsa, Fayetteville Technical Community College, and Jefferson Community College.
Graduated in 1998 from Tulsa Community College; majored in Business.

PERSONAL　　Can provide excellent personal and professional references from all previous employers.

Magazine & book sales

Date

Exact Name of Person
Title or Position
Name of Company
Address
City, State, Zip

SALES CLERK   Dear Exact Name of Person: (or Dear Sir or Madam if answering a blind ad.)

With the enclosed resume, I would like to make you aware of the considerable management, problem-solving, and customer service experience I could put to work for you. I am currently in the process of relocating permanently to Michigan, where most of my family lives.

As you will see from my resume, I am currently involved in sales, customer service, and inventory control for a major book and magazine center in Georgia. In my prior position in one of the southeast's largest malls, I managed all aspects of store operations for a prominent retailer of fine jewelry. Prior to that, I excelled in a track record of promotion to increasing responsibilities with the county clerk's office where I completed four years of college studies in Communication Arts.

In addition to my strong customer service and operations management skills, I am skilled with Windows, including Word, Excel, and Access. I am also experienced in setting up and utilizing spreadsheets and in handling accounting including accounts receivable, accounts payable, and inventory control. In my job at the county clerk's office, I was praised for the leadership and initiative I displayed in transforming a troubled billing function with a pattern of chronic late payments into a punctual and accurate accounts payable operation.

A resourceful and enthusiastic individual, I have always found resourceful ways to contribute to increased efficiency in all of my jobs. For example, I have expressed my creativity in developing exciting point-of-sale displays that have multiplied inventory turnover. Known as a cheerful and enthusiastic team player with unlimited personal initiative and resourcefulness, I can provide outstanding personal and professional references at the appropriate time.

If you can use a versatile young professional known for an excellent attitude as well as superior work habits including reliability, dependability, and honesty, I hope you will contact me to suggest a time when we might meet to discuss your needs. I can assure you in advance that I could rapidly become an valuable permanent asset to your organization.

Sincerely,

Marcella Brown

MARCELLA BROWN

1110½ Hay Street, Fayetteville, NC 28305   •   preppub@aol.com   •   (910) 483-6611

OBJECTIVE   To contribute to an organization that can use a skilled professional with extensive customer service and operations management experience along with an ability to expertly operate all office machines and equipment.

EDUCATION   **Communication Arts**, Georgia State University, Atlanta, GA, 1997.
- Worked in numerous part-time jobs in order to finance my college education as well as volunteer and leadership positions; those jobs and activities included working in the Student Life Office, the Registrar's Office, serving as Secretary of the GSU Student Union, working as Advertising Manager of the Student Newspaper, acting as Secretary to the department head of the Communications Department, and working in the Psychology Department.
- Received the Communications Arts Award for contributions to the drama department through my acting, directing, and managerial services.

Theatre Arts and Internship, Morehouse College, Atlanta, GA, 1995.
Received Certificates of Completion from courses in Windows XP, Morehouse College, 2005. On my own initiative, have completed numerous courses related to computer operations, personal development, communication skills, and other areas in order to improve my poise and confidence.
- Completed Success 2005 Seminar which focused on motivational techniques.

SPECIAL   Skilled with Windows including Word, Excel, Access, PowerPoint
SKILLS
- Experienced in setting up/utilizing spreadsheets
- Experienced in accounts receivable and payable as well as inventory control

HONORS   Have received numerous awards and honors including the following:
- Numerous Certificates of Achievement for contributions to employers

EXPERIENCE   **SALES CLERK.** Georgian Magazine and Book Center, Atlanta, GA (2003-present). Have been credited with making significant contributions to store profitability through my ability to create and implement exciting point-of-sale displays as well as my skills in sales and customer service.
- Am involved in purchasing and controlling inventory.
- Maintain a wide range of records pertaining to sales and inventory control.

OFFICE ASSISTANT II. Fulton County Clerk and Recorder, Atlanta, GA (1997-02). Began working for this organization as a temporary worker and was offered a full-time job and continuously promoted to increasing responsibilities.
- Received, set up, and tracked jobs and the status of multiple jobs.
- Set up and maintained spreadsheets and prepared monthly billing and time sheets.
- Inventoried office supplies and micrographic supplies on a monthly basis and placed orders for products and equipment needed.
- Assisted my boss in producing the statewide Clerk and Recorder's Newsletter.
- Was crosstrained as a Microtechnician, and learned to prep and film documents.
- Was praised for the leadership and initiative I displayed in taking over a troubled billing function in which the organization was sending out its quarterly bills late; after a short time, the bills were being produced on time and our accounts balanced to the penny.

PERSONAL   Can provide outstanding references. Am known as a very outgoing and enthusiastic professional who prides myself on attention to detail and organizational skills.

Banking & auto dealership support

Date

Exact Name of Person
Title or Position
Name of Company
Address
City, State, Zip

SALES FINANCE
RELATIONSHIP
MANAGER

Dear Exact Name of Person: (or Sir or Madam if answering a blind ad.)

    With the enclosed resume, I would like to make you aware of my exceptional skills in areas which include establishing strong customer relationships, providing top-notch financial support for businesses, and managing operations and accounts for maximum profitability.

    As you will see from my enclosed resume, I have excelled in a track record of accomplishment with Wellington Bank. In my current position I am the Relationship Manager to 55 active automotive dealerships in seven counties. Because of my strong customer service orientation as well as my ability to identify problems and opportunities, I have generated a commercial pipeline of $21 million during 2001, and I increased retail loan volumes from $250,000 to $1,200,000 a week.

    In a previous position with Wellington, I took over the management of a 10-employee branch and transformed it into a branch ranked at #1 in production status based on loans/deposits in a network of 9 branches. Prior to my taking over as manager, the branch was designated to be closed but, through my aggressive leadership and customer service, top management revised its strategic plan and the branch remains open and is prospering to this day.

    You will see from my resume that, in every job I have held, I have been ranked "the best" or in the top 5% of producers.

    If you feel you can use a dynamic producer who offers a sophisticated understanding of sales and finance as it relates to businesses of all sizes, I hope you will contact me to suggest a time when we could meet to discuss your needs. I can provide exceptional references at the appropriate time.

Yours sincerely,

John Ginman

JOHN GINMAN

1110½ Hay Street, Fayetteville, NC 28305 • preppub@aol.com • (910) 483-6611

OBJECTIVE

To benefit an organization that can use a strong bottom-line producer who excels in developing relationships, delivering exceptional sales results, and solving business problems in ways that increase revenue, boost market share, and satisfy customers.

EXPERIENCE

With Wellington Bank, have excelled in a variety of challenging assignments that tested my sales ability, management skills, and executive problem-solving talents:
2001-present: SALES FINANCE RELATIONSHIP MANAGER. Wellington Bank, New York, NY. Am the Relationship Manager to 55 active automotive dealerships with individual sales of more than $60 million annually; identify commercial lending opportunities and solicit dealer use of a competitive consumer retail/lease plan.
- Have generated a commercial pipeline of $21 million in wholesale and commercial portfolio (the previous territory record was $6 million); increased retail loan volumes from $250,000 to $1,200,000 a week.
- As of this year-to-date, my territory and I are ranked #2 among 78 counterparts in six states in production within the Sales Finance Division.
- Identify customer needs that would allow the integration of a complete financial services package; have excelled through my ability to identify and solve problems as well as my emphasis on customer service and building solid customer relationships.
- Within the Central Region of Wellington, have excelled at integrating other lines of business into my relationship base.

2000-01: SMALL BUSINESS RELATIONSHIP MANAGER. Wellington Bank, Boston, MA. Was ranked in top 5% in production among 75 relationship managers in three states.
- Generated more than $1 million a month in new small business credit; excelled in offering a broad range of credit, treasury services, and other instruments to businesses with sales of less than $2 million.

1999-00: BRANCH MANAGER. Wellington Bank, New York, NY. Managed and motivated 10 employees while establishing strong customer relationships.
- Achieved #1 production status in loans/deposits in a network of 9 branches; when I took over the management of this branch, it was ranked second to last.
- Although this branch was designated to be closed by mid-2000, I was credited with "turning around" a problem operation and restoring management's confidence.

1998-99: MORTGAGE (RESIDENTIAL) ORIGINATOR. Wellington Bank, New York, NY. Generated an average of $1 million a month in residential mortgages, and learned the characteristics of residential mortgage underwriting.

1995-98: SALES FINANCE DEALER CREDIT MANAGER. Wellington Bank of GA, Atlanta, GA. Generated $6 million monthly in consumer loans from automotive dealerships in middle and northeast Georgia; this exceptional productivity occurred as I simultaneously maintained an unusually low loan delinquency ratio of .53%.
- Nurtured a territory producing $300,000 in monthly sales to $3 million in monthly sales.

EDUCATION

B.A. in Finance, minor in Business, Georgia State University, Atlanta, GA, 1998.
A.A. in Government, Louisburg College, Louisburg, SC, 1995.
Extensive financial and sales training sponsored by Wellington on business accounting.

Nonprofit services

Date

Exact Name of Person
Title or Position
Name of Company
Address
City, State, Zip

SALES REPRESENTATIVE

Dear Exact Name of Person: (or Dear Sir or Madam if answering a blind ad.)

With the enclosed resume, I would like to make you aware of my desire to become affiliated with your organization in some capacity in which you could utilize my strong sales, marketing, and communication skills.

As you will see from my resume, I am a successful business manager who has been in business in the Miami market. Although I am highly successful in my current position and have established a loyal customer base, I am selectively exploring opportunities with companies that could utilize my sales and marketing strengths. I am certain I could positively and profitably impact the bottom line of an organization that can use a highly motivated self starter.

You will notice from my resume that I have extensive sales and marketing experience. I have worked tirelessly for area organizations in sales and marketing capacities as a volunteer, and I have raised money for organizations and charities including the American Cancer Society, Diabetic Association, and Ronald McDonald House. I have organized and trained other volunteers and sales representatives in techniques including closing the sale and overcoming objections. On numerous occasions both in my own business and in marketing situations, I have been told that I have a gift for establishing rapport with others.

If you can use a dynamic sales professional to represent your products, I would enjoy discussing suitable sales opportunities with your company. I can provide outstanding personal and professional references.

Yours sincerely,

Christina Wildes

CHRISTINA WILDES

1110½ Hay Street, Fayetteville, NC 28305   •   preppub@aol.com   •   (910) 483-6611

OBJECTIVE

I want to contribute to the growth in market share of the Sebastian product line through my extensive product knowledge as well as my strong sales abilities and communication skills.

EDUCATION

Completed nearly four years of college, Miami-Dade Community College, Miami, FL. Graduated from the **Cosmetology Program** at MDCC, 1999.
Completed extensive course work at the Dental Hygiene School, MDCC, before I changed my major and transferred into the beauty industry.
Graduated from Tropical High School and excelled academically; took college preparatory courses including Advanced Placement Biology and Chemistry, 1994.

PRODUCT KNOWLEDGE

Highly experienced in using products of all major hair products companies including Sebastian, Paul Mitchell, Aveda, and other major lines.

EXPERIENCE

SALES REPRESENTATIVE. Various charitable organizations, Miami, FL (2005-present). Have become known as a tireless and enthusiastic worker for numerous fundraisers and charity organizations.
- Use my "people skills" and my ability to communicate with others in a persuasive fashion in order to raise money for nonprofit organizations such as the American Cancer Society, the Diabetic Association, and Ronald McDonald House.
- Approach businesses in order to solicit their sponsorship of fundraising events such as golf outings and car washes.
- Have created flyers and sold door-to-door in order to promote worthy causes.
- Have developed a proven ability to exceed ambitious sales goals; have a personal style which is effective in establishing rapport and gaining trust.
- Have trained and organized other volunteers to cold call, make door-to-door sales, implement effective marketing presentations, and overcome objections in sales.

SEBASTIAN EDUCATOR, SEBASTIAN ADVOCATE, & HAIR DESIGNER. Earl's Hair Design, Miami, FL (2001-present). Am a self-employed professional in a salon with three hair designers; the three of us have worked together for more than 10 years.
- Am respected all over Miami, which has 400 salons, for my extensive knowledge; am sought out for my product knowledge.
- Act as the in-house inventory ordering contact for the Sebastian line.
- Worked as **Sebastian Educator** with the Cox Distributorship; traveled seasonally to undergo training, and then taught classes in Miami, Fort Lauderdale, and Coral Springs related to product knowledge and color.
- Also worked as a **Sebastian Advocate**; received advanced training about Sebastian techniques and products and then shared my knowledge with my colleagues.
- Played a key role in organizing a major hair show in Miami; organized the show, sold tickets, coordinated regional designers, and helped to manage the show held at the Miami Center.
- Worked numerous hair shows in Orlando and Tampa.

SALON MANAGER. Virginia Hair & Boutique, Miami, FL (1995-01). Managed a hair salon while also providing manicures.

PERSONAL

Single with no children. Will cheerfully travel as extensively as my employer's needs require. In my spare time, enjoy running marathons. Can provide outstanding references.

Cable services sales

Date

Exact Name of Person
Title or Position
Company Name
Address
City, State, Zip

SALES REPRESENTATIVE

Dear Exact Name of Person: (or Dear Sir or Madam if answering a blind ad.)

With the enclosed resume, I would like to make you aware of my interest in exploring employment opportunities with your organization. Although I am excelling in my current position and can provide outstanding references at the appropriate time, I am selectively exploring other opportunities.

I have excelled in both inside sales and outside sales jobs which required exceptionally strong customer service skills. In my current inside sales position, I am one of the company's top two "closers." I close 50% of sales whereas most of the 40 sales professionals have a closing percentage of 25%. Although the quota is 45 accounts weekly, I average 70 accounts weekly. I have come to believe that consistency is the key to success in sales and, if you want to excel, you have to be highly self-motivated and set very high personal goals.

I was recruited for my previous job as a Finance Manager by an industry colleague, and I continuously set new standards for myself in terms of resourcefulness and productivity as I discovered new ways to find financing for customers with credit problems.

In prior outside sales positions, I received nearly every honor given by my employers for sales effectiveness. I was named a Five Star Employee and Gold Certified Professional and I consistently ranked in the top five of 40 sales professionals. My written and oral communication skills are excellent; I was a regular contributor of articles to a national monthly internal newsletter, and I was selected as the company's specialist in charge of communicating with potential customers by Internet.

If you can use a dynamic and ambitious professional who offers an exceptional ability to satisfy customers in sales and customer service situations, I hope you will contact me to suggest a time when we might meet to discuss your needs. Thank you in advance for your time.

Yours sincerely,

Robert L. Wright

ROBERT L. WRIGHT

1110½ Hay Street, Fayetteville, NC 28305   •   preppub@aol.com   •   (910) 483-6611

OBJECTIVE

I want to join an organization that can use an award-winning sales professional who offers extensive experience in customer service, problem solving, and financial management.

SALES PHILOSOPHY

I believe that consistency is the key to success in sales. If you want to excel, you have to be self-motivated and set very high *personal* goals.

EXPERIENCE

SALES REPRESENTATIVE. Time Warner Cable, Savannah, GA (2005-present). Am excelling in a sales role with the largest distributor of TWC in the US; the company I work for is responsible for 80% of TWCs sales.

- **Inside sales:** In this inside sales role, am one of the company's top two in "closing percentage" (closing the sale); I close 45%-50% of sales whereas most salespeople close 25%-30%. My normal sales volume is 70 accounts weekly; the quota is 45.
- In our business, we usually have to convince customers to switch from cable to TWC; and all customers we deal with must have credit cards.

FINANCE MANAGER. Saturn of Savannah, Savannah, GA (2002-05). Was recruited for this job by an industry colleague; I became very skilled in securing financing for people with serious credit issues.

- Continuously set new standards for myself in terms of resourcefulness and productivity; oversaw and administered contracts to various banks and finance companies. Established strong working relationships with financial institutions all over the country, and followed up aggressively with finance companies to ensure funding of dealer contracts.

SALES CONSULTANT & INTERNET SPECIALIST. CarMax, Savannah, GA (1999-02). Was **"Salesman of the Month"** numerous times, and always ranked in the top five of 40 sales professionals. I typically sold 18 autos monthly compared to the average of 12.

- Was ranked as a **Five Star Employee** and **Gold Certified Professional;** was among the top three salespeople and maintained a 98% in customer and sales satisfaction.
- Helped train and develop new employees in the sales department.
- This dealership was the largest privately owned dealership in the U.S. with 75 locations nationwide. I developed and promoted the dealership through various articles I wrote in the company's monthly newsletter "Teammates."
- As **Internet Specialist,** worked closely with Internet customers to ensure a positive experience.

SALES CONSULTANT. Skeeter Ford-Lincoln-Mercury, Savannah, GA (1996-99). Was a **Gold Certified Professional** and received multiple plaques and honors for sales achievements.

- On my own initiative, developed a protocol for working with new customers and implemented new process.

EDUCATION & TRAINING

Completed **Computer Drafting and Business Administration** courses, Savannah State University, Savannah, GA.
Completed numerous training programs and seminars related to sales, customer service, and financial management through providers selected by Saturn of Savannah, Skeeter, and other companies.

PERSONAL

Outstanding written and oral communication skills. Offer a working knowledge of the Italian language. Computer knowledge includes Word, Access, and Excel. Internet proficient.

Automotive sales and service

Exact Name of Person
Title or Position
Name of Company
Address
City, State, Zip

SALES REPRESENTATIVE

Dear Exact Name of Person: (or Dear Sir or Madam if answering a blind ad.)

With the enclosed resume, I would like to make you aware of my interest in applying my strong sales and customer service skills to benefit your organization.

As you will see from my resume, I am currently excelling as a Sales Representative with an automobile dealership which sells 150 cars monthly. Although I have excelled in this job and am making a solid living in the automotive industry, I am interested in becoming involved in the sale of even bigger-ticket items. I have found that my sunny disposition as well as my aggressive and persistent style of follow through are well suited to the sale of expensive items. Although I am young, customers enjoy my fresh approach and I am able to rapidly establish trust and rapport. I have become respected by the senior sales professionals at the dealership because of my good attitude, reliability, and strong work ethic.

You will see from my resume that I completed a semester of college at Indiana University East after graduating from River Creek High School. I excelled academically but was unable to finance my education. I am planning on completing further college courses in my spare time, and I can assure you that I offer a high degree of intelligence and can succeed in any training program required.

If you can use an ambitious self-starter who thrives on high goals related to sales and profitability, I hope you will contact me to suggest a time when we might meet to discuss your needs. Although I can provide outstanding references at the appropriate time, I would appreciate your not contacting my current employer until after we speak. Thank you in advance for your time.

Yours sincerely,

Nellie Turlington

NELLIE TURLINGTON

1110½ Hay Street, Fayetteville, NC 28305   •   preppub@aol.com   •   (910) 483-6611

OBJECTIVE

To contribute to a company that can use an aggressive and persistent young professional who seeks to be challenged by ambitious goals related to sales, customer service, and profitability.

EXPERIENCE

SALES REPRESENTATIVE. Freeman Toyota, Indianapolis, IN (2005-present). Am excelling in the sale of "big-ticket" items and, although I am making a solid living in selling new and used cars, I have decided that I want to move into sales of even bigger-ticket items.

- Have become certified in Toyota sales after extensive training; excelled in all training provided by the company and manufacturers, and have rapidly become knowledgeable of product features.
- On numerous occasions, have been commended by customers for my sunny disposition, and have earned the respect of veteran sales professionals for my persistence and follow through with customers, even with those who do not buy a car now. Am continuously developing and building relationships.
- Have learned that I enjoy selling large, expensive items, and thrive on the challenge of helping the dealership meet its monthly sales goal of 150 cars.

WAITRESS. Marriott and Hilton Hotel, Indianapolis, IN (2004-05). Worked as a waitress in two quality hotels which aimed for the highest standards of customer service and customer satisfaction.

- Was encouraged to remain with Marriott and was groomed for rapid advancement into a supervisory position because of my leadership and problem-solving ability.

CASHIER. CVS, Cincinnati, OH (2004). Worked briefly for this national drug store chain before relocating to Indianapolis, my home town.

CASHIER. Hardees, Noblesville, IN (2003). After completing a semester of college, was rehired by Hardees because of my previous outstanding work performance when I worked for Hardees during my senior year of high school.

- Also held a simultaneous job as a Factory Worker at Johnson & Johnson.

EDUCATION

Completed half a year of college studies, Indiana University East, Indianapolis, IN, 2003.

- Although I was excelling academically, I had to abandon my plans to attend college full-time because of financial reasons; am planning on completing my degree in my spare time.

Graduated from River Creek High School, Noblesville, IN, 2002.

- Ran track in high school.

Have completed extensive training sponsored by my employers related to sales, customer service, and quality control.

PERSONAL

In my spare time, enjoy movies and bowling. Have a knack for providing top-quality customer service and enjoy helping customers.

Telecommunications services

Exact Name of Person
Title or Position
Name of Company
Address
City, State, Zip

SALES REPRESENTATIVE

Dear Exact Name of Person: (or Dear Sir or Madam if answering a blind ad.)

With the enclosed resume, I would like to make you aware of my interest in exploring employment opportunities which require a vibrant go-getter with a proven ability to excel in any task I take on.

As you will see from my enclosed resume, I have excelled in sales and customer service within the Nortel organization. After establishing a distinguished track record of results in sales and customer service with Nortel in Louisiana, I was specially recruited to relocate to Kentucky to open up the Nortel LTD store in Bowling Green. I have trained three employees in sales and customer service, and I have provided leadership by maintaining the top sales position in the store. I am very proud that the Bowling Green store is ranked #2 in customer service among all stores in the U.S. while maintaining top rankings in sales.

Prior to joining the Nortel organization, I won numerous awards and incentives for outstanding performance related to sales and customer service within financial institutions and banking environments. At U.S. Bank, I won the bank's award for Top Salesperson and was named Customer Service Representative of the Year. I believe the key to my success is my work ethic combined with my attitude that customer satisfaction is the number one priority. Although that may seem like simple philosophy, I have found that success always follows from hard work and that attitude.

If you have a position in which you can use my dynamic, make-it-happen style, I hope you will contact me. I would welcome the opportunity to tackle new challenges which require highly professional skills in sales and customer service along with an intense personal desire to achieve superior bottom-line results.

Yours sincerely,

Helena Christianson

HELENA CHRISTIANSON

1110½ Hay Street, Fayetteville, NC 28305   •   preppub@aol.com   •   (910) 483-6611

OBJECTIVE   To contribute to the success and growth of an organization that can use a vibrant and enthusiastic professional who offers a proven ability to excel in sales and customer service while solving difficult problems and discovering new business opportunities.

EXPERIENCE   **SALES REPRESENTATIVE.** Nortel LTD Store, Shreveport, LA and Bowling Green, KY (2004-present). Because of my exceptional sales results with Nortel in Louisiana, was specially recruited to relocate to Kentucky to open up the Nortel LTD store in Bowling Green.
- Trained three employees on Spice sales techniques and Nortel Systems.
- Provide leadership by example; have maintained the top sales position in the store.
- Have led the store to achieve top rankings nationally in sales and to earn the designation as the #2 store in customer service in the U.S.
- Won many prizes and awards including a cruise trip to Anchorage, AK.
- Established outstanding customer relations and tried to satisfy customers the first time.

SALES REPRESENTATIVE/EXECUTIVE ASSISTANT. U.S. Bank, Shreveport, LA (1998-02). Because of my outstanding reputation and exceptional results at Wachovia Bank, was specially recruited by the President, Morgen Crow, for a highly visible job of raising start-up capital for a proposed new bank.
- Worked with the directors of the bank and followed up on their leads for stock sales.
- Placed in charge of analyzing/recommending software packages for the new bank.
- As the trusted "right arm" of the bank president, displayed an ability to choose my words carefully in public when marketing the concept of this new financial institution.

CUSTOMER SERVICE REPRESENTATIVE & HEAD TELLER. Wachovia Bank, Shreveport, LA (1994-98). Rapidly advanced to handle greater and greater responsibilities while playing a major role in leading our branch to win the "Prime 50" campaign for bottom-line results and to be singled out for recruiting more new customers than any other branch; became known for my aggressive and strategic sales instincts.
- As Customer Service Representative, trained and managed up to five tellers.
- In 1998, was recruited by MetLife Insurance and became licensed to sell Life and Health insurance; rapidly became successful in selling auto and homeowners insurance and life/health insurance, and won several bonuses for top sales results.

CUSTOMER SERVICE REPRESENTATIVE/TELLER. U.S. Bank, Shreveport, LA (1992-94). Won the bank's award for **Top Salesperson** and was named **Customer Service Representative of the Year**; won the Top Commissions award every month for product sales, and was the major reason why we won the "Branch of the Year" award.

CUSTOMER SERVICE REPRESENTATIVE/TELLER. American National Bank, Shreveport, LA (1988-92). Excelled in sales, and led my branch to win the 1991 award for most product sales within the entire region through my personal sales production.

EDUCATION   Completed courses in accounting and banking, Louisiana State University, Shreveport, LA. Numerous college-level management development programs and technical seminars; gained valuable knowledge from seminars including "Keeping the Customer," "Dealing with the Problem Customer," "Cross Selling Products," and other areas.

PERSONAL   Am very physically fit and disciplined about my exercise program. Have run in several 10K runs. Have a knack for mastering new software and am very computer proficient.

Hospital and medical services

Date

Exact Name of Person
Title or Position
Name of Company
Address
City, State, Zip

Dear Exact Name of Person: (or Dear Sir or Madam if answering a blind ad.)

I would appreciate an opportunity to talk with you soon about how I could contribute to your organization through my knowledge of claims processing, office management, and customer service gained while earning a reputation as a congenial and well-informed professional.

With more than 20 years experience at Twin Cities Hospital in Minneapolis, MN, I have advanced while building on and expanding my skills and knowledge during departmental reorganizations and rapid growth. Presently a Customer Service Representative, I coordinate a number of functional areas including insurance billing, correspondence department management, refund processing, and customer and patient relations.

As you will see from my enclosed resume, I have advanced consistently from File Clerk, to Patient Representative, to Assistant Supervisor, to my current position. In 2005 I played a key role in establishing the Correspondence Department and am its first supervisor. I trained the staff and now guide them in responding to inquiries from third-party insurance billers in order to expedite the turnaround time for paying claims.

I am a diplomatic, congenial professional with strong motivational and mentoring skills to complement my knowledge, skills, and abilities. I am certain that through my versatility and knowledge of business operations I would be a valuable asset to any organization seeking a mature, dependable individual.

I hope you will call or write me soon to suggest a time convenient for us to meet and discuss your current and future needs and how I might serve them. Thank you in advance for your time.

Sincerely,

Stella Lloyd

STELLA LLOYD

1110½ Hay Street, Fayetteville, NC 28305   •   preppub@aol.com   •   (910) 483-6611

OBJECTIVE

To offer extensive experience in office management and special knowledge of medical claims processing to an organization that can use a mature professional known for diplo- macy, mediating skills, and a thorough understanding of business operations.

SPECIAL SKILLS & KNOWLEDGE

Through experience and training, have gained well-developed knowledge of the business concepts of collections, billing, accounts receivable, and bad debts.
Am familiar with standard office machines including typewriters, calculators, and computers using the Windows operating system.
Hold current certification in CPR and Emergency First Aid.

EXPERIENCE

SENIOR CUSTOMER SERVICE REPRESENTATIVE. Twin Cities Hospital, Minneapolis, MN (1985-present). Advanced to increasingly more responsible positions and developed a wide range of customer service, finance, and office management skills while displaying my versatility as internal operations were reorganized and expanded through the years.

- Processed refunds and credit balances for Twin Cities Hospital and St. Paul Hospital patients. Became a specialist at troubleshooting patient and customer complaints and providing high quality customer services as supervisor of a nine-person staff.
- Was frequently cited for my attention to detail, knowledge of regulations and guidelines, and ability to ensure compliance.
- Developed and maintained excellent working relations with key personnel in other departments so that services and support activities could be coordinated.
- Ordered supplies and controlled inventories of equipment and supplies as well as arranging maintenance and repairs on office machines.
- Gained the respect and trust of my peers, superiors, and hospital management and during a 2005 reorganization was promoted to my current position which built on my skills and knowledge gained in earlier positions.
- Helped structure the correspondence department, trained personnel, coordinated the information receiving process with other departments.
- As **ASSISTANT SUPERVISOR** of billing and audit adjustments, took on these additional duties in 2000 as well as billing claims to private institutions and contractual services as the control clerk for these activities.
- Promoted to **PATIENT REPRESENTATIVE** (1985-91) from **FILE CLERK,** was selected during a department reorganization to become involved in cost reimbursement recording for Medicare and Medicaid.

Highlights of earlier experience: As an **ASSISTANT SUPERVISOR** for a furniture showroom and catalog sales store, was known for my accuracy as a cashier as well as my attention to detail and thoroughness in processing receipts and filling orders for an K-Mart satellite store in Memphis, TN.

EDUCATION & TRAINING

Was certified as a **Home Health Aide**, Minneapolis Community & Technical College, MN, 2005; completed a 75-hour program.
- Completed courses in Introduction to Microsoft Windows XP.
Attended training programs in areas including updated Medicare regulations, updated Worker's Compensation regulations, and collections, MN Hospital Association.

PERSONAL

Enjoy volunteering my time in church activities which have included secretary for the Board of Trustees and as a leader in community outreach activities.

Hospital supplies and services

Date

Exact Name of Person
Title or Position
Name of Company
Address
City, State, Zip

SENIOR CUSTOMER SERVICE REPRESENTATIVE

Dear Exact Name of Person: (or Dear Sir or Madam if answering a blind ad.)

I would appreciate an opportunity to talk with you soon about how I could contribute to the school system through my purchasing, customer relations, office management, and accounting experience and personal qualities. Consider this letter application for the positions of Purchasing Agent and Administrative Assistant.

As you will see from my resume, I have skills and abilities that could make me a valuable part of your team. In addition, I feel certain that you would find me to be a hardworking and reliable professional who prides myself on always giving "110%" to every job I undertake. I can provide excellent personal and professional references on request.

I hope you will call or write me soon to suggest a time convenient for us to meet and discuss your current and future needs and how I might serve them. Thank you in advance for your time.

Yours Sincerely,

Karen Duffy

KAREN DUFFY

1110½ Hay Street, Fayetteville, NC 28305   •   preppub@aol.com   •   (910) 483-6611

OBJECTIVE

To contribute experience in the areas of purchasing, customer service, and sales to an organization that can use my specialized knowledge related to all aspects of medical supply procurement, storage, and distribution as well as my technical computer operations skills.

EXPERIENCE

Became known for my outstanding communication skills and inventory management knowledge and advanced with Nationwide Hospital Supply Co., Houston, TX:

SENIOR CUSTOMER SERVICE REPRESENTATIVE. (2005-present). Advanced to this "team management" position to handle a wide range of activities including training and overseeing junior customer service specialists, working with purchasing agents, solving invoice and inventory-related problems, and taking care of billing discrepancies.

- Work closely with sales reps and hospital purchasing agents while servicing approximately 80 accounts. Receive and process phone orders as well as working with shipping and receiving clerks to find solutions for difficulties.
- Gained a broad base of knowledge of products from 350 vendors in the medical supply products field. Earned recognition for my calm and polite manner when dealing with demanding and difficult customers.
- Became proficient in solving problems and working against deadline pressure.
- Increased my computer operating skills while using automated systems.
- Accompany sales representatives on calls to hospital purchasing agents and help in meetings with customers through my product knowledge and communication skills.
- Chosen to represent the company at meetings for purchasing agents held in both Texas and California; also attended meetings with sales and manufacturing personnel in order to gain a better understanding of the products marketed by the company.

CUSTOMER SERVICE SPECIALIST. (1999-04). Became well acquainted with the needs of purchasing agents unique to the medical products field and improved my customer service abilities and computer operating skills.

- Contributed to my company's reputation for high-quality service while becoming known to customers throughout Texas.
- Developed highly refined telephone communication skills.

CONTRACT COMPLIANCE AND REVISION CLERK. (1993-99). Accepted orders from customers in seven states, then checked each order and made revisions so that units of measurements were standardized for easier and faster filling.

- Became familiar with the availability of rebates offered by each manufacturer.
- Learned the products offered by 350 vendors and how each product was marketed.

Highlights of other experience: As a Purchasing Agent for an optical company, learned the sources and qualities for a variety of products including lenses and eyeglass frames.

EDUCATION

Earned an **associate's degree in Industrial and Business Management**, Texas Southern University, Houston, TX.

COMPUTERS & OFFICE SKILLS

Am experienced in operating PC computer for word processing, inventory control and record keeping. Operate office equipment including dictaphones, copiers, fax, other machines.

PERSONAL

Handle pressure, stress, and deadlines with "a cool head." Am a skilled problem solver who works well with others. Am familiar with shipping, billing, and inventory control.

Retail sales and service

Date

Exact Name of Person
Title or Position
Name of Company
Address
City, State, Zip

SENIOR SALES ASSOCIATE

Dear Exact Name of Person: (or Dear Sir or Madam if answering a blind ad.)

With the enclosed resume, I would like to make you aware of my interest in joining your organization in some capacity which could use my strong background in sales and customer service as well as my solid training in accounting and bookkeeping.

Sales Distinctions

I am 25 years of age and have worked since I was 18 years old for AAFES, the Army and Air Force Exchange Service. During that time I have excelled in every assignment and have received numerous cash bonuses as well as several Sales Recognition Awards (SRAs). I am proud to say that I have increased sales in every department in which I have worked, and while in Fort Bragg, NC, in 2003-04, I earned the distinction of the #1 electronics sales representative in the U.S. while leading my department to a 25% sales increase.

Accounting and Bookkeeping Knowledge

In my spare time, I have nearly completed an Associate's degree in Accounting and Bookkeeping, and my degree program included coursework in financial reporting, accounts receivable and payables management, budget analysis, financial statement analysis, and other similar areas. I excelled academically while also performing with distinction in my full-time day job. My experience with AAFES includes some accounting and bookkeeping, as I have handled responsibilities as a Head Teller and Cashier. In one assignment, I was responsible for balancing all money received daily from 16 cash registers, and it was my job to assure the correct balancing of more than $75,000.

I am a very well organized individual with superior problem-solving abilities who rapidly masters new tasks and activities. I am certain that you would find me in person to be a congenial individual who would represent your company with poise and professionalism. I hope you will contact me soon to suggest a time when we could meet to discuss your needs and how I might be of service to you. I can provide outstanding personal and professional references at the appropriate time.

Yours sincerely,

Lauren Fern

LAUREN FERN

1110½ Hay Street, Fayetteville, NC 28305 • preppub@aol.com • (910) 483-6611

OBJECTIVE   To benefit an organization that can use a skilled young professional who has excelled in every aspect of sales and customer service, and who also offers outstanding accounting and bookkeeping knowledge along with experience as a teller and head cashier.

EDUCATION   **Accounting and Bookkeeping:** Am pursuing completion of an **Associate's degree in Accounting**; thus far have completed more than one year of course work in Accounting (77 hours) and Bookkeeping (267 hours), Fayetteville Technical Community College, Fayetteville, NC, 2003-04.
- Studied courses including Budget Analysis, Cost Reporting, Financial Reporting, Financial Statement Analysis, Accounts Receivable and Payable Analysis and Management, Cash Flow Analysis, and Cost Accounting.
- Was only two months short of graduating from this program and receiving my diploma when my husband was transferred to Fort Riley, KS; am transferring credits to Kansas State University in order to complete my studies at night.

Sales and Customer Service: Through the Army and Air Force Exchange Service (AAFES), completed numerous training programs and workshops related to sales, retail merchandising, customer service, cash handling, and bookkeeping.

HONORS   Received several AAFES Sales Recognition Awards (SRAs) and numerous cash bonuses in recognition of my superior sales and customer service results.

EXPERIENCE   *Have been promoted in the following track record of promotion as an employee of AAFES while increasing sales in every department in which I have worked:*
SENIOR SALES ASSOCIATE. Fort Riley, KS (2005-present). Based on my consistently outstanding Personnel Evaluation Reports (PERs), was offered a position by AAFES immediately after relocating to Fort Riley.
- Handle the sales of housewares and hardware items. Was designated as a Senior Sales Associate based on my excellent performance and service to AAFES.

CASHIER/SALES ASSOCIATE. Fort Bragg, NC (2003-04). Earned the distinction of #1 electronics seller in all of the U.S. while playing a key role in increasing sales by 25%.
- Assisted customers with the sales of stereo and computer items.
- Updated customer files on the computer.
- Received several Sales Recognition Awards (SRAs).

SALES ASSOCIATE. Fort Bragg, NC (2000-03). Assisted customers in the selection of linens and housewares; received numerous awards for superior sales performance.

SALES ASSOCIATE/CASHIER. Italy (1999-00). Assisted customers in the selection of shoes and men's clothing.

HEAD TELLER, CASHIER'S CAGE. Italy (1999). Handled the responsibility of balancing all money received daily from 16 cash registers; assured the correct balancing of approximately $75,000 daily. Handled responsibilities similar to those of a teller in a credit union; cashed payroll and personal checks.

CASHIER. (1998-99). Acted as Cashier for purchases in all departments.

PERSONAL   Can provide outstanding personal and professional references.

Product warranty services

Date

Exact Name of Person
Title or Position
Name of Company
Address
City, State, Zip

**SENIOR SERVICE
REPRESENTATIVE**

Dear Exact Name of Person: (or Dear Sir or Madam if answering a blind ad.)

With the enclosed resume, I would like to make you aware of my background as an experienced customer service professional and order management supervisor with highly polished skills related to supervising employees as well as solving complex customer problems.

As you will see from my resume, I have excelled in a track record of advancement with a Fortune 500 company, and I have been involved in resolving customer problems related to the ordering, manufacturing, and shipment of industrial products including motor controls. I began with the company in an entry-level position after briefly serving my country in the U.S. Navy, and I was quickly promoted to a role which involved production planning. I then supervised a 20-person department involved in the assembly, wiring, and shipment of half a million dollars in industrial products monthly.

As my career within Roberts Manufacturing progressed, I was promoted to senior positions which involved managing orders and handling customer service. Because of my understanding of product manufacturing and engineering as well as my highly effective communication skills, I excelled in coordinating the often-complex process of customer ordering and order fulfillment. I established and maintained cordial relationships with customers worldwide while expertly performing liaison with all functional areas involved in filling the customer's order including sales, engineering, manufacturing, and quality control.

In my most recent position I significantly reduced costs for Roberts through my ability to handle product warranty inquiries and claims. In 2002, I reduced by 50% the cost of product warranty claims compared to 2001, and I have greatly reduced the company's response time to product warranty inquiries. I am proud that the Pocatello facility now responds to 90% of inquiries within 24 hours.

If you can use a versatile and experienced professional who offers extensive knowledge of manufacturing, production, and sales functions, I hope you will contact me to suggest a time when we might meet to discuss your needs. I would be committed to helping your company achieve the highest customer satisfaction levels.

Sincerely,

Ned Lawrence Arabia

NED LAWRENCE ARABIA

1110½ Hay Street, Fayetteville, NC 28305 • preppub@aol.com • (910) 483-6611

OBJECTIVE

I want to contribute to an organization that can use a dedicated professional with experience in product line engineering, and manufacturing and customer service supervision.

EDUCATION

Bachelor of Science in **Marketing**, Pocatello State University, Pocatello, ID, 1982. Associate's degree in **Business Administration**, Pocatello Community College, Pocatello, ID. Extensive company-sponsored professional training related to **customer service, statistical process control, manufacturing supervision, production planning**, other areas.

EXPERIENCE

After a distinguished career with Roberts Manufacturing, have taken an early retirement in order to pursue other opportunities; advanced in the following track record of promotion at this company's Pocatello, ID location:

1999-present: PRODUCT WARRANTY COORDINATOR & SENIOR CUSTOMER SERVICE REPRESENTATIVE. For a state-of-the-art manufacturing facility, handled product warranty inquiries and claims; determined correct action after extensive problem analysis which involved coordinating local and field engineering personnel.
- In 2002, reduced by 50% the cost of product warranty claims compared to 2001.
- Improved the department's response time so that 90% of inquiries are responded to within 24 hours.

1997-99: SENIOR CUSTOMER SERVICE REPRESENTATIVE. In a very fast-paced job, coordinated the shipping of expedited orders and obtained outsourced material while also maintaining the manufacturing schedule for a department of 50 people; coordinated scheduling with field personnel and performed liaison with customer service on orders.

1990-97: SENIOR ORDER MANAGEMENT REPRESENTATIVE. Worked closely with engineering, manufacturing, and materials departments to optimize scheduling for customers; processed changes to orders including pricing changes. Coordinated customer visits for the review of engineering work and the inspection of equipment.

1987-90: MANAGER OF ORDER MANAGEMENT. Managed three people while supervising a department which performed scheduling of manufacturing; acted as the Customer Service Representative for field inquiries and interfaced with engineering, marketing, and manufacturing in achieving the highest quality product and turnaround time for customers.

1985-87: ASSOCIATE PRODUCT LINE ENGINEER. Utilized technical catalogs for quoting prices and delivery times of aftermarket parts and assemblies; provided customer service once the orders were received from the field sales organization.

1982-85: MANUFACTURING SUPERVISOR. Supervised a 20-person department involved in the assembly, wiring, and shipment of $500,000 in parts and assemblies monthly.
- Supervised hourly employees and became skilled at preparing performance reports.

1982: ASSOCIATE PRODUCTION PLANNER. After beginning as a Manufacturing Technician making wiring harnesses from engineering wiring diagrams and schematics, was promoted after 3 months to be in charge of reviewing material and engineering content of orders to be scheduled for manufacturing; scheduled work to ensure level production while managing on-time shipments to customers.

PERSONAL

Serve on the Board of Directors for Junior Achievement of Eastern ID-Pocatello.

Shipping services

Date

Exact Name of Person
Title or Position
Name of Company
Address
City, State, Zip

Dear Exact Name of Person: (or Dear Sir or Madam if answering a blind ad.)

With the enclosed resume, I would like to make you aware of my interest in exploring employment opportunities with your organization.

Extensive experience in customer service

As you will see from my resume, I have worked for only one employer for the past ten years, and I was steadily promoted to positions of increasing responsibility while earning numerous awards for quality results. As the main point of contact for numerous customers including Nextel, Bellsouth, and Cingular, I became known as an individual who could be trusted totally to make sure finished goods got to the right people on time and at the lowest possible cost. When the telecommunications industry began to experience demand problems, my employer—Crosstel—aggressively downsized, but I was the only employee in Crosstel's Twin Falls facility who was offered a transfer to Boise rather than become downsized. I can provide outstanding references at the appropriate time from Crosstel, but I have decided to explore employment opportunities outside the telecommunications industry.

Expertise in shipping management and computer operations

During much of the 1990s, Crosstel was in a tremendous growth phase, and I managed the shipping of finished goods valued at up to $8 million a week. I scheduled carriers including UPS, FedEx, and trucking companies, and I also became knowledgeable of air regulations and documentation related to the air transport of electronic products. I am familiar with the equipment of FedEx, UPS, and Emery systems, and I have utilized Oracle applications software and spreadsheets for shipping management.

Experience in employee training and supervision

Since 1997, I routinely provided oversight for six junior employees including forklift operators and production assistants. Through training sponsored by Crosstel, I became a certified trainer and facilitator for *Habits of Highly Effective People,* and I trained many employees at the Twin Falls facility in that positive philosophy.

I am seeking an employer who can use a versatile and loyal employee who is known for attention to detail and strong problem-solving ability. Through my experience in shipping management, I have learned that aggressive follow-through is often the key to quality results. I hope you will contact me to discuss any current openings you may have, and I thank you in advance for your time.

Yours sincerely,

Valerie Dillinger

VALERIE DILLINGER

1110½ Hay Street, Fayetteville, NC 28305 • preppub@aol.com • (910) 483-6611

OBJECTIVE

To contribute to an organization that can use a vibrant and enthusiastic young professional who offers strong sales and customer skills along with extensive technical knowledge related to shipping management, traffic documentation, and manufacturing operations.

EDUCATION

Associate Degree, Business Administration, College of Southern Idaho, Twin Falls, ID, 1994.
Completed numerous management training programs sponsored by Crosstel in these and other areas:

    Oracle Applications   Quality Control   Shipping Management

Certified Trainer and Facilitator for *Habits of Highly Effective People.*
- Trained small groups at Crosstel in the positive approach known as *The Habits.*
  TL 9000 Auditor. Trained to perform quality control auditing in telecommunications companies.

COMPUTERS & EQUIPMENT

Proficient with the Windows operating system and software including Word and Excel.
Have utilized equipment of FedEx, UPS, and Emery systems.

EXPERIENCE

For the past ten years, worked for a leading company in the telecommunications field, Crosstel, and received exemplary evaluations in all areas, 1995-present:
1997-present: SHIPPING MANAGER & CUSTOMER SERVICE REPRESENTATIVE.
Twin Falls and Boise, ID. Became skilled in all aspects of shipping management; was promoted to Assistant Shipping Manager in 1997 and then progressed to handle full responsibility for shipping management in the absence of the Warehouse Manager.
- **Shipping management:** In the mid and late nineties, the telecommunications industry was booming, and I managed shipping of $8 million in electronics products weekly. Scheduled carriers including UPS, FedEx, and logistic carriers. Worked with large specialized trucking companies as well as LTL carriers. Became knowledgeable of all air regulations and airport procedures/documentation related to the shipment of goods.
- **Customer service:** Communicated with customers including Nextel, Bellsouth, Cingular, and many others. On my own initiative, used my organizational and planning skills to consolidate customer weekly shipments so that freight costs could be minimized and customer satisfaction maximized. Provided excellent customer service to internal customers, too, who included Crosstel in Montana. Worked with the Repair and Return Department to assure that customers in the field got needed equipment on time.
- **Employee training and supervision:** Managed six people who included forklift operators and production assistants. Trained employees in *Habits of Highly Effective People* and trained employees to operate the Axiom computer system and the Oracle computer system.
- **Awards and honors:** Received numerous Quality plaques given by the company to employees who exemplified a quality attitude and produced quality results.
- **Company downsizing:** I survived the massive layoffs which the company implemented in 2004 and 2005, and I was the only salaried employee in the Twin Falls facility who was asked to relocate to the shipping office in Boise when Crosstel closed down the shipping operation in Twin Falls.

1996-97: INVENTORY CONTROL SPECIALIST. Twin Falls, ID. Processed inventory transactions and was responsible for the transfer of material to various sites.
1995-96: PRODUCTION CONTROL PLANNER ASSISTANT. Twin Falls, ID. Processed work orders for the manufacturing floor; prepared documents; handled timekeeping and payroll.

Retail services

Date

Exact Name of Person
Title or Position
Name of Company
Address
City, State, Zip

STORE MANAGER

Dear Exact Name of Person: (or Dear Sir or Madam if answering a blind ad.)

With the enclosed resume, I would like to express my interest in exploring employment opportunities with your organization.

As you will see from my resume, I am an experienced retailer with store management experience. Although I am held in the highest regard by my current employer and am being groomed for further promotion, I am selectively exploring other opportunities. I can provide outstanding references at the appropriate time, but I would appreciate your not contacting my current employer until after we talk.

I was handpicked for my current position which involved starting up a One Stop Store for Fielding Drug, Co. There are now 21 One Stop Stores in NM and AZ, and they offer discounted front-end drug store products as well as the expanded One Stop trademarked line. We have also integrated clothing lines including Lauren Forbes and name brand "first quality" overruns into the One Stop Stores. Because of my outstanding communication skills and reputation as an innovative retailer, I was chosen as the spokesperson for the "Southwestern Managers Think Tank," and I communicate the views of my peers to upper management in the parent organization. My store won the Customer Service Award of the Year, and I am also proud that the turnover in my store has been practically non-existent. I have retained nearly all the employees I hired when I started the store, and I believe those employees would say that they feel well treated. Prior to my current position I excelled as an Assistant Manager in a large Fielding Drug store which included a pharmacy.

In prior experience, I excelled in outside sales positions in the business equipment industry and as a Realtor Associate. I offer exceptionally strong customer service and problem-solving skills.

If you can use an astute problem solver who is accustomed to contributing to the bottom line in an environment in which there is stiff competition and constant pressure on the profit margin, I hope you will contact me to suggest a time when we might meet. I would certainly enjoy discussing your needs.

Sincerely,

Angelique Sommers

ANGELIQUE SOMMERS

1110½ Hay Street, Fayetteville, NC 28305   •   preppub@aol.com   •   (910) 483-6611

OBJECTIVE	To contribute to an organization that can use an experienced manager with exceptionally strong sales and communication skills along with a proven ability to identify new trends, solve complex problems, and develop junior employees.
EXPERIENCE	*Have been promoted in the following "track record" based on accomplishments; am being groomed for further promotion:* **2005-present: STORE MANAGER.** One Stop Store (a division of Fielding Drug, Co.), Las Cruces, NM. Was specially selected to assume the responsibility of starting up a new One Stop Store within the Fielding organization; Fielding now operates One Stop Stores in NM and AZ which offer discounted frontend drug store products and the expanded One Stop trademarked line.

- Managed the transition when the Fielding Drug store at this location relocated six blocks away and the site became the home of the One Stop Store; handled hiring and merchandising of this new value store.
- Integrated clothing lines including Lauren Forbes and other national chain brands' first quality overruns into the store's merchandising mix.
- Hired and trained the store's eight employees and have maintained exceptionally low turnover; the staff feels well treated and they respond with loyalty.
- Received the **Customer Service Award of the Year.** My store has also received exceptionally high evaluations of merchandising and maintenance.
- Am the spokesperson for the **"Southwestern Managers Think Tank,"** a brainstorming tool used by Fielding; am widely respected for my strong communication skills.
- Utilize a computer daily to access reports related to sales, gross margin percentages, UPCs, merchandise availability, and other matters. However, the One Stop Stores still rely on the store manager to order all merchandise since there is no automated reordering system. Am extensively involved in ordering merchandise, verifying invoices, and maintaining store records.

2002-05: ASSISTANT MANAGER. Fielding Drug, Co., Las Cruces, NM. Was rapidly promoted in a store with 12 employees which included a pharmacy.

- Made contributions to the success of the store in special promotions and other areas.

OUTSIDE SALES REPRESENTATIVE & MAJOR ACCOUNT REPRESENTATIVE. Crestwood, Inc., Albuquerque, NM (1990-01). Was a top producer in this company which was bought in the 1990s by Hinkle Solutions.

- Set up numerous major new accounts including the Kellogg's account; managed the local Stryker account.
- Won numerous awards for sales achievements and customer service performance.

ASSISTANT TO THE MANAGER. Central Office Supplies, Inc., Las Cruces, NM (1984-89). Became the owner's managerial "right arm" as I ordered all office supplies for resell, typeset documents, and sold office supplies/equipment.

Other experience: Was a highly successful Realtor Associate in Las Cruces, NM, where I was a member of the Las Cruces Board of Realtors.

EDUCATION	Extensive training in sales and management sponsored by Fielding Drug, Co.; Crestwood, Inc.; and other organizations. Have attended numerous motivational and time management. Completed one year of college course work, New Mexico State University, Las Cruces, NM.

Retail sales and service

Date

Exact Name of Person
Title or Position
Name of Company
Address
City, State, Zip

**STORE MANAGER &
CUSTOMER SERVICE
SUPERVISOR**

Dear Exact Name of Person: (or Dear Sir or Madam if answering a blind ad.)

With the enclosed resume, I would like to make you aware of my interest in exploring opportunities with your organization.

As you will see from my enclosed resume, for nearly 10 years I have excelled in retail store management, and I have won numerous awards which recognized my outstanding sales and customer service skills. Prior to working in retail store management, I worked in the banking field for 14 years, and I was promoted to supervise computer operations and data entry operations. I am comfortable in any organization which requires attention to detail as well as strong customer service skills.

Although I have excelled most of my life in management positions, I am seeking to transition from retail store management into an area in which I can utilize my strong customer service and sales skills. Being a retail store manager has had its satisfactions, but I am ready to trade in the responsibilities of store management for responsibilities related to sales and customer service.

I sincerely hope you will not view me as overqualified for the positions which your organization may have to offer. I am at the point in my life and career where I am eager to downsize my supervisory responsibilities in order to become a part of an outstanding organization with ambitious goals for sales and customer service. I truly enjoy working with others—both co-workers and customers—and I am confident that my seasoned public relations and problem-solving skills would allow me to become an asset to any organization.

I hope you will contact me to suggest a time when we might meet to discuss your needs. I would be willing to consider any position within your organization which would make me a valuable part of your team.

Yours sincerely,

Adeline Alston

ADELINE ALSTON

1110½ Hay Street, Fayetteville, NC 28305   •   preppub@aol.com   •   (910) 483-6611

OBJECTIVE   To contribute to an organization that can use a strong customer service professional who offers a proven ability to manage financial transactions while applying highly effective sales and communication skills.

EXPERIENCE   **STORE MANAGER & CUSTOMER SERVICE SUPERVISOR.** Payless Shoes, Sacramento, CA (1996-present). Have gained outstanding sales and customer service skills while managing all aspects of shoe stores which produced sales of $350,000 annually.

- **Customer relations:** Maintain outstanding relationships with customers and have cemented customer loyalties to Payless through my hands-on management style and approachability: customers know they can always approach me when they have a problem they feel I should know about.
- **Cash control and financial management:** Operate a cash register. Process payroll via computer.
- **Employee management and teamwork:** Continuously train and encourage employees, and have developed numerous employees who have become outstanding professionals.
- **Computer operations:** Utilize a computer daily in order to manage inventory levels, access information related to product availability, and submit data related to sales and productivity.
- **Quality control:** Continuously manage key areas of quality control and profitability.
- **Awards and honors:** Have received the following awards, honors, and recognitions during the past ten years:
  Store Manager of the Year, 1998, 2001, 2005
  Best Payroll Control, 1998, 2002, 2004
  Best Shrink Performance, 1998, 2002, 2004, 2005
  Outstanding Overall Store Sales, 1998, 1999, 2000, 2001, 2004, 2005

Highlights of prior experience:
SUPERVISOR & DATA ENTRY OPERATIONS MANAGER. Bank of America, Portland, OR. For 14 years prior to moving to Sacramento, CA, I was employed by Bank of America in Sacramento.

- Began as an Assistant Supervisor and was promoted to Supervisor in charge of all aspects of banking for computer operations within Bank of America.
- Supervised all data entry operations for the bank.
- Gained an understanding of how retail banking works, and enjoyed working in this environment which emphasizes customer service and customer satisfaction.

EDUCATION   Have completed numerous courses and seminars related to financial management, customer service, sales, and management reporting.
Completed training programs related to computer operations.
Completed numerous management training programs sponsored by employers.

PERSONAL   Known for my ability to establish warm working relationships. Outstanding reputation.

You may already realize that applying for a federal government position requires some patience and persistence in order to complete rather tedious forms and get them in on time. Depending on what type of federal job you are seeking, you may need to prepare an application such as the SF 171 or OF 612, or you may need to use a Federal Resume, sometimes called a "Resumix," to apply for a federal job. But that may not be the only paperwork you need.

Many Position Vacancy Announcements or job bulletins for a specific job also tell you that, in order to be considered for the job you want, you must also demonstrate certain knowledge, skills, or abilities. In other words, you need to also submit written narrative statements which microscopically focus on your particular knowledge, skill, or ability in a certain area. The next few pages are filled with examples of excellent KSAs. If you wish to see many other examples of KSAs, you may look for another book published by PREP: "Real KSAs--Knowledge, Skills & Abilities--for Government Jobs."

Although you will be able to use the Federal Resume you prepare in order to apply for all sorts of jobs in the federal government, the KSAs you write are particular to a specific job and you may be able to use the KSAs you write only one time. If you get into the Civil Service system, however, you will discover that many KSAs tend to appear on lots of different job announcement bulletins. For example, "Ability to communicate orally and in writing" is a frequently requested KSA. This means that you would be able to use and re-use this KSA for any job bulletin which requests you to give evidence of your ability in this area.

What does "Screen Out" mean? If you see that a KSA is requested and the words "Screen out" are mentioned beside the KSA, this means that this KSA is of vital importance in "getting you in the door." If the individuals who review your application feel that your screen-out KSA does not establish your strengths in this area, you will not be considered as a candidate for the job. You need to make sure that any screen-out KSA is especially well-written and comprehensive.

How long can a KSA be? A job vacancy announcement bulletin may specify a length for the KSAs it requests. Sometimes KSAs can be 1-2 pages long each, but sometimes you are asked to submit several KSAs within a maximum of two pages. Remember that the purpose of a KSA is to microscopically examine your level of competence in a specific area, so you need to be extremely detailed and comprehensive. Give examples and details wherever possible. For example, your written communication skills might appear more credible if you provide the details of the kinds of reports and paperwork you prepared.

KSAs are extremely important in "getting you in the door" for a federal government job. If you are working under a tight deadline in preparing your paperwork for a federal government position, don't spend all your time preparing the Federal Resume if you also have KSAs to do. Create "blockbuster" KSAs as well!

FEDERAL RESUME OR RESUMIX

TAMEIKA L. JACKSON
SSN: 000-00-0000
1110 1/2 Hay Street
Boston, MA 28305
Home Phone: 910-483-6611
Work Phone: 910-483-2439

Country of Citizenship: USA
Veterans' Preference:
Reinstatement Eligibility:
Highest Federal Civilian Grade Held:

**Federal Resume
CUSTOMER SERVICE
MANAGER**

**SUMMARY
OF SKILLS**

Over ten years of experience in office management and personnel management, customer service and public relations, as well as computer operations and office equipment operation. Extensive knowledge of specialized terminology needed to type correspondence, reports, and memoranda along with knowledge of grammar, spelling, capitalization, and punctuation. Ability to type 40 words per minute.

EXPERIENCE

CUSTOMER SERVICE MANAGER. Jun 2003-present. 40 hours per week. Prep Personnel, 1110 Hay Street, Boston, MA 28305. Ms. Frances Sweeney, (910) 483-6611. Manage office operations, customer service, and the organization of accounting information for the company accountant. Type correspondence, memoranda, and reports in final form. Utilize my excellent knowledge of functions, procedures, and policies of the office.

- Have become known for my gracious manner when answering the phone.
- Utilize my communication skills while speaking with potential customers as well as existing clients by phone and in person to answer their technical questions about the company's cleaning services.
- Manage both commercial and residential accounts.
- Schedule appointments for company services and determine correct prices.
- Handle a wide range of bookkeeping functions; investigate and analyze previous invoices in order to attach them to current work orders.
- Have been commended for my ability to deal graciously with the public and have been credited with increasing company revenue through my public relations and customer service skills.

PERSONNEL ADMINISTRATIVE SPECIALIST. Apr 1991-Jun 2003. 40 hours a week. HHC, 93rd TRANSCOM, Ft. Kobbe, Panama APO AE 28305. SFC F. Sweeney, (telephone unknown). Expertly performed a wide range of office duties, and was selected as Noncommissioned Officer In Charge (NCOIC) when my unit was deployed to Somalia.

- Was specially selected as Rear Detachment S-1 NCOIC as a Specialist (E-4) even though this position is normally held by an SFC (E-7).
- Utilized a computer with Microsoft Office for word processing.

The Position Vacancy
Announcement specified a
three-page limit for this
Federal Resume.

- Handled personnel administration activities including processing hundreds of soldiers in and out of our 400-person organization.

PERSONNEL ADMINISTRATION SPECIALIST & UNIT CLERK.
Feb 1987-Apr 1991. 40 hours a week. HHC, COSCOM, Frankfurt, Germany, APO AE 28305. 1SG Franc Sweeney, (telephone unknown). Utilized my skills in office procedures while excelling in a job as a Unit Clerk (1987-90) and then as a Personnel Administration Specialist (1990-91) within the same organization.
- Received a special award for my leadership as Unit Clerk in reducing a large backlog of personnel documents (SIDPERS) to zero—our unit was the first one to achieve that goal within 2d Army. The citation for the Army Achievement Medal which I received praised my efforts in "reducing 347 critical data blanks on the SIDPERS System to zero, allowing Headquarters Company to become the first of 16 units to reach this target." **Was commended for dedication and self-sacrificing devotion to duty.**
- As Personnel Administration Specialist, provided administrative support to Headquarters and Headquarters Company; posted changes to personnel files for 298 personnel, maintained personnel records including medical and dental records for hundreds of employees; and assisted personnel in coordinating appointments for annual physicals, immunizations, dental exams, photographs.
- Became known for excellent written and oral communication skills.
- On a formal evaluation of my performance during this period, **was commended for my "ability to adapt to changing requirements" and recommended for "rapid promotion to increased supervisory responsibility."**

ADMINISTRATIVE SPECIALIST & PERSONNEL SPECIALIST.
Mar 1983-Jan 1987. 40 hours a week. 5th Engineering Battalion, Ft. Drum, NY 28305. MSG Francis Sweeney (telephone unknown). Excelled in a job as a Clerk Typist and advanced because of my cheerful attitude and ability to handle large volumes of work.

EDUCATION & TRAINING

Certificate, USAR Unit Administration Basic Course, 1998.
Certificate, Administrative Specialist Course, U.S. Army, 1997.
Certificate, Primary Leadership Course, U.S. Army, 1997.
Certificate of Training, Battalion Training Management Course, U.S. Army, 1997.
Certificate of Training, Maintenance Management Course, 1994.
Certificate of Completion, Clerk-Typist Course, U.S. Army, 1984.
Graduate of Steadfast High School, Oakland, CA, June, 1982.

CLEARANCE & OFFICE SKILLS

While in military service, held a Secret clearance.
Proficient with all office equipment: computers, typewriters, copiers.

MEDALS & AWARDS

While in military service, received numerous awards and medals including Army Service Ribbon, Army Reserve Components Overseas Training Ribbon, Army Achievement Medal, NCO Professional Development Ribbon, Army Good Conduct Medal, Army Commendation Medal, National Defense Service Medal, Rifle M16 Sharpshooter Badge.

Her experience is in office management and administrative support. She will be applying for jobs at the GS-05 level.

You will notice that a Federal Resume is different from the "civilian" resume. You don't provide your employers' names and phone numbers, or your salary history, on a "civilian" resume!

FEDERAL RESUME OR RESUMIX

VICTOR A. NEILSON

1110 ½ Hay Street

Fayetteville, NC 28305

Home: 910-483-6611

Cell: 910-483-6611

E-mail: preppub@aol.com

SSN: 123-45-6789

Date of birth: 01/01/1973

Country of Citizenship: United States

Veteran's Preference: 5%

CUSTOMER SERVICE REPRESENTATIVE & EQUIPMENT COORDINATOR

EXPERIENCE

May 2005-present: **EQUIPMENT COORDINATOR & CUSTOMER SERVICE REPRESENTATIVE.** PRP, Inc., 1110½ Hay Street, Dallas, TX 28305. $48,000 per annum. Supervisor: Corey Bailey, 910-483-6611. Am a key member of the management team of a company which leases critical industrial equipment including power generators, temperature control equipment, and air compressors to customer organization which include chemical plants, manufacturing plants, building contractors, military organizations, and other customers. Perform major functions including the following:

- **Quality Assurance:** Perform analysis/investigations to ensure proper maintenance of power generators, temperature control equipment, and air compressors. Assure that leased equipment is in quality operating condition prior to delivery to customers. When leased equipment is returned, check material for evidence of carelessness or misuse of equipment or property. Determine liability for property that is damaged, lost, or destroyed. Conduct and document safety and environmental inspections. Coordinate all labor for normal or emergency repair of equipment.
- **Customer Service:** Coordinate with customers. Manage delivery schedules of leased equipment.
- **Logistics Management:** Coordinate the logistics involved in providing customers with leased equipment. Organize transportation of equipment via commercial carriers and expertly prepare and review all paperwork and documentation to assure completeness for future audits.
- **Contract Negotiation:** Negotiate contracts with customers for leased equipment. Negotiate key details of leases including price, delivery, customer support services, and other issues.
- **Experience with Military Contracting:** Coordinate with military contracting representatives and have become knowledgeable of the process of responding to solicitations as well as providing quality assurance information to contract specialists.

Oct 2001-Apr 2005: **CUSTOMER SERVICE REPRESENTATIVE & CONTRACT SPECIALIST.** United Rentals, 1110½ Hay Street, Dallas, TX 28305. $40,000 per annum. Supervisor: Chris Turner, Phone 910-483-6611. Prospected for new accounts while servicing existing customers. Coordinated with all levels of management in various industries including manufacturing and construction. Negotiated long-term and short-term leases for major pieces of construction equipment. Was handpicked to train new customer service representatives.

Aug 1999-Oct 2001: **EQUIPMENT COORDINATOR & CONTRACT SPECIALIST.** John Equipment, 1110½ Hay Street, Dallas, TX 28305. $30,000. Supervisor: Richard Stone, Phone 910-483-6611. For a $6 million fleet of construction equipment, prepared and maintained rental/lease agreements and handled collections as needed. Edited and filed all rental agreement reports, customer reports, and equipment reports for business operations.

Dec 1997-Jul 1999: **ENGINEERING WORK-STUDY.** Smith Memorial Hospital, 1110½ Hay Street, Dallas, TX 28305. Supervisor: Al Morris, Phone 910-483-6611. While completing requirements for my Bachelor of Business Administration degree, excelled in a work-study program with the Smith Memorial Hospital during which I repaired and maintained all mechanical hospital equipment. Worked without supervision while repairing and maintaining ceiling tile, sinks, and drains throughout the hospital. Also worked in the X-ray room, where I prepared and maintained records for customers and agency use while interacting with all levels of hospital personnel.

Jul 1995-Nov 1997: **POWER GENERATION EQUIPMENT REPAIR SUPERVISOR.** Dallas Army National Guard, Detachment, 125th Engineer BN, 1110½ Hay Street, Dallas, TX 28305. Rank: E-5. Supervisor: Chief Warrant Officer Caleb Lonestar, Phone 910-483-6611. As a proud member of the National Guard, maintained and repaired diesel generator systems and vehicles throughout the unit. Handled extensive responsibility for quality assurance as I inspected and repaired all equipment in order to assure 100% serviceability. Became highly experienced in inspecting and operating all types of vehicles ranging from quarter-ton trucks, to five-ton cargo trucks, to forklifts. Trained junior employees.

Sept 1992-Jun 1995: **GENERATOR REPAIR SPECIALIST & QUALITY ASSURANCE TECHNICIAN.** U.S. Army, Fort Hood, TX 28305. Rank E-4. Supervisors: Multiple. Phone unknown. On active duty with the U.S. Army, maintained 40 generator systems while continuously performing quality assurance inspections. Inspected paperwork to ensure that correct repair and maintenance procedures were followed. Trained and supervised junior employees, and assigned specific duties as well as tools and equipment to employees.

COMPUTER EXPERTISE

Experienced in utilizing custom software programs for procurement, supply management, logistics management, and accounting management.
Skilled in utilizing Microsoft Word and the MS Office including Excel and PowerPoint.
Completed computer training in Windows and Word.

EDUCATION & TRAINING

Completed the Bachelor of Business Administration (B.B.A.) degree, Southern Methodist University, Dallas, TX, 2000.
Graduated from Primary Leadership Development Course, Reserve Component Noncommissioned Officers Course, Fort Hood, 1997.
Graduated from the Ordnance Center and School, Power Generation Equipment Repairer Course, Fort Bragg, NC, 1993. Completed training in these and other areas:

Arc Welder Repair	Gas Engine Repair	Circuit Board Repair
Exciter and Exciter Regulator Repair	Ignition Systems	Starter Motor Repair
Liquid Cooling	Fuel Circuits	Battery Charging

Completed Basic Training, U.S. Army Training Center, Fort Benning, GA, 1992.
Completed Airborne Course, U.S. Army Infantry School, Fort Leonard Wood, MO, 1993.
Completed formal and hands-on training related to Reserve Component (RC) and National Guard policies and procedures as a member of the TX National Guard working in Dallas and Houston, TX, 1996-2004.
Graduated from Texas Senior High School, Dallas, TX, 1991.

MEDALS

Certificates of Achievement; Army Commendation Medal; numerous letters of commendation.

FEDERAL RESUME OR RESUMIX

GRACE GREELY

1110½ Hay Street
Fayetteville, NC 28305
Phone: 910-483-6611
Work: 910-483-6611
E-mail: preppub@aol.com

SSN: 111-11-1111
Date of birth: January 1, 1965
Country of Citizenship: United States
Veteran's Preference: 10 point compensable

PATIENT ADMINISTRATION CLERK

EXPERIENCE

12/11/2002 to present. **PATIENT ADMINISTRATION CLERK.** Military Medical Center Patient Administration Division, Fort Campbell, KY 28305. 40 hours per week. Supervisor: Mrs. Janet Smith, 910-483-6611. Began in this position in 12/11/2002 and continued until 05/01/2004, at which time I was called back to active duty when my National Guard unit was reactivated and mobilized for service in Afghanistan. In May 2004, returned to my position with Military Medical Center. Have earned respect for my outstanding customer service and patient relations skills as I handle multiple tasks as a receptionist, recordkeeping specialist, and clerk in a busy medical clinic providing a variety of medical specialties. Have become very knowledgeable of medical equipment, medical forms, and medical terminology. Kept accountability of records as well as inputting data into the CHCS software.

Office automation: Operate a computer and provide office automation support. Apply my training related to the CHCS software.

Medical recordkeeping: Assemble and maintain records in strict compliance with federal and military regulations. Maintain patient records and file results of laboratory tests, X-rays, EKGs, other tests.

Written communication: Compile data for a variety of reports, and ensure correct grammar, spelling, and format. Prepare releases of information for patients.

Customer service and patient relations: Have been commended for my outgoing personality and cheerful disposition as I serve patients and work resourcefully to solve their problems.

05/01/2004 to 11/30/2005. **AUTOMATED LOGISTICS SPECIALIST.** The Army National Guard, 1110½ Hay Street, Fayetteville, NC 28305. 40 hours per week. Rank: SPC E-4. Supervisor: Mr. John Johnson, 910-483-6611. During my employment with Military Medical Center from 2002-present, was recalled to active duty for 15 months when my National Guard unit was mobilized for deployment to Afghanistan in support of Operation Enduring Freedom. Worked as a Supply Clerk and Motor Pool Clerk, and resolved numerous problems related to transportation problems and fleet management issues.

09/10/1999 to 04/30/2002. **SUPPLY TECHNICIAN.** Upstate Construction, Co., Watertown, NY 28305. 40 hours per week. Supervisor: Mr. Casey Cameron, 910-483-6611. Utilized a computer to create shipping supply documents. Responsible for hand receipts while maintaining records and accounting for property book items.

10/15/1997 to 09/10/1999. **WAREHOUSE CLERK.** TRF Map Depot, Fort Drum, NY 28305. 40 hours per week. Supervisor: Mr. Nathan White, 910-483-6611. Received a Top Secret security clearance while working at this facility which maintained and stored maps for various units on the Fort Drum installation.

11/12/1988 to 10/01/1997. **MATERIEL STORAGE AND HANDLING SPECIALIST.** U.S. Army, Fort Drum, NY 28305. After completing Basic Training at Fort Leonard Wood, MO, and Advanced Individualized Training (AIT) at Fort Bragg, NC, assumed my first position in the materiel storage and handling field in Fort Campbell, KY in 1988. Became skilled in issuing and receiving parts for vehicles, and provided outstanding customer service to all units within a battalion. Became an inhouse expert on hazardous materials (HAZMAT) procedures.

From 1994-1997, with the C/123rd Support BN, performed Item Manager functions related to the documentation and fiscal control of non-expendable items by requisitioning, receiving, and issuing equipment such as vehicle parts. Utilized an automated property control program and applied my clerical skills in performing complex transactions. Edited requests for non-expendable supplies and equipment including regular, special, and high-value items. Operated word processing equipment to prepare a variety of material including correspondence, forms, reports, and other documents.

From 1988-1993, worked as a Materiel Storage and Handling Specialist for the Supply Company at Fort Campbell, KY, where I issued and received Class IX parts for vehicles and heavy equipment. Earned rapid promotion from private to E-4.

Logistics Management accomplishments: Gained experience as a Supply System Analyst while working with the USAR automated supply system.

Storage and Distribution accomplishments: Conducted physical inventories and location audits to reconcile manual and automated inventory records. Screened incoming customer order cycles for accuracy and completeness.

CLEARANCE

Held a Top Secret security clearance while working at TRF Map Depot, Fort Drum, NY.

EDUCATION

Completed one year of college course work in Early Childhood Education, Jefferson Community College, Watertown, NY. GPA 3.0.
Completed Primary Leadership Development Course, U.S. Army, 1995.
Graduated from Bill Apple Senior High School, New York, NY, 1986.

TRAINING

Medical terminology and medical equipment training: Trained in Composite Health Care Systems (CHCS), Military Medical Center, Fort Drum, NY, 2002. Extensive on-the-job training related to medical terminology and medical equipment at Military Medical Center, 2002-present.

Computer training: Microsoft training, 1998. Trained in the QAD system, 1997. Completed one week of training related to Enable, 1992. On-the-job training from 1991-94 related to SAMS, SARS, and ULLS computer programs used in the supply and logistics field.

Supply, logistics, and materials management training: Completed Advanced Individualized training as a Materiel Storage and Handling Specialist, Fort Jackson, SC, 1988. Learned materiel storage handling procedures. Completed Hazardous Cargo Procedures Training, 1992.

MILITARY AWARDS & MEDALS

Military: Bronze Star Medal (two awards). Army Good Conduct Medal (two awards). National Defense Service Medal (two awards). Global War on Terrorism Service Medal. Southwest Asia Service Medal with two Bronze Service Star (BSS). Army Forces Reserve Medal and Mobilization. Noncommissioned Officer's Professional Development Ribbon. Army Service Ribbon. Overseas Service Ribbon.

FEDERAL RESUME or RESUMIX

MICHAEL A. WHITE
1110½ Hay Street
Fayetteville, NC 28305 USA
Home Phone: 910-483-6611
www.prep-pub.com
E-mail: preppub@aol.com

SSN: 000-11-2222
Date of birth: January 01, 1959
PROGRAM ANALYST   Country of Citizenship: United States
Veteran's Preference: 10 point compensable

EXPERIENCE   01/01/2004-present: **PROGRAM ANALYST.** U.S. Army, S-3, 5th Special Forces Group, Fort Hood, TX 48361. 40 hours per week. Rank: SFC. Supervisor: MSG Woodrow, 910-483-6611. In the intensive environment of special operations during wartime, worked with the S-3/Program Manager (a Major) as I performed complex financial analysis and statistical accounting in support of the 5th Special Forces Group's training program. While acting as a consultant, obtained input from managers in three battalions and three companies in order to develop—and annually revise—a five-year plan which forecast training and personnel needs. Conducted detailed analyses of cost effectiveness, identified potential problems, and predicted future efficiency of programs. Data and predictions I developed were used to create the five-year plan that became the "master plan" and "training bible" to ensure that 1,000 Special Forces team members received on-time training in areas such as SCUBA, electronics, communications, and airborne operations. Performed cost-benefit analyses and trend analyses. Developed cost data and performed cost analyses of expenditures.

- Developed Excel spreadsheets, Access databases, and reports that monitored spending monthly and quarterly. Utilized the Army Training, Readiness, and Resource System (ATRRS). Developed a new Access database that forecast future training deficiencies and other problems. Created and delivered PowerPoint presentations praised for clarity.

- When training needs exceeded resources, procured funding for specialty training. Established strong working relationships with the Marines, Air Force, and Navy. Became the "go-to" professional when program managers from other services sought guidance about coordinating specialty training. Helped the Schools program become the best within USASOC.

- In my spare time, attended college in the evenings and earned my B.S. in Accounting with a 3.67 GPA as I completed courses including cost accounting, managerial accounting, and statistics. In my senior year, served as a company's Chief Financial Officer on a two-month project. Prepared balance sheets, profit and loss statements, cash flow statements, and other documents.

- Received Tax Preparer's ID issued by the IRS in 2004 (have prepared tax documents since 1984).

01/01/2002-12/31/2003: **RESOURCES MANAGER.** U.S. Army, S-3, 5th Special Forces Group, Fort Hood, TX 48361. 40 hours per week. Rank: SFC. Supervisor: SGM Heinz, 910-483-6611. When I took this job, inherited a situation in which key Special Forces individuals were unaware of their specific training requirements, which jeopardized their ability to remain ready to deploy on highly specialized teams.

- Because of my analytical skills and ability to use software programs as a management tool, I was handpicked to assume responsibility for PERSTEMPO projections. Developed a new software program that monitored PERSTEMPO projections so that unit deployments could occur on time and in compliance with regulatory and legal requirements. Developed a PERSTEMPO tracking database system that accommodated the new Global Forces Management Database System (GFMDS). Instructed personnel in the use of the new GFMDS Report.
- Expertly utilized Excel spreadsheets, Access databases, PowerPoint software, and the ATRRS system while analyzing resources and forecasting training needs. Utilized a classified software program to perform accounting and control functions. Processed over 303 school allocations with a 98.4% utilization rating. Performed research, statistical analysis, and cost analyses while making adjustments based on recommendations from staff and commanders. Established and maintained an automated school database that controlled expenditures by unit. Analyzed and evaluated personnel and equipment authorizations using Tables of Organization and Equipment (TOES) and Modified Tables of Organization and Equipment (MTOES).
- Developed and delivered outstanding PowerPoint presentations. Prepared written justifications of resource requirements.
- Maintained accountability of NBC equipment and supplied valued at $1 million, and directed the storage and monitoring of radioactive materials.

01/01/2000-12/31/2001: **OPERATIONS MANAGER.** U.S. Army, 75th MSB, 3rd Infantry Division, Fort Benning, GA 28305. 40 hours per week. Rank: SFC. MSG Mitchell, phone unknown. For a 655-person battalion, coordinated battalion operations while also supervising intelligence gathering and analysis. Was continuously involved in budgetary analysis and cost analysis as I ensured that funds were properly allocated to meet training needs. On a formal performance evaluation, was praised for "unparalleled technical expertise; always provides sound recommendations."

- On my own initiative, developed and implemented standard operating procedures (SOPs) for the schools program and for the Standard Army System program.
- Developed training plans using the software program known as the Standard Army Training (SATS) program. Initiated the SATS program in the battalion and trained Training NCOs on the SATS program, which became a model within the 3rd Infantry Division.
- On my own initiative, developed a tracking system to track all on-post and off-post schools.
- Prepared PowerPoint presentations and conducted briefings.
- Analyzed personnel and equipment authorizations using Tables of Organization and Equipment (TOES) and Modified Tables of Organization and Equipment (MTOES) for each company.

09/15/1998-12/31/1999: **FIRST-LINE SUPERVISOR.** U.S. Army, 3rd Chemical Company, 3rd Infantry Division, Fort Benning, GA 28305. 40 hours per week. Rank: SFC. 1LT Patrick, phone unknown. As Platoon Sergeant for the only forward deployed dual-purpose chemical company in the Pacific Basin, trained and supervised 27 people. With 100% accuracy, accounted for $2 million in equipment. Performed detailed research and cost analyses in order to ensure that training was complete within the projected budget.

PROGRAM ANALYST

- Assessed proficiency of platoon during NBC operations. Routinely anticipated and resolved a wide range of problems using my strong analytical and problem-solving abilities.
- Mentored three soldiers who were selected as Soldiers of the Month and Battalion Operator of the Quarter. Trained the platoon to achieve outstanding results on the Physical Fitness Test and on numerous decon and smoke missions. Was commended for my ability to establish strong working relationships with people at all levels.
- Became skilled in utilizing Excel spreadsheets as a management tool in conducting research and in developing recommendations for future courses of action.

01/01/1997-09/14/1998: **OPERATIONS MANAGER & COST ANALYST.** U.S. Army, 3rd Infantry Division, Fort Benning, GA 28305. 40 hours per week. Rank: SFC. CPT Sweeney, phone unknown. As Force Integration NCO, determined requirements and established priorities while providing guidance to various activities in the formulation, planning, and execution of the Command operating budget. Tracked funds distribution while also reconciling commitments/ obligations and reallocating organizational funds as directed. Monitored costs and prepared reports projecting use of available resources. Used advanced office automation skills to support budget operations such as updating, revising, sorting, calculating, manipulating, and converting spreadsheet data into various formats, programs, and reports. Prepared written justification of resource requirements, and prepared data in support of requirements. Analyzed and evaluated the documentation of personnel and equipment authorizations and requirements in Tables of Organization and Equipment (TOES) and Modified Tables of Organization and Equipment (MTOES) for a five-year window. Analyzed and reviewed trends in battlefield capability and determined cost factors related to the brigade's long-range plan.

- Acted as the Brigade Chemical NCO for a 2,400-person Brigade Combat Team. Developed standard operating procedures related to nuclear, biological, and chemical (NBC) matters and integrated all NBC equipment. Developed standard operating procedures (SOPs) related to contaminated casualty treatment, and trained personnel in proper contaminated casualty handling procedures. Improved the brigade's readiness and safety postures through my development of garrison SOPs and radiation safety SOPs.
- Was praised for my ability to prepare and deliver effective PowerPoint presentations on a wide variety of subjects. Conducted conferences and presentation and briefs pertaining to USR, NBC, Force Modernization, and the Quarterly Training Brief.

01/01/1995-12/31/1996: **OPERATIONS MANAGER.** U.S. Army, 483rd Maintenance Battalion, 3rd Infantry Division, Fort Benning, GA 28305. 40 hours per week. Rank: SFC. Supervisor: CPT Gibbs, Phone unknown. Established reporting methods to monitor costs involved in operating the training program for six separate companies with more than 800 personnel. Automated manual procedures to improve the timeliness of information provided to management. Served as the central point of authoritative information on administrative policies, NBC training, and chemical defense supplies and equipment. Developed and implemented plans for fielding new equipment. Planned and supervised the issuing and training related to the M40A1 protective mask. Compiled a variety of statistical data and information requiring research into reports, guidance memorandums, and data charts for incorporation into briefings, presentations, talking papers, information summaries, and impact statements. Reviewed budget data and recommended movement of funds based on analysis of historical execution rates, planning programmatic decisions, program manager input, and justification by key managers. Frequently performed duties of a Budget Analyst as I examined all phases of program, planning, and analysis necessary to formulate and support the budgetary needs of activities related to battalion operations and NBC Schools. Analyzed, maintained, gathered, compiled, and verified all data required to produce reports, charts, graphs, information papers, and briefings. Checked accuracy of budget justification data. Advised program managers of cost effectiveness, problems found, and future operational efficiency of programs.

EDUCATION	**B.S. degree in Accounting**, Central Texas College, Killeen, TX, awarded Dec 2004. Excelled academically with a 3.67 GPA. Total credit hours earned: 157. Graduated from Ladybug Senior High School, Houston, TX, 1977. Extensive on-the-job training in tax preparation since 1987.
TRAINING	**NBC training:** (1) Technical Escort, Killeen, TX, 15 Jan-10 Feb 2004: Became skilled in performing Tech Escort duties involving field sampling, detection, identification, limited decontamination, and mitigation/remediation of hazards associated with chemical, biological, and radiological materials. (2) Chemical Advanced Noncommissioned Officer Course (54B40), Fort Bragg, NC, 02 Jan-02 Mar 1997. (3) Chemical Basic Noncommissioned Officer Course (54B30), Fort Benning, GA, 10 Aug-12 Sep 1988. (4) Chemical Recon Course, Fort Benning, GA, June 1992. **Computer training:** Army Training, Readiness, and Resource System (ATRRS), 2001. Extensive training since 1993 related to Word, Excel, PowerPoint, Access, and other programs. **Battlefield operations:** Battle Staff Noncommissioned Officer Course, Fort Bragg, NC, 10 May-20 Jun 1998. Training focused on the BN and BDE level, and task performance standards are from ARTEP Mission Training Plans for light and maneuver forces and all battlefield operating systems. **Other:** Master Fitness Trainer Course, Germany, July 1996. Equal Opportunity Course, Jan 2001. Administrative Specialist Course, Fort Riley, KS, 20 Oct-15 Nov 1986.
AWARDS	**Academic:** Inducted into Alpha Beta Business Honor Society, Nov 2004. Inducted into Beta Kappa Evening College Honor Society, Nov 2003. **Military:** Meritorious Service Medal; Army Commendation Medal (8); Army Achievement Medal (4); Good conduct Medal (7); Korean Defense Service Medal; Kuwait Liberation Medal; Southwest Asia Medal; National Defense Medal; Overseas Ribbon (4).
OTHER INFORMATION	**Computer expertise:** Highly proficient with Word, Excel, Access, and PowerPoint. Skilled in utilizing specialized databases including the Global Forces Management Database System (GFMDS) and the Army Training, Readiness, and Resource System (ATRRS). Have utilized computer programs daily for 15 years. **Accounting expertise:** Highly experienced tax preparer since 1987. Hold an official Tax Preparer's ID issued by the IRS. Skilled at preparing balance sheets, profit and loss statements, cash flow statements, and other financial documentation. Skilled at analyzing financial documentation to determine problems and flaws. **Volunteer experience:** Volunteer Income Tax Assistance (VITA) Volunteer for 2003 and 2004, Central Texas College. **Security clearance:** Secret security clearance

Date

Exact Name of Person
Title or Position
Name of Company
Address
City, State, Zip

Dear Exact Name of Person: (or Dear Sir or Madam if answering a blind ad.)

I am writing to express my interest in the Career Management Program. I received your application for entry-level management positions and am sending my resume, interest sheet, and transcripts.

I would like to mention a few things about my experience and background that would be of importance as you consider my application. For approximately 15 months I have been a volunteer Procurement Clerk with the Directorate of Contracting at Fort Campbell, KY, where I have been given the opportunity to strategically build on my education and experience while gaining exposure to how the contracting process works. Contracting and acquisition are areas of strong interest for me and I have wanted to get into this field for as long as I can remember.

In looking at the career opportunities listed on the application, I find that I am especially interested in receiving consideration for positions as a "Contracting and Acquisition Specialist" and would also be interested in receiving consideration for "Comptroller — Budget, Management, and Program Analysis" positions. I am a very service-oriented professional with a strong desire to grow in settings where service and customer satisfaction are considered of high importance.

I am presently a student at Hopkinsville Community College where I am pursuing a bachelor's degree in Business Administration. I completed two associate's degrees at Hopkinsville Community College — Business Administration and Public Administration.

I hope you will contact me soon to arrange a brief meeting to discuss your current and future needs and how I might serve them. Thank you in advance for your time.

Sincerely,

Abigail Wright

KSA #1: Knowledge of claims procedures.

Overview of knowledge in this KSA

I have a great deal of experience in developing and maintaining information files and records, reviewing material for specific information, utilizing automated data processing equipment, and communicating with professionals in various settings which would all readily transfer to the medical care recovery claims process. I am certain that through my ability to easily learn and follow new methods and procedures and my office skills, I offer experience which would allow me to quickly learn the specifics of medical care recovery claim processing.

Experience related to this KSA

As a Sales Associate at Hecht's Department Store in Hopkinsville, KY, from 08/03 to 08/04, I gained knowledge of claims procedures in situations where items had to be returned to vendors or manufacturers because of obvious flaws. There were standard forms which had to be filled in and very specific procedures which had to be followed to ensure the store received credit for damaged merchandise or merchandise it hadn't received.

As a Sales Store Checker (05/97 to 09/98) and as a Store Worker (01/97 to 05/97) in the Italy commissary I worked in the administrative section where situations arose when items had to be refused or returned because they were defective, faulty, or the wrong quantity. Again there were specific forms and procedures to follow to properly complete the claims process in order to receive credit or be reimbursed.

Education and training related to this KSA

Attend Hopkinsville Community College, KY, where I am pursuing a bachelor's degree in Business Administration.

Earned **A.A.S. degrees in Business Administration and Public Administration** from Hopkinsville Community College, KY, in 2004 and 2003. Course work which would give me the type of skills and knowledge to process medical insurance claims have included accounting and government accounting, finance and budgeting, policy analysis, business communications, and data processing,

I received my Notary Public License from the State of Kentucky in September 2002.

EXAMPLE OF A KSA

ABIGAIL WRIGHT

SSN: 987-65-4321

CLAIMS CLERK (OA), GS-0000-05, Announcement #P-P-4-83

KSA #2: Ability to communicate both orally and in writing.

CLAIMS CLERK (OA),
GS-0000-05,
Announcement
#P-P-4-83
KSA #2

Overview of knowledge in this KSA

Throughout my career which has included a great deal of time spent in customer service, office operations, sales, pre-school and day care settings, and general office/data entry, I have always been called on to communicate orally with a wide range of co-workers, the public, peers, and superiors. Of course in office settings, being able to communicate in written form was also of prime importance for record keeping.

Experience related to this KSA

Since 9/03 I have been a volunteer Procurement Clerk in the Directorate of Contracting at the headquarters of the 101ˢᵗ Airborne Division and Fort Campbell, KY, where one of my main responsibilities is communicating on a regular basis with potential vendors. I instruct these potential vendors on how the initial bid contract process works. I also respond to frequent inquiries from vendors who wish to bid for government contracts.

As a Test Data Collector/Ram Data Entry Clerk for Ramcom, Fort Campbell, KY, from 06/04 to 03/05; as a Sales Associate for Hecht's Department Store in Hopkinsville, KY, from 08/03 to 08/04; and as a Sales Store Checker for the Post Commissary at Fort Campbell, KY, from 04/99 to 09/99, I used my verbal communications skills extensively while working in close cooperation with customers, peers, and superiors.

As a Sales Store Checker (05/97 to 09/98) and as a Store Worker (01/97 to 05/97) in the Italy commissary I used my verbal and written communication skills mainly to help me work in close cooperation with others to provide good customer service. For example, I responded to customers' questions regarding product availability, location, price, and other related information.

From 11/96 to 01/97 as a Child Care Giver in a military child development center in Italy, I used my oral communication skills on a regular and frequent basis. I provided instructional training in a variety of subjects and activities while interacting with the children by singing and dancing with the children as well as reading to them and using my written skills to prepare educational aids.

As an Army Community Services (ACS) volunteer from 02/96 to 12/97, I applied verbal communication skills regularly while making calls to prospective employers and talking with them about employment opportunities as well as assisting job applicants by answering their questions about the available services. My written communication skills were used to help in the preparation of correspondence such as editing.

Education and training related to this KSA

Attend Hopkinsville Community College, KY, where I am pursuing a bachelor's degree in Business Administration.

Through college courses and training programs, studied subject matter which enhanced oral and written communications skills while completing **A.A.S. degrees in Public Administration and Business Administration**, Hopkinsville Community College, KY. Degrees received in 2004 and 2003.

ABIGAIL WRIGHT
SSN: 987-65-4321
CLAIMS CLERK (OA), GS-0000-05, Announcement #P-P-4-83

KSA #3: Ability to maintain records.

Overview of knowledge in this KSA

The ability to maintain records with accuracy and thoroughness has been an integral part of many of my jobs in areas including positions in commissary offices, child development centers, Army Community Services centers, retail department stores, a college faculty computer lab, an automotive warehouse, and a public school system.

Experience related to this KSA

Since 09/03 I have been a volunteer Procurement Clerk in the Directorate of Contracting at the headquarters of the 101st Airborne Division and Fort Campbell, KY, where an important part of my job is to maintain documentation and records. I add and delete vendors so that the bidder's mailing list is accurate and up to date as well as extracting proper documentation from purchase requests. Nearly half of my time is spent reviewing, maintaining, and processing file documentation.

As a Test Data Collector/RAM Data Entry Operator for Ramcom, Fort Campbell, KY, from 06/04 to 03/05, maintaining accurate records was a main focus. I performed general office routines and office support procedures relative to the completion of test forms and data collection. I utilized lap top computers and other ADP equipment.

As a Sales Associate at Hecht's Department Store in Hopkinsville, KY, from 08/03 to 08/04, one important aspect of my job in addition to sales and customer service was operating computerized cash registers and assisting with daily audits and cash drawer reconciliations.

Maintaining detailed records was also an important part of my job as a Sales Store Checker at the Post Commissary, Fort Campbell, KY, from 04/99 to 09/99. In addition to verifying prices and item classifications, figuring total amount of purchase, and collecting money on each purchase, was also responsible for assisting customers and processing credit slips. I operated a 10-key electronic adding machine at the end of each shift to count cash, checks, coupons, and other cash items. Prepared cash reconciliation and accountability reports and turned in cash, reports, and other material to my supervisor at the end of each shift.

As a Sales Store Checker at the Italy commissary from 05/97 to 09/98, performed responsibilities in record keeping as described in the 1999 job at Fort Campbell. Additional responsibilities included working in the Administrative and Accounting Section where I performed such duties as processing requisitions which I reviewed, edited, and checked for compliance with all applicable government regulations. Operated a computer terminal to code data for requisitioning. Maintained and prepared records, reports, and files including inventory and balance-on-hand adjustments for discrepancies.

Education and training related to this KSA

Attend Hopkinsville Community College, KY, pursuing B.S. in Business Administration. Completed **A.A.S. degrees in Public Administration and Business Administration,** Hopkinsville Community College, KY, 2004 and 2003.

MORE EXAMPLES OF KSAs

MELISSA A. WHITE
SSN: 000-00-0000
CUSTOMER SERVICE REPRESENTATIVE, GS-6611-05 (Training to GS-07)
Announcement #AM-00-000

KSA #1: Ability to review, research, and coordinate work order requests.

**CUSTOMER SERVICE
REPRESENTATIVE,
GS-6611-05
(Training to GS-07)
Announcement
#AM-00-000
KSA #1**

In my current position as an Office Automation Clerk for A Co., HHC Bn., P.I.R., I receive and respond to a large number of inquiries both over the phone and in person. Provide information to resolve their questions and concerns immediately or perform research to locate the information they need. Receive, validate, investigate, and resolve customer complaints. Schedule preventive maintenance and repairs on office equipment, telecommunications systems, and other essential office systems; make service calls and obtain necessary permissions from my supervisor and other management personnel. Place project requests for required major repairs, such as repairs to HVAC equipment, using DA Form 4283, the Engineer Work Request, or Work Order. Continue to follow up on any requested repairs in order to ensure that the work order is processed and the repairs are completed in a timely and accurate manner.

In an earlier position as a Customer Service Representative for Bank of America (2000), answered a large volume of incoming customer complaints and inquiries. Directed customers to the appropriate person and department necessary to ensure that their concerns were addressed in a timely manner. Where possible, personally provided information to resolve the customers question or complaint, or researched their inquiry on my own initiative in order to obtain the information needed to provide a timely resolution. Handled repair and service orders for office automation equipment, communications equipment, and air conditioning/HVAC equipment, as well as the physical location itself. Scheduled and coordinated with the Branch Manager, regional facilities management, and other personnel to ensure that the required permissions were secured prior to approving the work. Contacted service technicians, plumbers, carpenters, subcontractors, etc. in order to schedule and coordinate the scheduling and completion of repairs.

Education and Training Related to this KSA:
Completed nearly three years of college-level course work towards a Bachelor's degree, West Virginia State College, Institute, WV; was recently evaluated, and now need only 12 courses to obtain a Bachelor of Science in Human Resources.

Completed a number of training courses, including:
- Microsoft Word, Excel, PowerPoint, and Access, 2005
- Time Management course, 2005
- Habits of Highly Effective People, 2005
- FormFlow, 2005

MELISSA A. WHITE

SSN: 000-00-0000

CUSTOMER SERVICE REPRESENTATIVE, GS-6611-05 (Training to GS-07)

Announcement #AM-00-000

KSA #2: Ability to operate automated data processing systems.

The main emphasis of my job is using a variety of word processors and other computer software to prepare a variety of narrative and tabular material according to prepared formats, form letters, standard paragraphs, and mail lists. Utilize Microsoft Word to prepare the full range of letters, memos, and other correspondence. Familiar with the features and functions of the program, including but not limited to spell check and online thesaurus; toolbars for drawing, forms, formatting, and borders; block commands for cutting, copying, and pasting text; and other advanced features used for page layout, setting margins, and text formatting. Provide assistance during the production and distribution of periodic performance evaluations, narratives for awards and medals, and memorandums, using word processors and other software to prepare these materials. Share my extensive knowledge of Word, Form Flow, and PageMaker. Utilize Local Area Network (LAN), providing training and assistance to office personnel in the operation of these and other automated data processing systems. Troubleshoot and assist in resolving problems with computer systems and software.

CUSTOMER SERVICE REPRESENTATIVE, GS-6611-05 (Training to GS-07) Announcement #AM-00-000 KSA #2

In a previous temporary position as Office Automation Clerk for the Directorate of Civilian Personnel, I operated word processing computer equipment in order to produce a wide variety of office documents such as letters, memos, and other correspondence; position descriptions, tracker reports, and other narrative and tabular data. Employed a wide range of advanced functions in software programs which included Access, Adobe PageMaker, and Word. Updated, revised, reformatted, entered, sorted, calculated, and retrieved a variety of information in databases. Utilized the resulting information for reports, to provide my supervisor with requested information, and to make revisions. Used a variety of word processing software and printing equipment to create, store, copy, retrieve, and print documents and formats. Used graphics software to produce charts and graphs for briefings and presentations as well as for preparing SOPs.

As Administrative Assistant for the Department of Defense Schools at Wuerzburg Elementary School, I used Word, Adobe PageMaker, and a variety of other software to prepare letters, memos, and other correspondence, as well as to create, update, and maintain student files containing information concerning medications, remediation, and behavioral disorders. At my recommendation, the school purchased updated software, resulting in greater efficiency overall for the recordkeeping system.

Education and Training Related to this KSA:

Completed nearly three years of college-level course work towards a Bachelor's degree, West Virginia State College, Institute, WV; was recently evaluated, and now need only 12 courses to obtain a Bachelor of Science in Human Resources.

Completed a number of training courses, including:
- Microsoft Word, Excel, PowerPoint, and Access, 2005
- Time Management course, 2005
- Habits of Highly Effective People, 2005
- FormFlow, 2005

ABOUT THE EDITOR

Anne McKinney holds an MBA from the Harvard Business School and a BA in English from the University of North Carolina at Chapel Hill. A noted public speaker, writer, and teacher, she is the senior editor for PREP's business and career imprint, which bears her name. Early titles in the Anne McKinney Career Series (now called the Real-Resumes Series) published by PREP include: *Resumes and Cover Letters That Have Worked, Resumes and Cover Letters That Have Worked for Military Professionals, Government Job Applications and Federal Resumes, Cover Letters That Blow Doors Open,* and *Letters for Special Situations.* Her career titles and how-to resume-and-cover-letter books are based on the expertise she has acquired in 25 years of working with job hunters. Her valuable career insights have appeared in publications of the "Wall Street Journal" and other prominent newspapers and magazines.

PREP Publishing Order Form

You may purchase our titles from your favorite bookseller! Or send a check, money order or your credit card number for the total amount*, plus $4.00 postage and handling, to PREP, 1110 1/2 Hay Street, Fayetteville, NC 28305. You may also order our titles on our website at www.prep-pub.com and feel free to e-mail us at preppub@aol.com or call 910-483-6611 with your questions or concerns.

Name: _____

Address: _____

E-mail address:_____

Payment Type: ☐ Check/Money Order   ☐ Visa   ☐ MasterCard

Credit Card Number: _____ Expiration Date: _____

Put a check beside the items you are ordering:

☐ $16.95—REAL-RESUMES FOR RESTAURANT, FOOD SERVICE & HOTEL JOBS. Anne McKinney, Editor

☐ $16.95—REAL-RESUMES FOR MEDIA, NEWSPAPER, BROADCASTING & PUBLIC AFFAIRS JOBS. Anne McKinney, Editor

☐ $16.95—REAL-RESUMES FOR RETAILING, MODELING, FASHION & BEAUTY JOBS. Anne McKinney, Editor

☐ $16.95—REAL-RESUMES FOR HUMAN RESOURCES & PERSONNEL JOBS. Anne McKinney, Editor

☐ $16.95—REAL-RESUMES FOR MANUFACTURING JOBS. Anne McKinney, Editor

☐ $16.95—REAL-RESUMES FOR AVIATION & TRAVEL JOBS. Anne McKinney, Editor

☐ $16.95—REAL-RESUMES FOR POLICE, LAW ENFORCEMENT & SECURITY JOBS. Anne McKinney, Editor

☐ $16.95—REAL-RESUMES FOR SOCIAL WORK & COUNSELING JOBS. Anne McKinney, Editor

☐ $16.95—REAL-RESUMES FOR CONSTRUCTION JOBS. Anne McKinney, Editor

☐ $16.95—REAL-RESUMES FOR FINANCIAL JOBS. Anne McKinney, Editor

☐ $16.95—REAL-RESUMES FOR COMPUTER JOBS. Anne McKinney, Editor

☐ $16.95—REAL-RESUMES FOR MEDICAL JOBS. Anne McKinney, Editor

☐ $16.95—REAL-RESUMES FOR TEACHERS. Anne McKinney, Editor

☐ $16.95—REAL-RESUMES FOR CAREER CHANGERS. Anne McKinney, Editor

☐ $16.95—REAL-RESUMES FOR STUDENTS. Anne McKinney, Editor

☐ $16.95—REAL-RESUMES FOR SALES. Anne McKinney, Editor

☐ $16.95—REAL ESSAYS FOR COLLEGE AND GRAD SCHOOL. Anne McKinney, Editor

☐ $25.00—RESUMES AND COVER LETTERS THAT HAVE WORKED. McKinney, Editor

☐ $25.00—RESUMES AND COVER LETTERS THAT HAVE WORKED FOR MILITARY PROFESSIONALS. McKinney, Editor

☐ $25.00—RESUMES AND COVER LETTERS FOR MANAGERS. McKinney, Editor

☐ $25.00—GOVERNMENT JOB APPLICATIONS AND FEDERAL RESUMES. Anne McKinney, Editor

☐ $25.00—COVER LETTERS THAT BLOW DOORS OPEN. McKinney, Editor

☐ $25.00—LETTERS FOR SPECIAL SITUATIONS. McKinney, Editor

☐ $16.95—REAL-RESUMES FOR NURSING JOBS. McKinney, Editor

☐ $16.95—REAL-RESUMES FOR AUTO INDUSTRY JOBS. McKinney, Editor

☐ $24.95—REAL KSAS--KNOWLEDGE, SKILLS & ABILITIES--FOR GOVERNMENT JOBS. McKinney, Editor

☐ $24.95—REAL RESUMIX AND OTHER RESUMES FOR FEDERAL GOVERNMENT JOBS. McKinney, Editor

☐ $24.95—REAL BUSINESS PLANS AND MARKETING TOOLS ... Samples to use in your business. McKinney, Editor

☐ $16.95—REAL-RESUMES FOR ADMINISTRATIVE SUPPORT, OFFICE & SECRETARIAL JOBS. Anne McKinney, Editor

☐ $16.95—REAL-RESUMES FOR FIREFIGHTING JOBS. Anne McKinney, Editor

☐ $16.95—REAL-RESUMES FOR JOBS IN NONPROFIT ORGANIZATIONS. Anne McKinney, Editor

☐ $16.95—REAL-RESUMES FOR SPORTS INDUSTRY JOBS. Anne McKinney, Editor

☐ $16.95—REAL-RESUMES FOR LEGAL & PARALEGAL JOBS. Anne McKinney, Editor

☐ $16.95—REAL-RESUMES FOR ENGINEERING JOBS. Anne McKinney, Editor

☐ $22.95—REAL-RESUMES FOR U.S. POSTAL SERVICE JOBS. Anne McKinney, Editor

☐ $16.95—REAL-RESUMES FOR CUSTOMER SERVICE JOBS. Anne McKinney, Editor

☐ $16.95—REAL-RESUMES FOR SAFETY & QUALITY ASSURANCE JOBS. Anne McKinney, Editor

_____ **TOTAL ORDERED**

_____**(add $4.00 for shipping and handling)**

_____**TOTAL INCLUDING SHIPPING *PREP** offers volume discounts. Call (910) 483-6611.*

THE MISSION OF PREP PUBLISHING IS TO PUBLISH
BOOKS AND OTHER PRODUCTS WHICH ENRICH
PEOPLE'S LIVES AND HELP THEM OPTIMIZE THE
HUMAN EXPERIENCE. OUR STRONGEST LINES ARE
OUR JUDEO-CHRISTIAN ETHICS SERIES AND OUR
REAL-RESUMES SERIES.

Would you like to explore the possibility of having PREP's writing
team create a resume for you similar to the ones in this book?

For a brief free consultation, call 910-483-6611
or send $4.00 to receive our Job Change Packet to
PREP, 1110 1/2 Hay Street, Fayetteville, NC 28305. Visit our
website to find valuable career resources: www.prep-pub.com!

QUESTIONS OR COMMENTS? E-MAIL US AT PREPPUB@AOL.COM